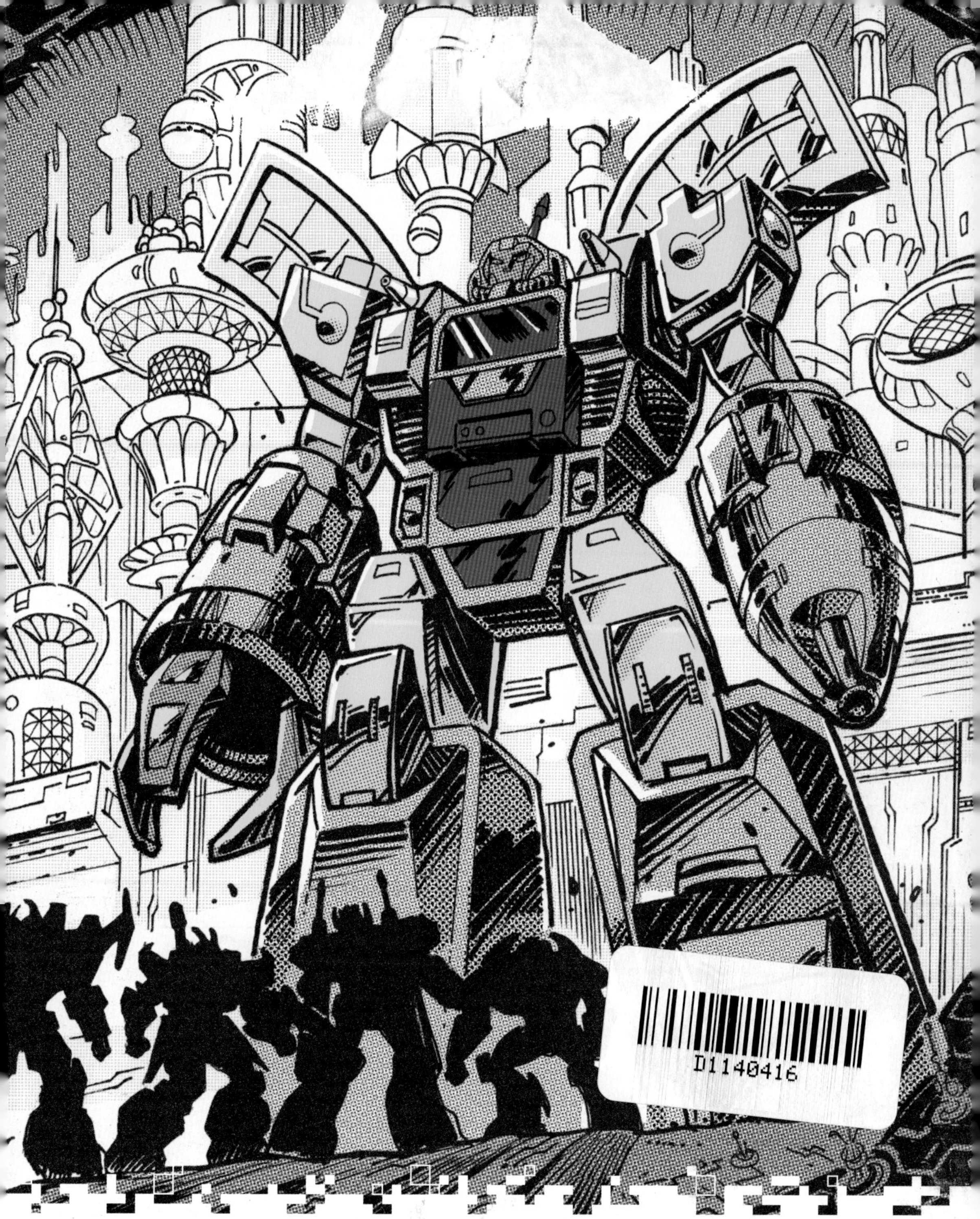



# THE TRANSFORMERS

## ROBOTS IN DISGUISE

VOLUME 3

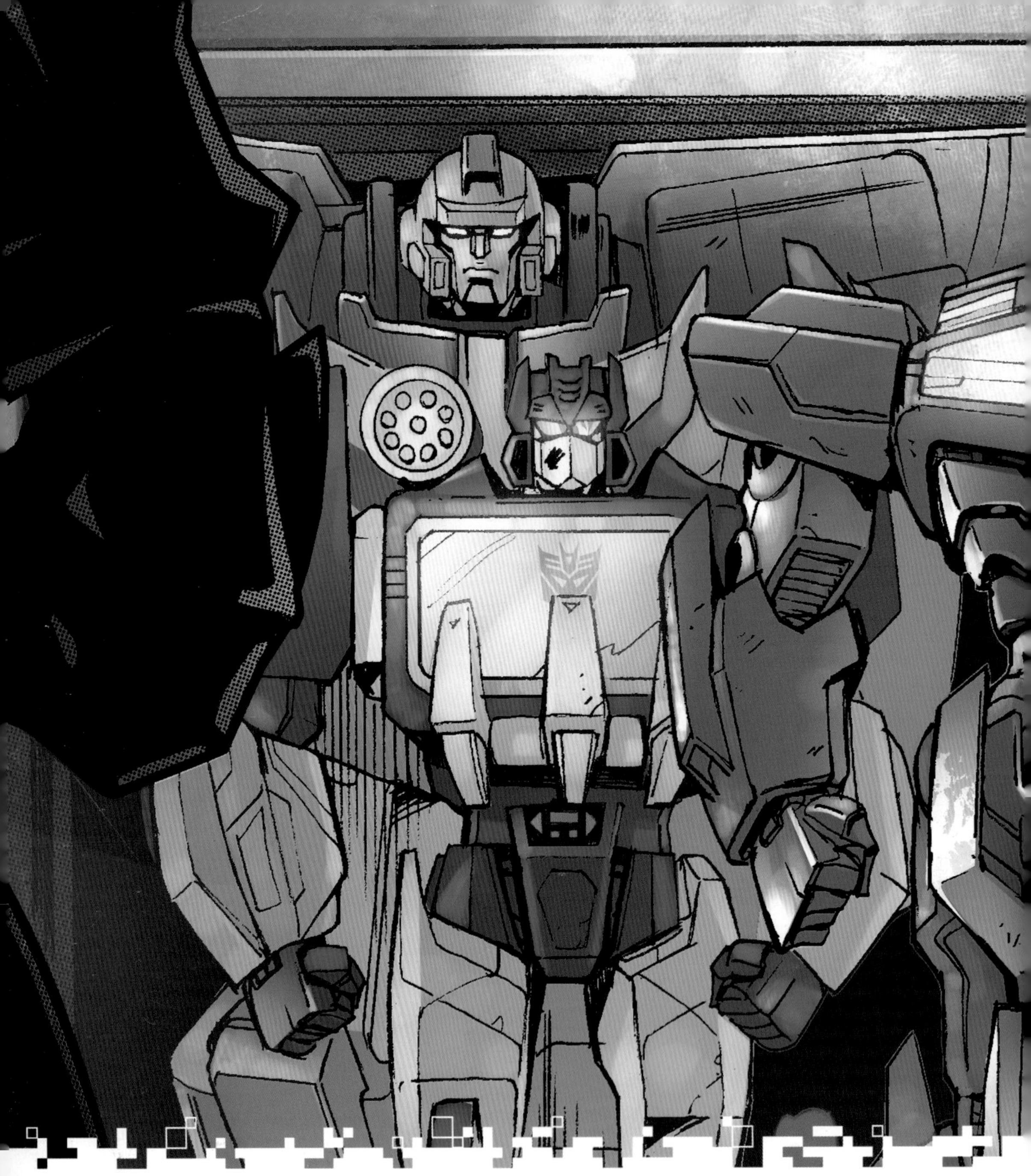

Collection Cover by Brendan Cahill • Cover Colors by Josh Perez
Series Edits by Carlos Guzman
Collection Edits by Justin Eisinger and Alonzo Simon
Collection Design by Chris Mowry

Special thanks to Hasbro's Aaron Archer, Jerry Jivoin, Michael Verret, Ed Lane, Joe Furfaro, Jos Huxley, Andy Schmidt, Heather Hopkins, and Michael Kelly for their invaluable assistance.

IDW founded by Ted Adams, Alex Garner, Kris Oprisko, and Robbie Robbins

ISBN: 978-1-61377-626-1

16 15 14 13 1 2 3 4

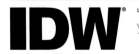

IDW®

Licensed By: Hasbro

Ted Adams, CEO & Publisher
Greg Goldstein, President & COO
Robbie Robbins, EVP/Sr. Graphic Artist
Chris Ryall, Chief Creative Officer/Editor-in-Chief
Matthew Ruzicka, CPA, Chief Financial Officer
Alan Payne, VP of Sales
Dirk Wood, VP of Marketing
Lorelei Bunjes, VP of Digital Services

Become our fan on Facebook **facebook.com/idwpublishing**
Follow us on Twitter **@idwpublishing**
Check us out on YouTube **youtube.com/idwpublishing**
**www.IDWPUBLISHING.com**



Originally published as THE TRANSFORMERS: ROBOTS IN DISGUISE Issues #10-11 and THE TRANSFORMERS: ROBOTS IN DISGUISE ANNUAL 2012.

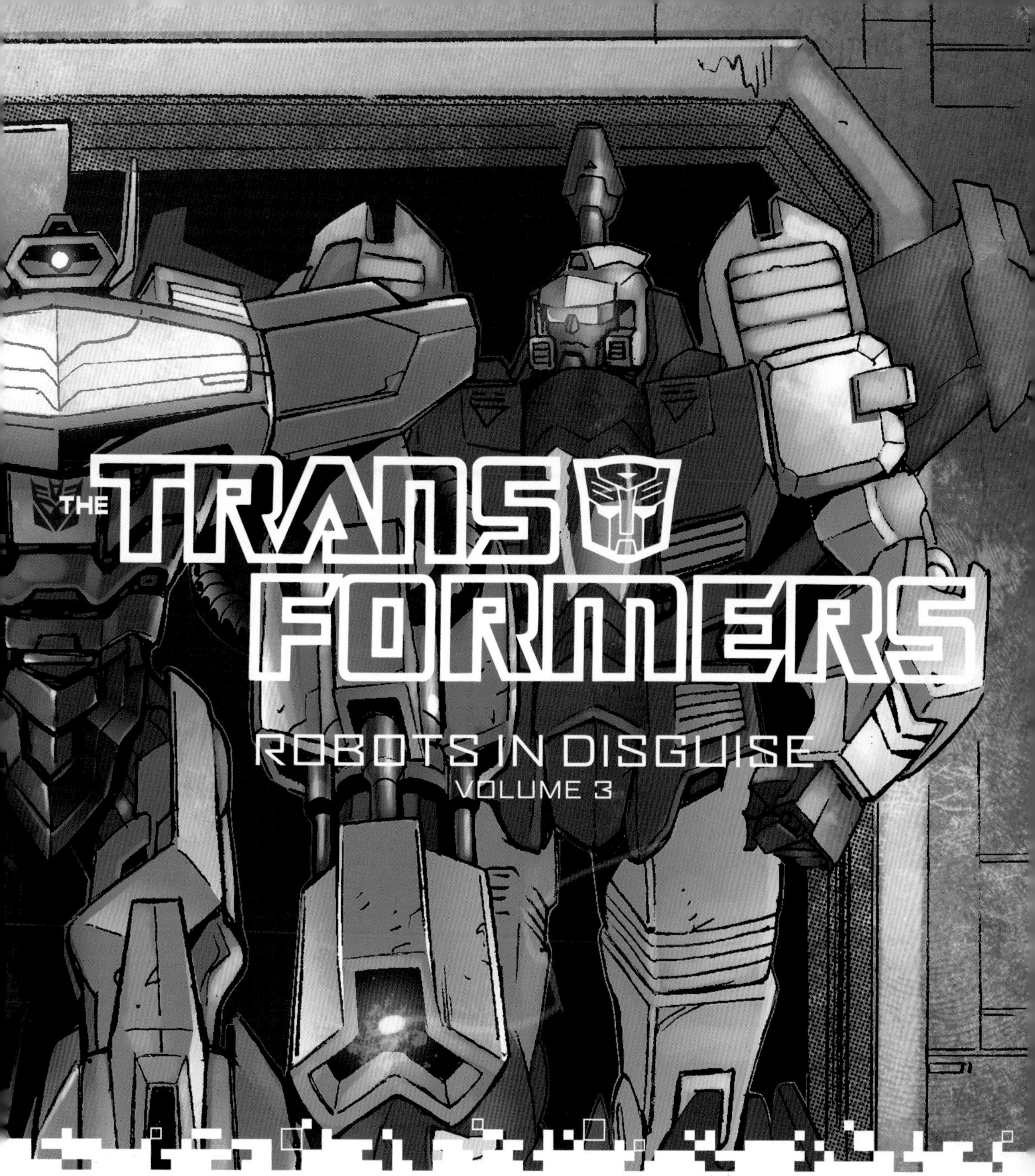

# THE TRANSFORMERS
## ROBOTS IN DISGUISE
### VOLUME 3

## ☐ SYNDROMICA [2]

WRITTEN BY **JOHN BARBER** ART BY **LIVIO RAMONDELLI**
LETTERS BY **SHAWN LEE**

## ☐ PRIMUS: ALL GOOD THINGS

WRITTEN BY **JOHN BARBER** ART BY **BRENDAN CAHILL**
COLORS BY **JOANA LAFUENTE** FLASHBACK ART AND COLORS BY **GUIDO GUIDI**
LETTERS BY **CHRIS MOWRY**

## ☐ THE END OF THE BEGINNING OF THE WORLD

WRITTEN BY **JOHN BARBER** ART BY **GUIDO GUIDI**
ADDITIONAL INKS BY **JOHN WYCOUGH** COLORS BY **PRISCILLA TRAMONTANO**
LETTERS BY **SHAWN LEE**

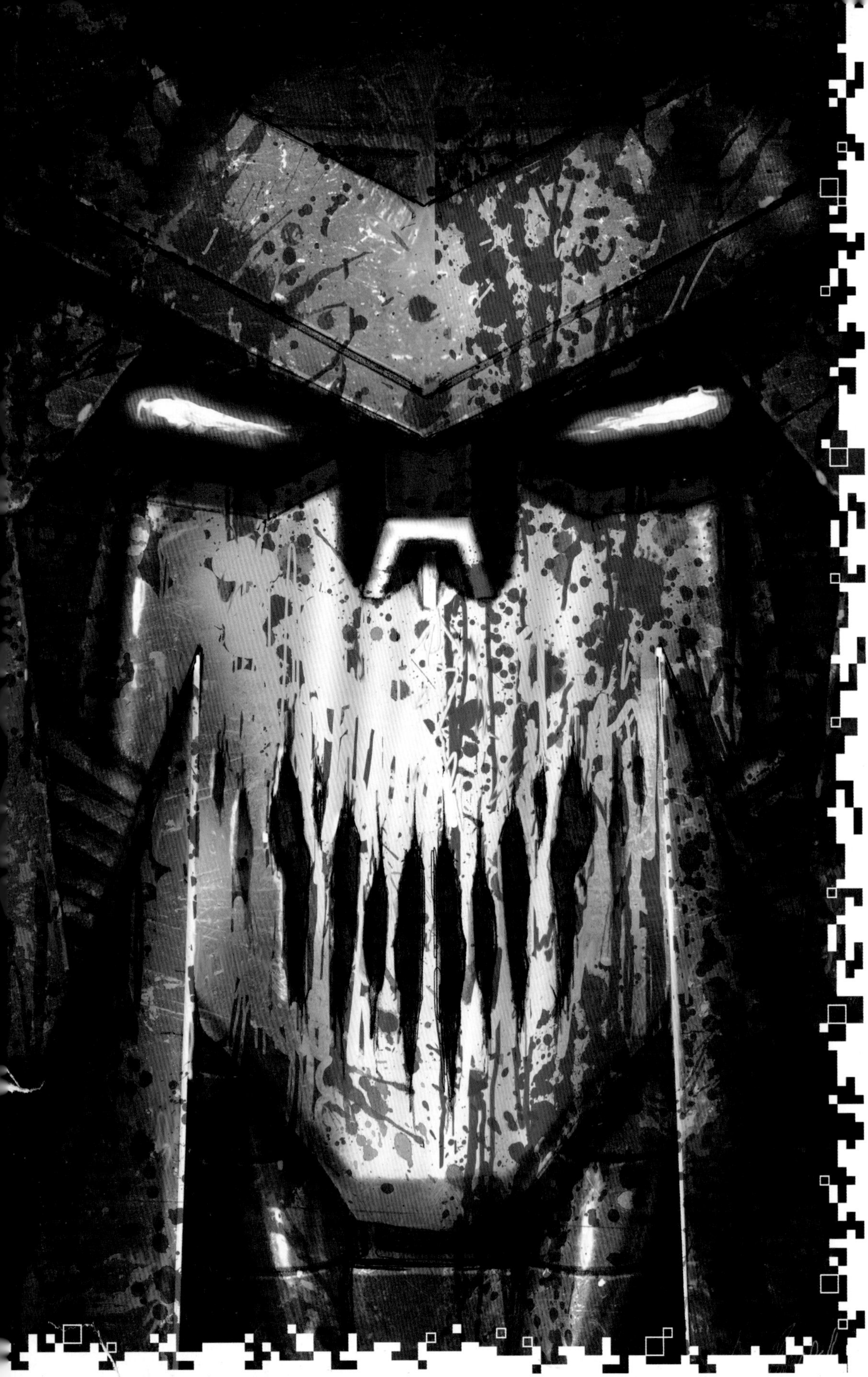

ROBOTS IN DISGUISE #10 COVER A
by **LIVIO RAMONDELLI**

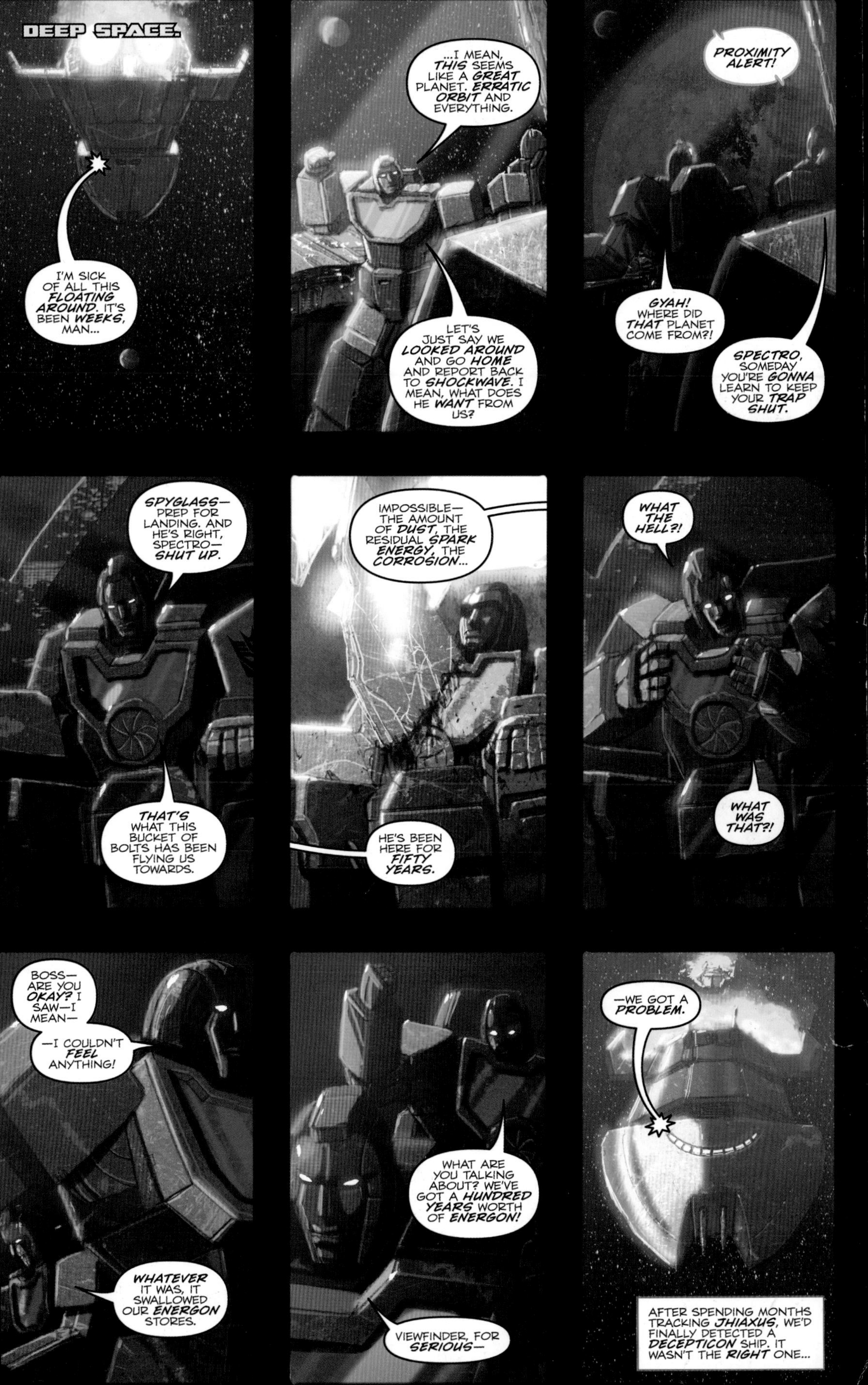
DEEP SPACE.
I'M SICK OF ALL THIS FLOATING AROUND. IT'S BEEN WEEKS, MAN...
...I MEAN, THIS SEEMS LIKE A GREAT PLANET. ERRATIC ORBIT AND EVERYTHING.
LET'S JUST SAY WE LOOKED AROUND AND GO HOME AND REPORT BACK TO SHOCKWAVE. I MEAN, WHAT DOES HE WANT FROM US?
PROXIMITY ALERT!
GYAH! WHERE DID THAT PLANET COME FROM?!
SPECTRO, SOMEDAY YOU'RE GONNA LEARN TO KEEP YOUR TRAP SHUT.
SPYGLASS— PREP FOR LANDING. AND HE'S RIGHT, SPECTRO— SHUT UP.
THAT'S WHAT THIS BUCKET OF BOLTS HAS BEEN FLYING US TOWARDS.
IMPOSSIBLE— THE AMOUNT OF DUST, THE RESIDUAL SPARK ENERGY, THE CORROSION...
HE'S BEEN HERE FOR FIFTY YEARS.
WHAT THE HELL?!
WHAT WAS THAT?!
BOSS— ARE YOU OKAY? I SAW—I MEAN—
—I COULDN'T FEEL ANYTHING!
WHATEVER IT WAS, IT SWALLOWED OUR ENERGON STORES.
WHAT ARE YOU TALKING ABOUT? WE'VE GOT A HUNDRED YEARS WORTH OF ENERGON!
VIEWFINDER, FOR SERIOUS—
—WE GOT A PROBLEM.
AFTER SPENDING MONTHS TRACKING JHIAXUS, WE'D FINALLY DETECTED A DECEPTICON SHIP. IT WASN'T THE RIGHT ONE...

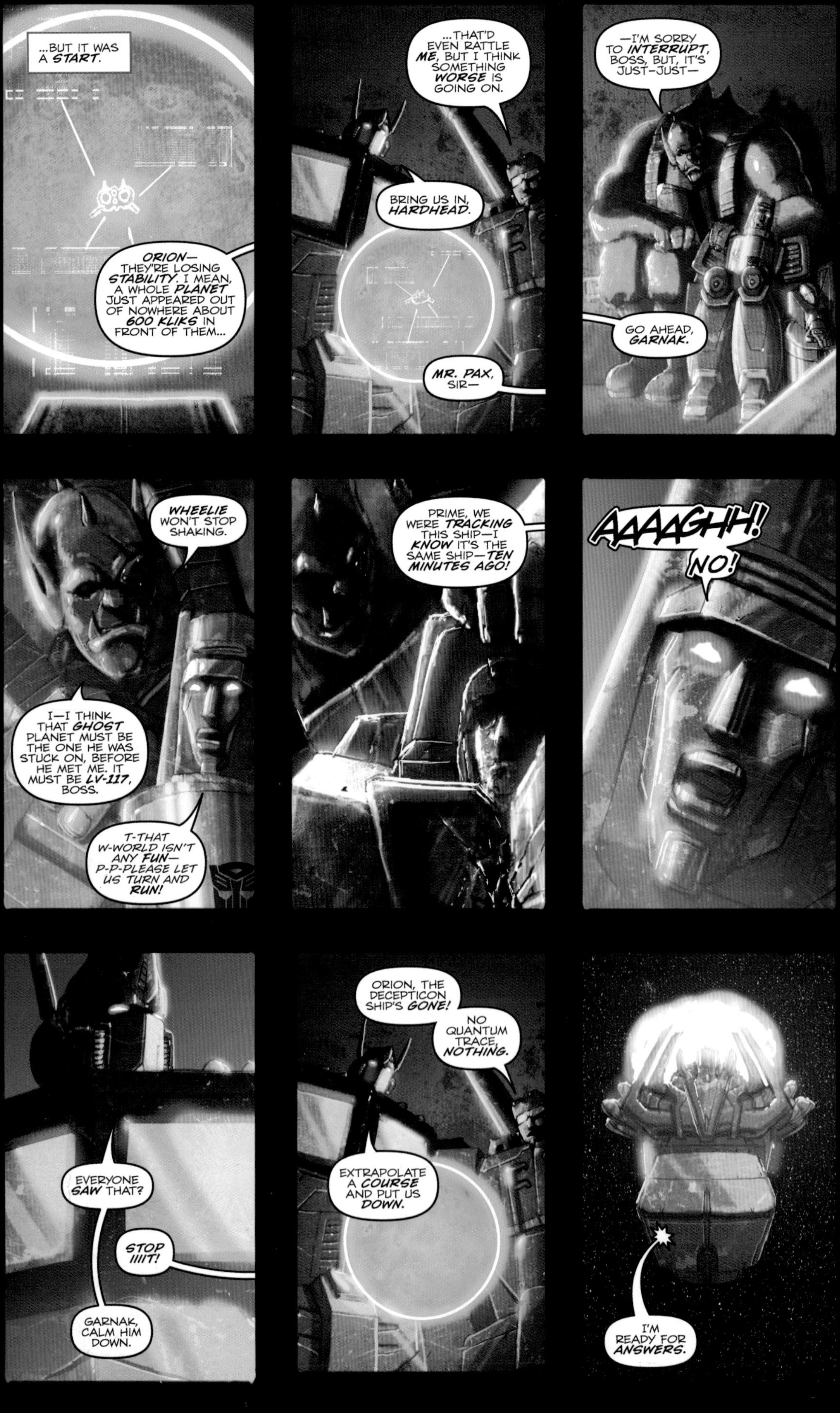

...BUT IT WAS A START.
ORION—THEY'RE LOSING STABILITY. I MEAN, A WHOLE PLANET JUST APPEARED OUT OF NOWHERE ABOUT 600 KLIKS IN FRONT OF THEM...
...THAT'D EVEN RATTLE ME, BUT I THINK SOMETHING WORSE IS GOING ON.
BRING US IN, HARDHEAD.
MR. PAX, SIR—
—I'M SORRY TO INTERRUPT, BOSS, BUT, IT'S JUST—JUST—
GO AHEAD, GARNAK.
WHEELIE WON'T STOP SHAKING.
I—I THINK THAT GHOST PLANET MUST BE THE ONE HE WAS STUCK ON, BEFORE HE MET ME. IT MUST BE LV-117, BOSS.
T-THAT W-WORLD ISN'T ANY FUN—P-P-PLEASE LET US TURN AND RUN!
PRIME, WE WERE TRACKING THIS SHIP—I KNOW IT'S THE SAME SHIP—TEN MINUTES AGO!
AAAAGHH!
NO!
EVERYONE SAW THAT?
STOP IIIIT!
GARNAK, CALM HIM DOWN.
ORION, THE DECEPTICON SHIP'S GONE!
NO QUANTUM TRACE, NOTHING.
EXTRAPOLATE A COURSE AND PUT US DOWN.
I'M READY FOR ANSWERS.

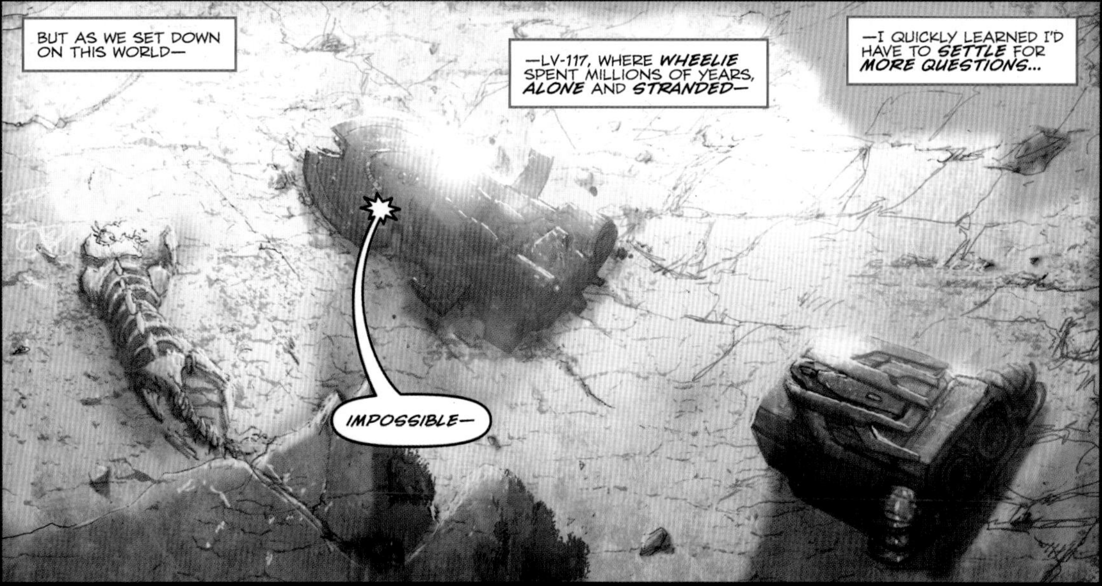
BUT AS WE SET DOWN ON THIS WORLD—
—LV-117, WHERE WHEELIE SPENT MILLIONS OF YEARS, ALONE AND STRANDED—
—I QUICKLY LEARNED I'D HAVE TO SETTLE FOR MORE QUESTIONS...
IMPOSSIBLE—

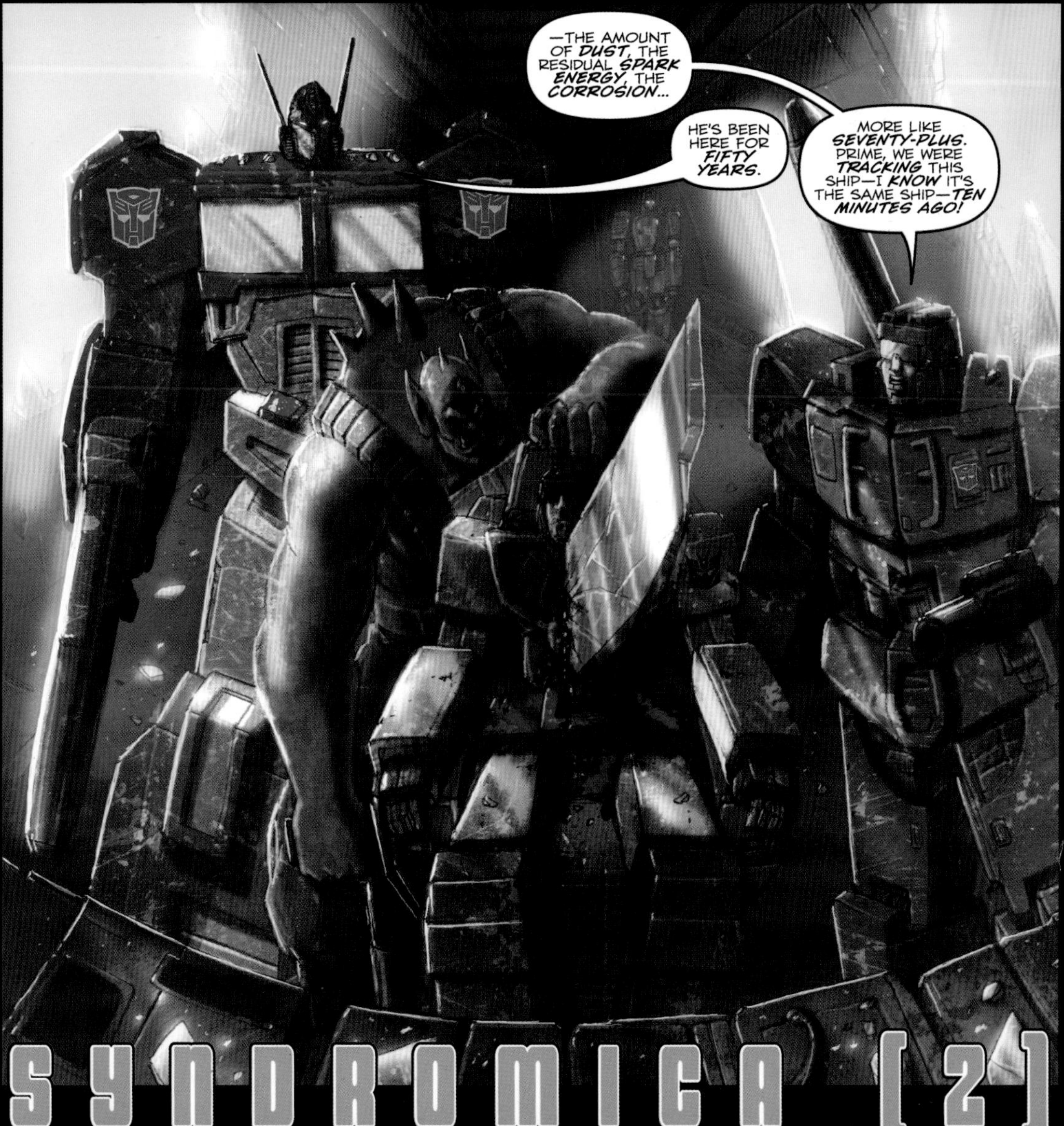
—THE AMOUNT OF DUST, THE RESIDUAL SPARK ENERGY, THE CORROSION...
HE'S BEEN HERE FOR FIFTY YEARS.
MORE LIKE SEVENTY-PLUS. PRIME, WE WERE TRACKING THIS SHIP—I KNOW IT'S THE SAME SHIP—TEN MINUTES AGO!
SYNDROMICA [2]

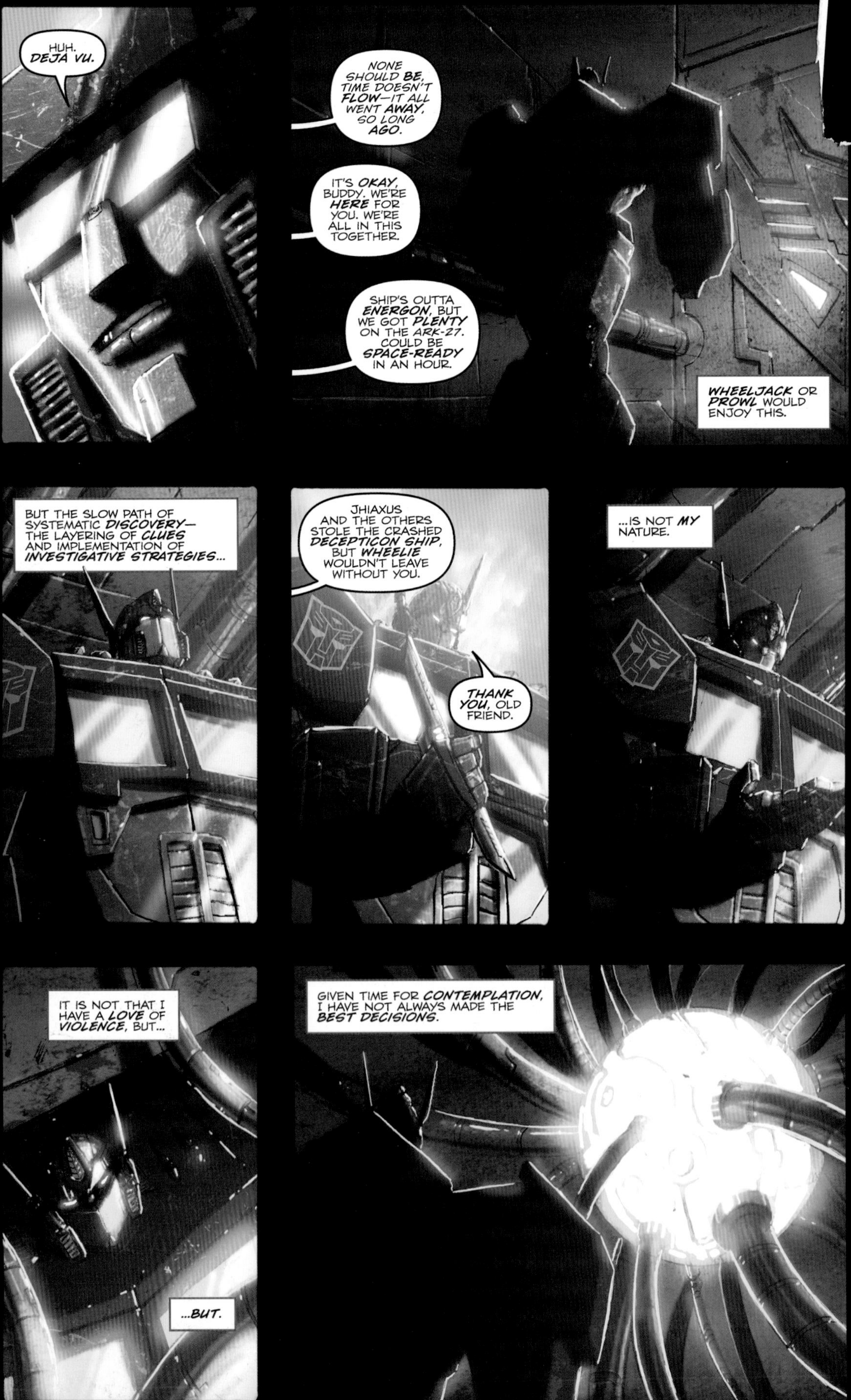
HUH. DEJA VU.
NONE SHOULD BE. TIME DOESN'T FLOW—IT ALL WENT AWAY, SO LONG AGO.
IT'S OKAY, BUDDY. WE'RE HERE FOR YOU. WE'RE ALL IN THIS TOGETHER.
SHIP'S OUTTA ENERGON, BUT WE GOT PLENTY ON THE ARK-27. COULD BE SPACE-READY IN AN HOUR.
WHEELJACK OR PROWL WOULD ENJOY THIS.
BUT THE SLOW PATH OF SYSTEMATIC DISCOVERY— THE LAYERING OF CLUES AND IMPLEMENTATION OF INVESTIGATIVE STRATEGIES...
JHIAXUS AND THE OTHERS STOLE THE CRASHED DECEPTICON SHIP, BUT WHEELIE WOULDN'T LEAVE WITHOUT YOU.
THANK YOU, OLD FRIEND.
...IS NOT MY NATURE.
IT IS NOT THAT I HAVE A LOVE OF VIOLENCE, BUT...
...BUT.
GIVEN TIME FOR CONTEMPLATION, I HAVE NOT ALWAYS MADE THE BEST DECISIONS.

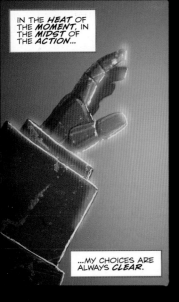

IN THE *HEAT* OF THE *MOMENT*, IN THE *MIDST* OF THE *ACTION*...

...MY CHOICES ARE ALWAYS *CLEAR*.

I JUST NEED SOMETHING TO *HAPPEN*.

FOLLOW ME— FOLLOW YOUR *MASTER*—

*RAAAGH—*

—YOU'RE TOO *LATE*—

—THE *DEVICE* IS ACTIVATED.

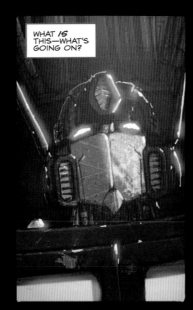

WHAT *IS* THIS—WHAT'S GOING ON?

MY GREATEST STUDENT, *SHOCKWAVE*, SENT *BLUDGEON* AND MONSTRUCTOR ON THIS QUEST.

FOLLOW!

UNN.

THE *SPHERE*... WHATEVER *HAPPENED* CAME FROM THE SPHERE... AND I FEEL AS I DID AFTER WE REVIVED *CYBERTRON*—AFTER THE *CHAOS* EVENT...

...AFTER I WAS *KNOCKED* THROUGH *TIME*.

HM.

*RRRRR—*

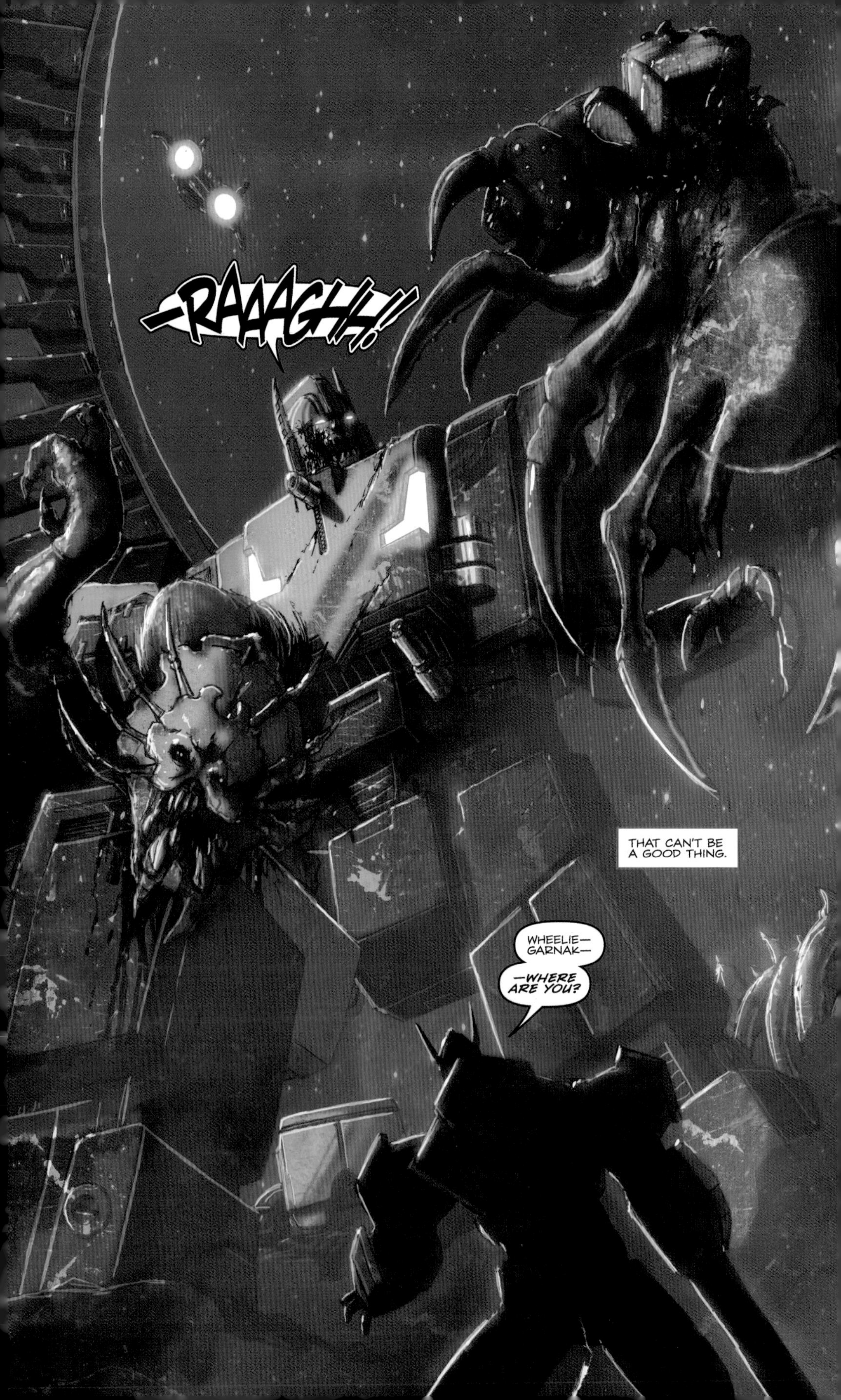
-RAAAGH!!
THAT CAN'T BE A GOOD THING.
WHEELIE—GARNAK—
—WHERE ARE YOU?

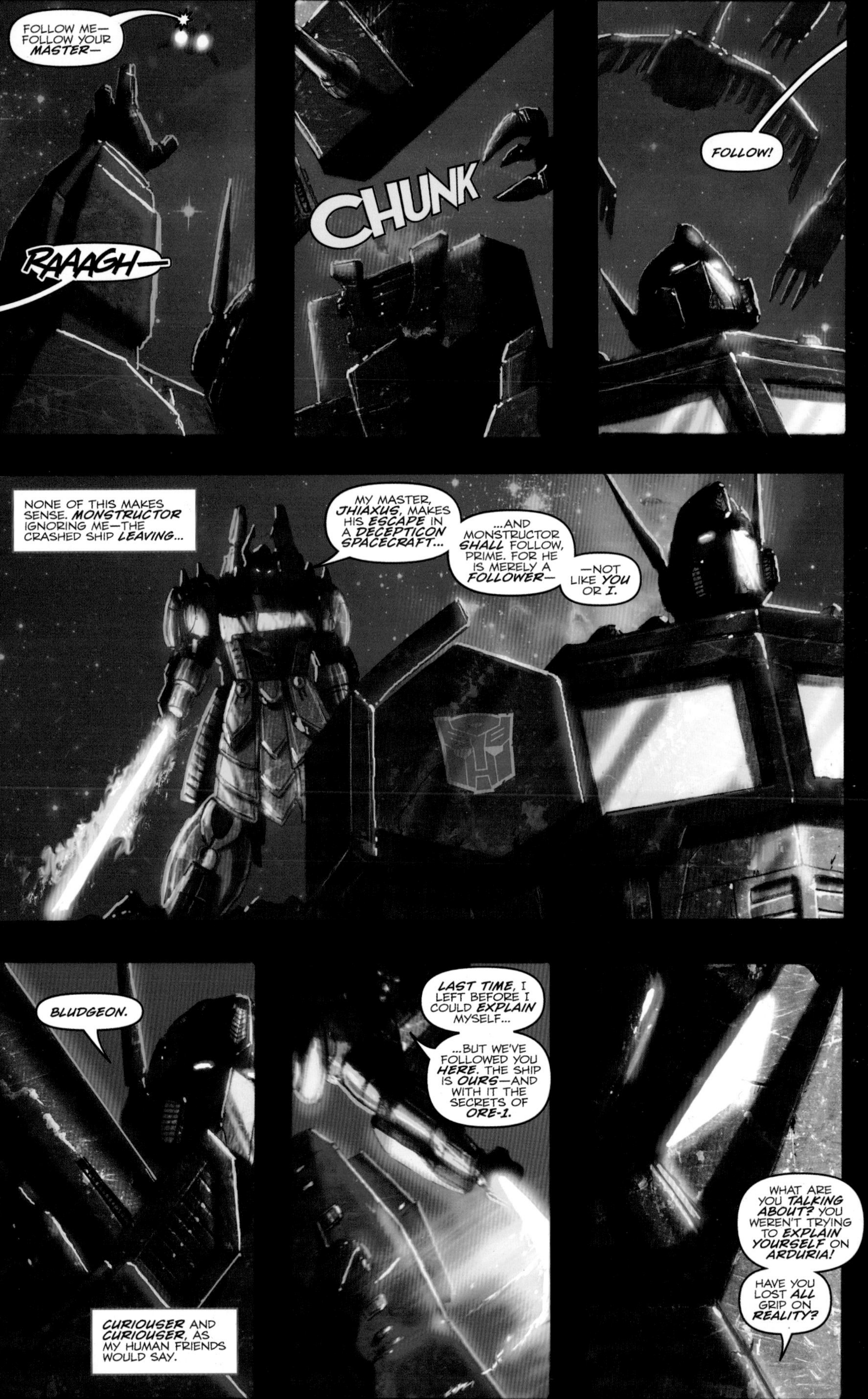
FOLLOW ME—FOLLOW YOUR MASTER—
RAAAGH—
CHUNK
FOLLOW!
NONE OF THIS MAKES SENSE. MONSTRUCTOR IGNORING ME—THE CRASHED SHIP LEAVING...
MY MASTER, JHIAXUS, MAKES HIS ESCAPE IN A DECEPTICON SPACECRAFT...
...AND MONSTRUCTOR SHALL FOLLOW, PRIME. FOR HE IS MERELY A FOLLOWER—
—NOT LIKE YOU OR I.
BLUDGEON.
CURIOUSER AND CURIOUSER, AS MY HUMAN FRIENDS WOULD SAY.
LAST TIME, I LEFT BEFORE I COULD EXPLAIN MYSELF...
...BUT WE'VE FOLLOWED YOU HERE. THE SHIP IS OURS—AND WITH IT THE SECRETS OF ORE-1.
WHAT ARE YOU TALKING ABOUT? YOU WEREN'T TRYING TO EXPLAIN YOURSELF ON ARDURIA!
HAVE YOU LOST ALL GRIP ON REALITY?

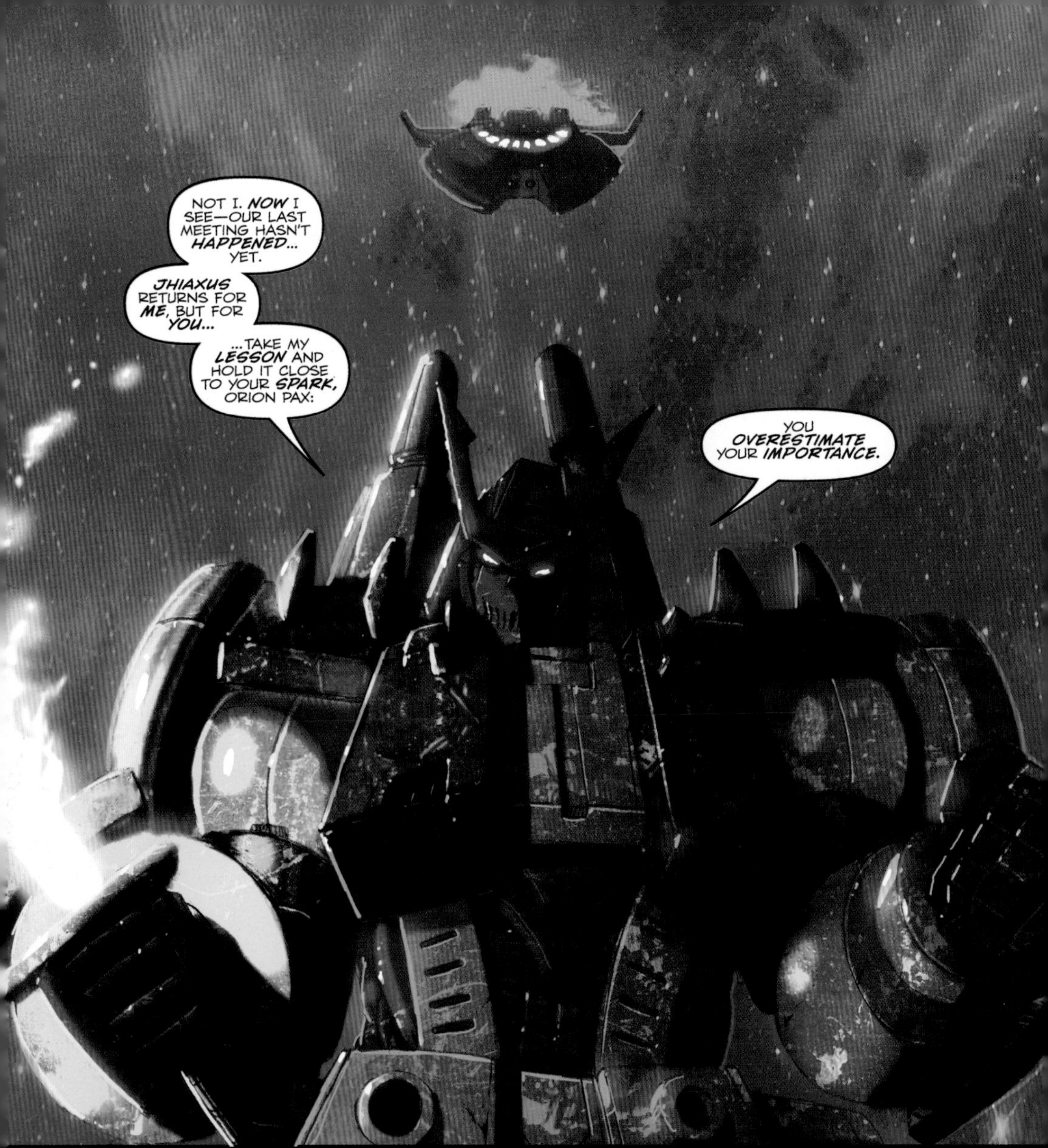
NOT I. NOW I SEE—OUR LAST MEETING HASN'T HAPPENED... YET.
JHIAXUS RETURNS FOR ME, BUT FOR YOU...
...TAKE MY LESSON AND HOLD IT CLOSE TO YOUR SPARK, ORION PAX:
YOU OVERESTIMATE YOUR IMPORTANCE.

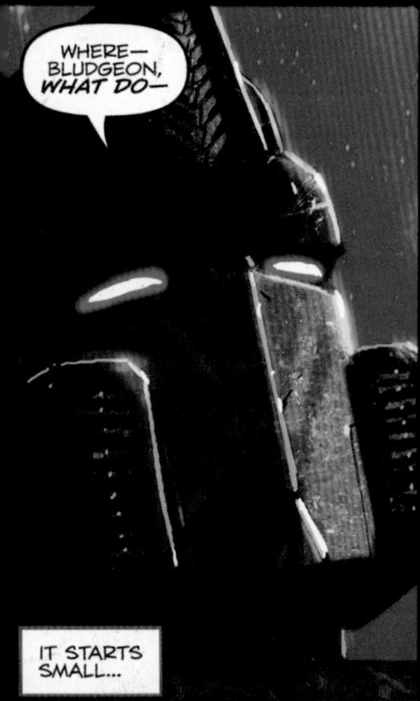
WHERE—BLUDGEON, WHAT DO—
IT STARTS SMALL...

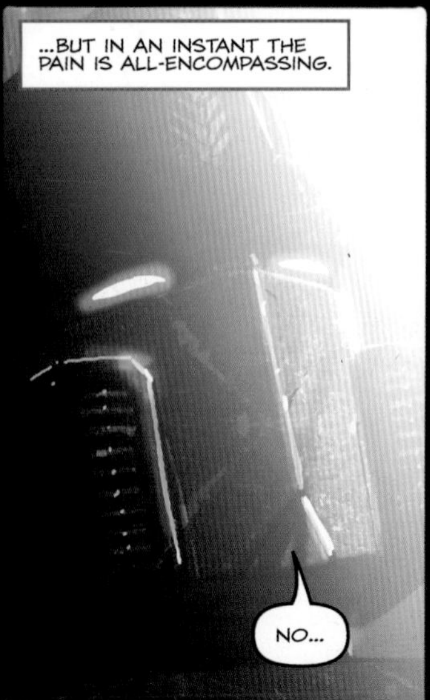
...BUT IN AN INSTANT THE PAIN IS ALL-ENCOMPASSING.
NO...

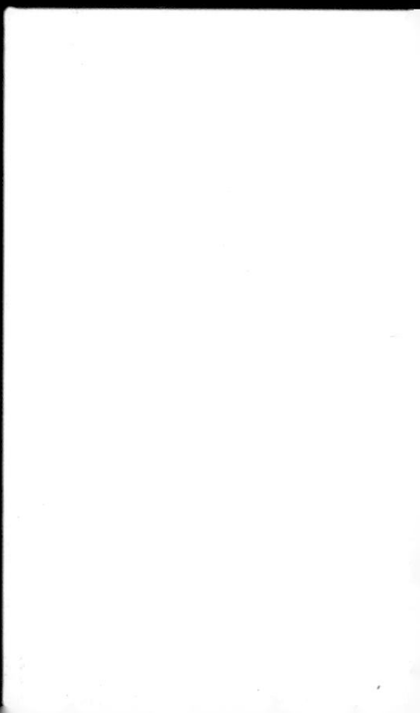

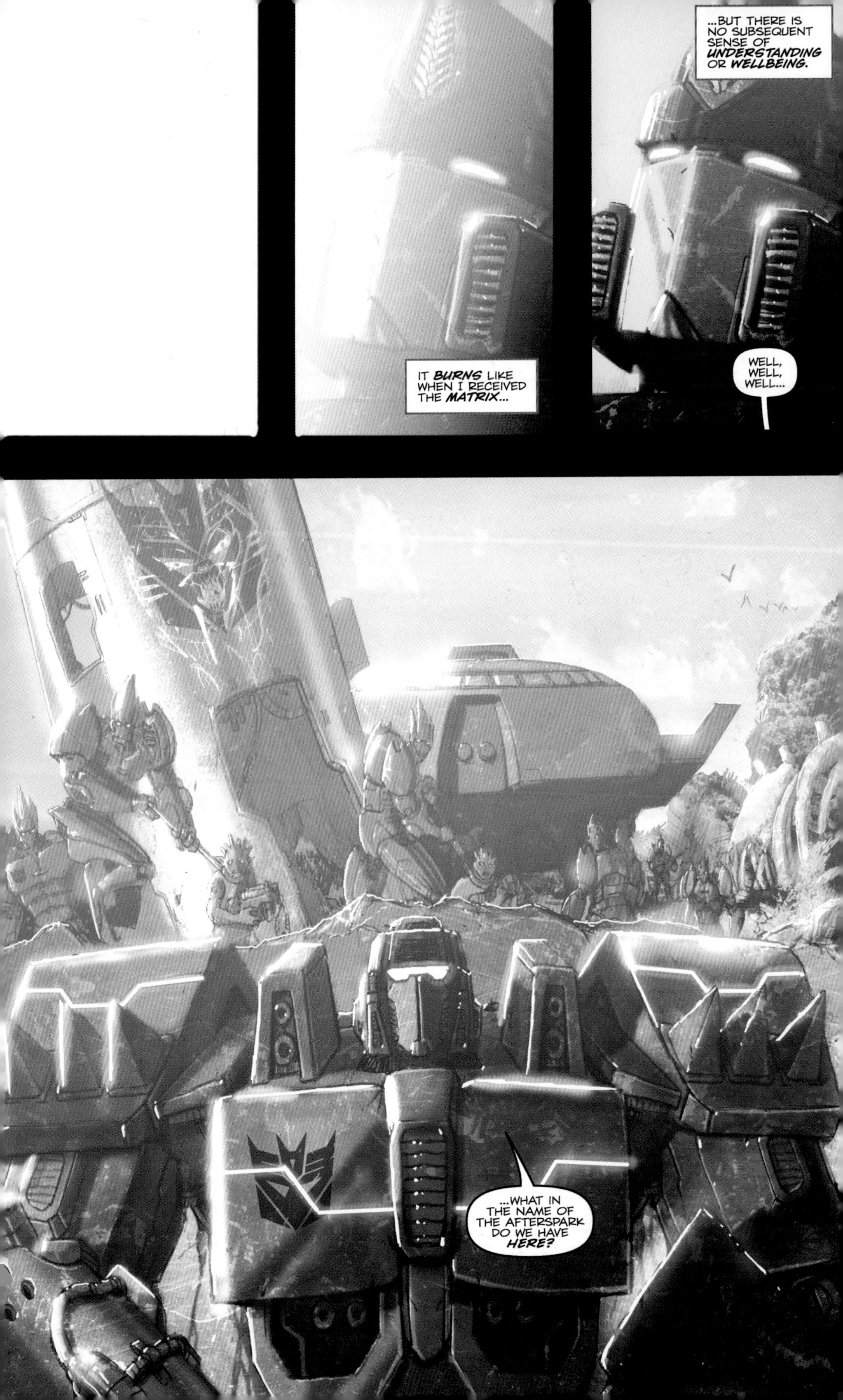
IT BURNS LIKE WHEN I RECEIVED THE MATRIX...
...BUT THERE IS NO SUBSEQUENT SENSE OF UNDERSTANDING OR WELLBEING.
WELL, WELL, WELL...
...WHAT IN THE NAME OF THE AFTERSPARK DO WE HAVE HERE?

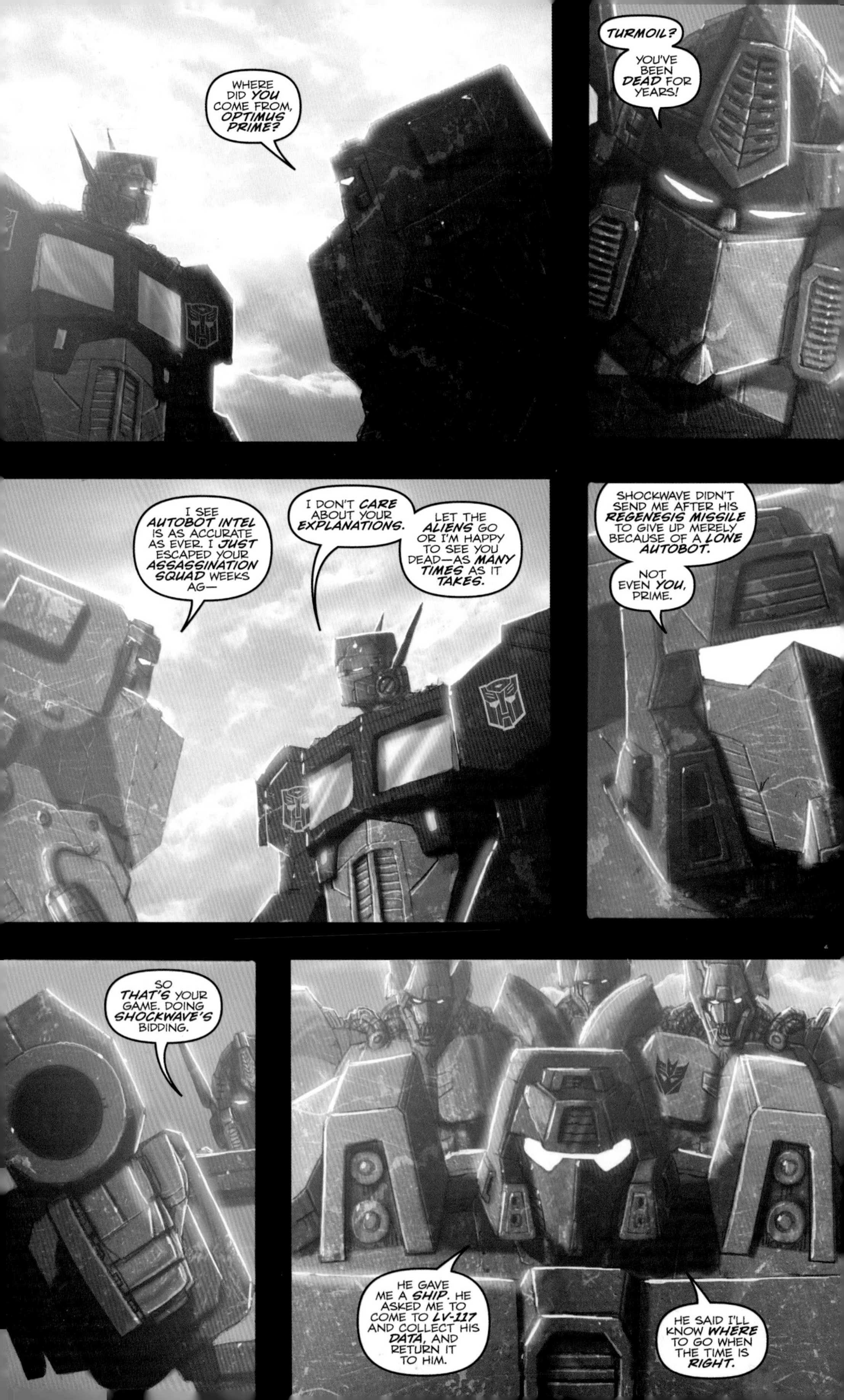
WHERE DID YOU COME FROM, OPTIMUS PRIME?
TURMOIL?
YOU'VE BEEN DEAD FOR YEARS!
I SEE AUTOBOT INTEL IS AS ACCURATE AS EVER. I JUST ESCAPED YOUR ASSASSINATION SQUAD WEEKS AG—
I DON'T CARE ABOUT YOUR EXPLANATIONS.
LET THE ALIENS GO OR I'M HAPPY TO SEE YOU DEAD—AS MANY TIMES AS IT TAKES.
SHOCKWAVE DIDN'T SEND ME AFTER HIS REGENESIS MISSILE TO GIVE UP MERELY BECAUSE OF A LONE AUTOBOT.
NOT EVEN YOU, PRIME.
SO THAT'S YOUR GAME. DOING SHOCKWAVE'S BIDDING.
HE GAVE ME A SHIP. HE ASKED ME TO COME TO LV-117 AND COLLECT HIS DATA, AND RETURN IT TO HIM.
HE SAID I'LL KNOW WHERE TO GO WHEN THE TIME IS RIGHT.

AND YOU TELL ME THIS *BECAUSE*...

BECAUSE HE SAID ANYTHING I *FIND* IS MINE TO DO WITH AS I *PLEASE*...

...ANYTHING I FIND.

TURMOIL ASSUMED A TRIBE OF *NATIVES* WHO'D SPENT GENERATIONS *MASTERING* SHOCKWAVE'S TECHNOLOGY WOULD BE ALL THAT WAS HERE—

—BUT THEN, TURMOIL IS A *FOOL*.

BLUDGEON—WITH *DEATH* AT HIS HEELS. BUT WHAT HAS HE *TAKEN* FROM THAT CREATURE?

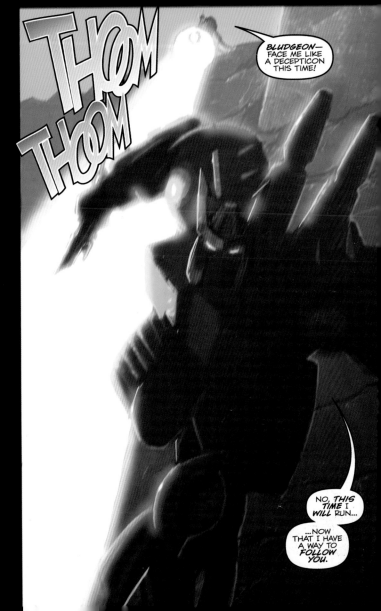

THOOM THOOM

BLUDGEON— FACE ME LIKE A *DECEPTICON* THIS TIME!

NO, *THIS TIME* I *WILL* RUN...

...NOW THAT I HAVE A WAY TO *FOLLOW* YOU.

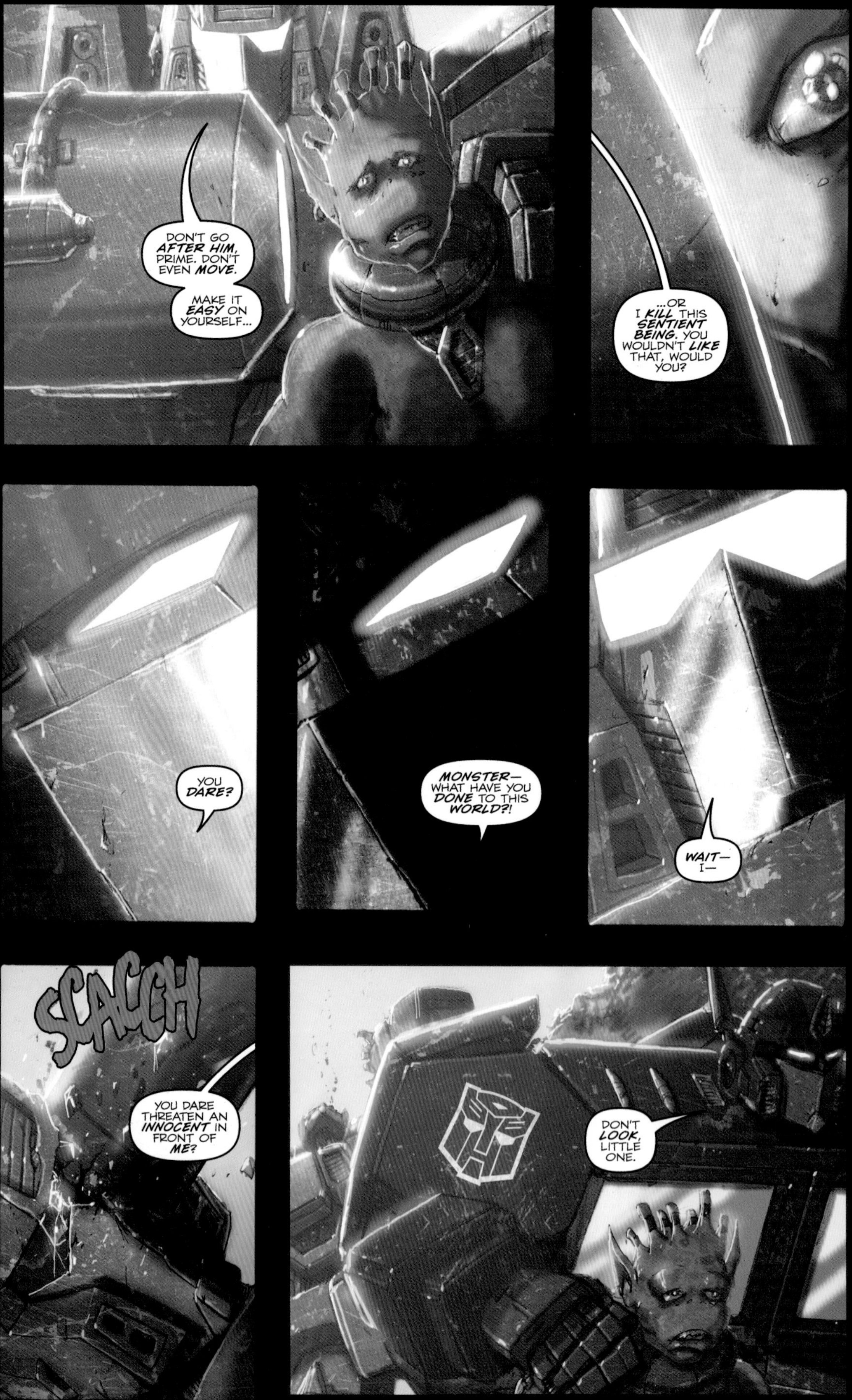
DON'T GO AFTER HIM, PRIME. DON'T EVEN MOVE.
MAKE IT EASY ON YOURSELF...
...OR I KILL THIS SENTIENT BEING. YOU WOULDN'T LIKE THAT, WOULD YOU?
YOU DARE?
MONSTER— WHAT HAVE YOU DONE TO THIS WORLD?!
WAIT— I—
SCACCH
YOU DARE THREATEN AN INNOCENT IN FRONT OF ME?
DON'T LOOK, LITTLE ONE.

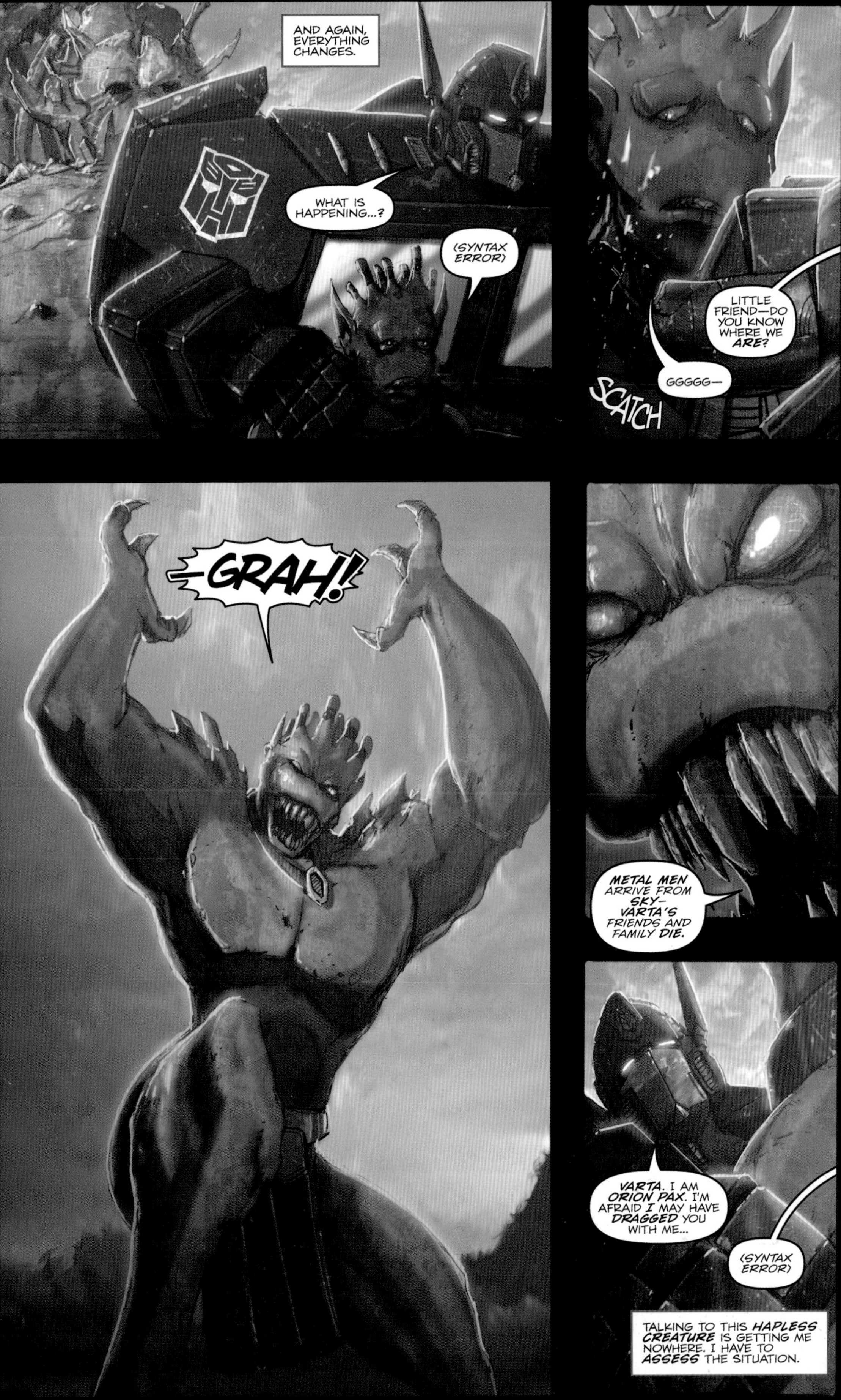
AND AGAIN, EVERYTHING CHANGES.
WHAT IS HAPPENING...?
(SYNTAX ERROR)
LITTLE FRIEND—DO YOU KNOW WHERE WE ARE?
GGGGG—
SCATCH
—GRAH!
METAL MEN ARRIVE FROM SKY—VARTA'S FRIENDS AND FAMILY DIE.
VARTA. I AM ORION PAX. I'M AFRAID I MAY HAVE DRAGGED YOU WITH ME...
(SYNTAX ERROR)
TALKING TO THIS HAPLESS CREATURE IS GETTING ME NOWHERE. I HAVE TO ASSESS THE SITUATION.

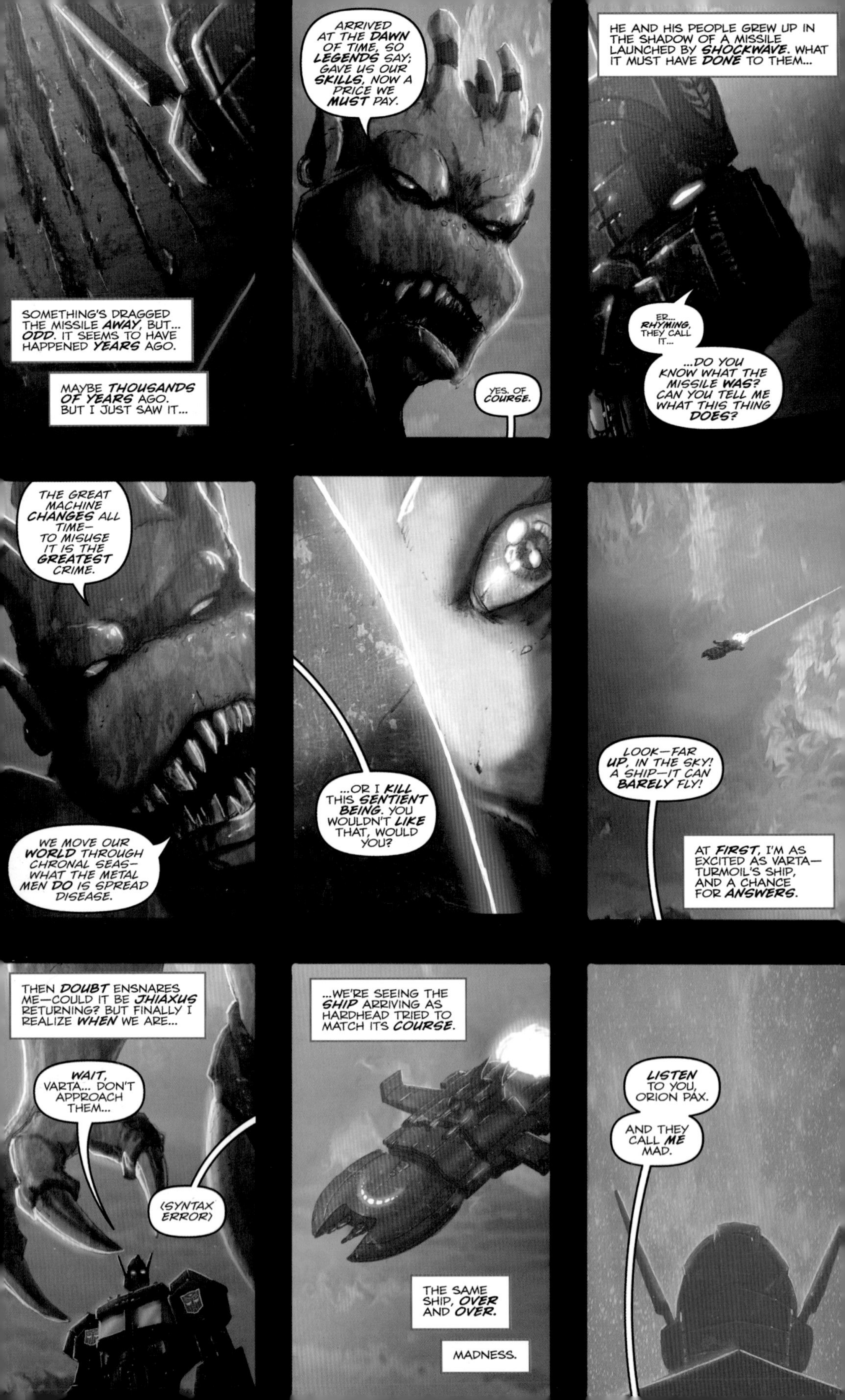
SOMETHING'S DRAGGED THE MISSILE AWAY, BUT... ODD. IT SEEMS TO HAVE HAPPENED YEARS AGO.
MAYBE THOUSANDS OF YEARS AGO. BUT I JUST SAW IT...
ARRIVED AT THE DAWN OF TIME, SO LEGENDS SAY; GAVE US OUR SKILLS, NOW A PRICE WE MUST PAY.
YES. OF COURSE.
HE AND HIS PEOPLE GREW UP IN THE SHADOW OF A MISSILE LAUNCHED BY SHOCKWAVE. WHAT IT MUST HAVE DONE TO THEM...
ER... RHYMING, THEY CALL IT...
...DO YOU KNOW WHAT THE MISSILE WAS? CAN YOU TELL ME WHAT THIS THING DOES?
THE GREAT MACHINE CHANGES ALL TIME— TO MISUSE IT IS THE GREATEST CRIME.
WE MOVE OUR WORLD THROUGH CHRONAL SEAS— WHAT THE METAL MEN DO IS SPREAD DISEASE.
...OR I KILL THIS SENTIENT BEING. YOU WOULDN'T LIKE THAT, WOULD YOU?
LOOK—FAR UP, IN THE SKY! A SHIP—IT CAN BARELY FLY!
AT FIRST, I'M AS EXCITED AS VARTA— TURMOIL'S SHIP, AND A CHANCE FOR ANSWERS.
THEN DOUBT ENSNARES ME—COULD IT BE JHIAXUS RETURNING? BUT FINALLY I REALIZE WHEN WE ARE...
WAIT, VARTA... DON'T APPROACH THEM...
(SYNTAX ERROR)
...WE'RE SEEING THE SHIP ARRIVING AS HARDHEAD TRIED TO MATCH ITS COURSE.
THE SAME SHIP, OVER AND OVER.
MADNESS.
LISTEN TO YOU, ORION PAX.
AND THEY CALL ME MAD.

BLUDGEON! I THOUGHT YOU RAN HOME, COWARD!
I NEVER RUN FROM AUTOBOTS.
YOU SET ME ADRIFT— YOU SENT US FALLING THROUGH TIME.
I DON'T KNOW WHAT—
—NO. I'M NOT PLAYING YOUR GAME, MADMAN.
WHERE DID VARTA GO? WHERE IS JHIAXUS? AND WHY DID YOU LEAD ME HERE?
WHY WAS JHIAXUS CALLING MY NAME WHEN HE WAS OUR PRISONER?
UHNF!
CALLING YOUR NAME...?
AH. YOU FLATTER YOURSELF, AUTOBOT.

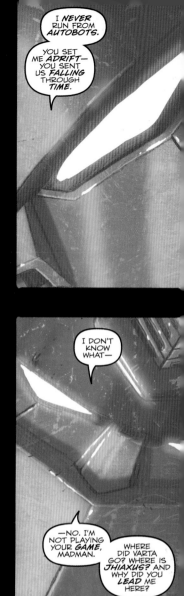

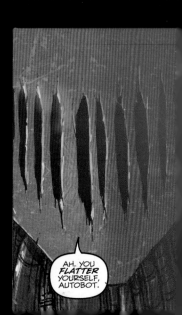

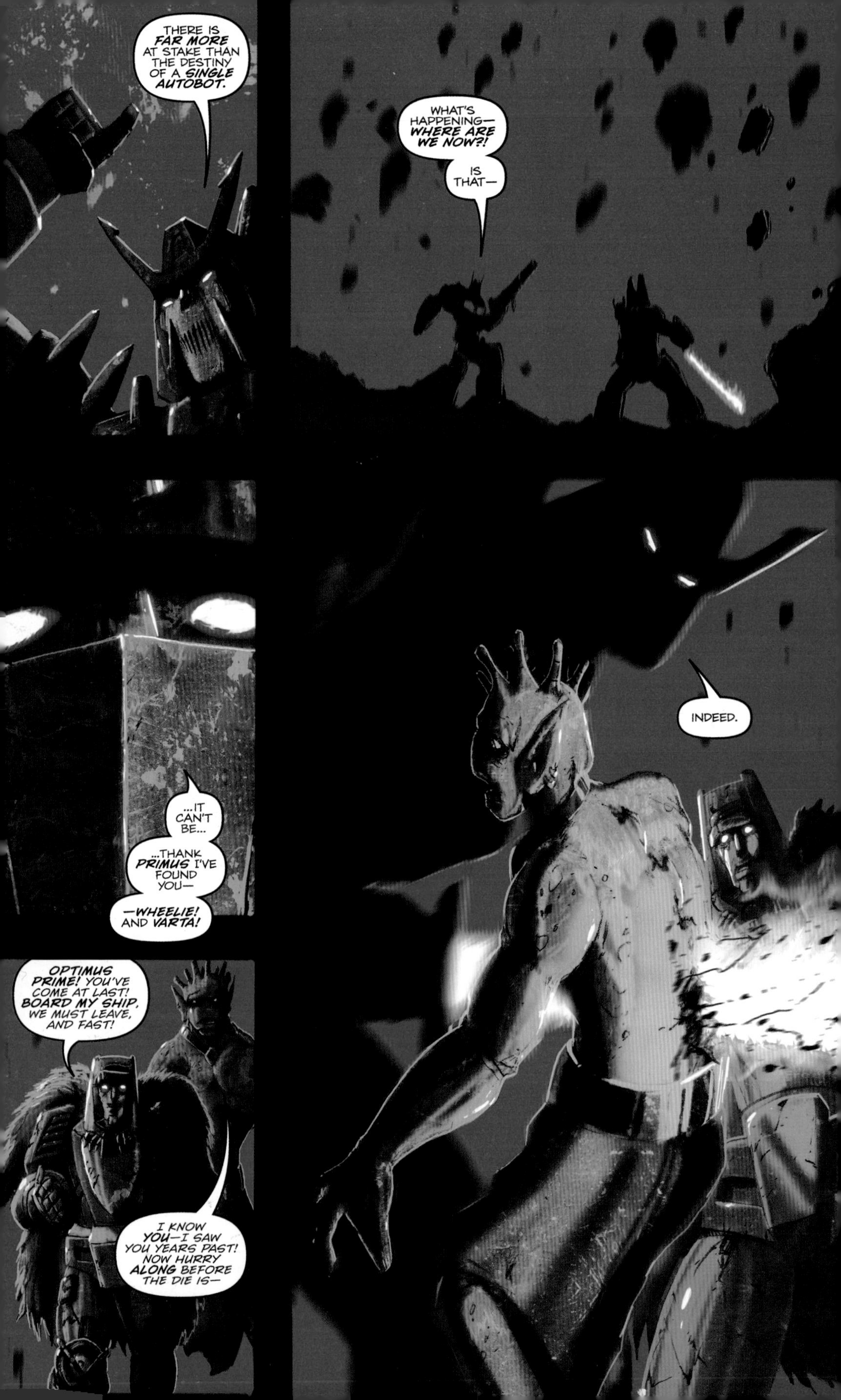
THERE IS FAR MORE AT STAKE THAN THE DESTINY OF A SINGLE AUTOBOT.
WHAT'S HAPPENING— WHERE ARE WE NOW?!
IS THAT—
...IT CAN'T BE...
...THANK PRIMUS I'VE FOUND YOU—
—WHEELIE! AND VARTA!
INDEED.
OPTIMUS PRIME! YOU'VE COME AT LAST! BOARD MY SHIP, WE MUST LEAVE, AND FAST!
I KNOW YOU—I SAW YOU YEARS PAST! NOW HURRY ALONG BEFORE THE DIE IS—

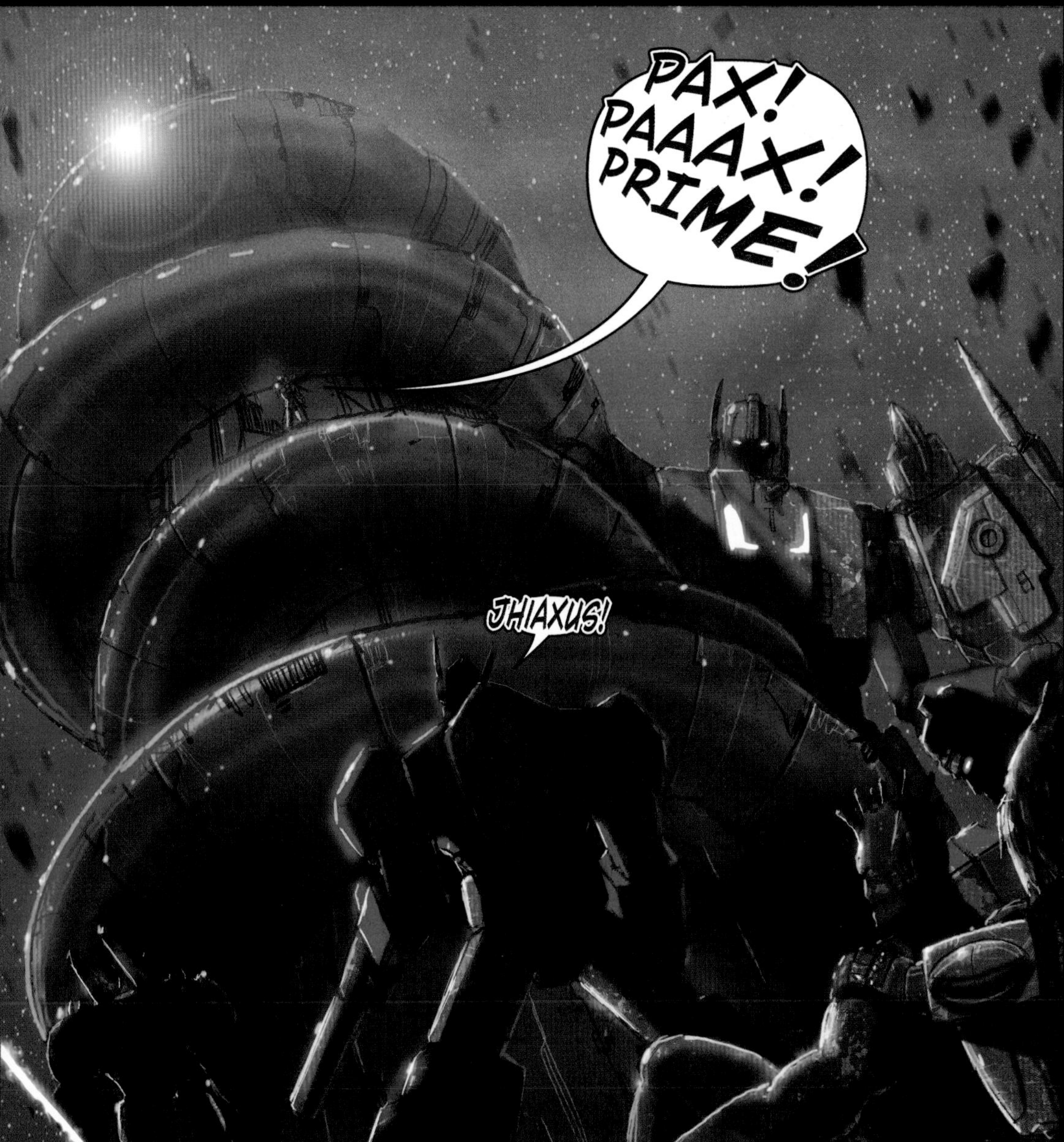
PAX! PAAAX! PRIME!
JHIAXUS!

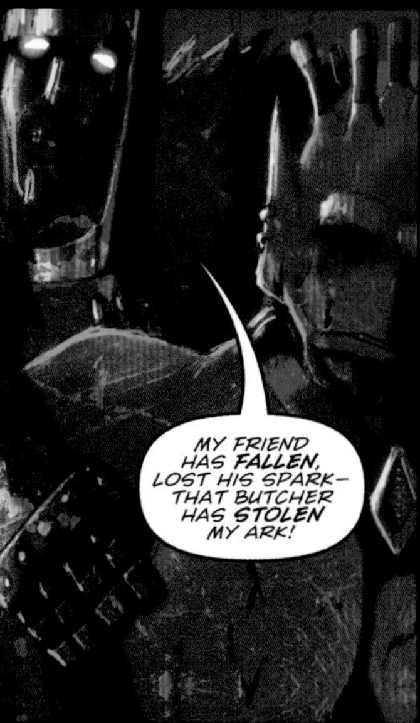
MY FRIEND HAS FALLEN, LOST HIS SPARK— THAT BUTCHER HAS STOLEN MY ARK!

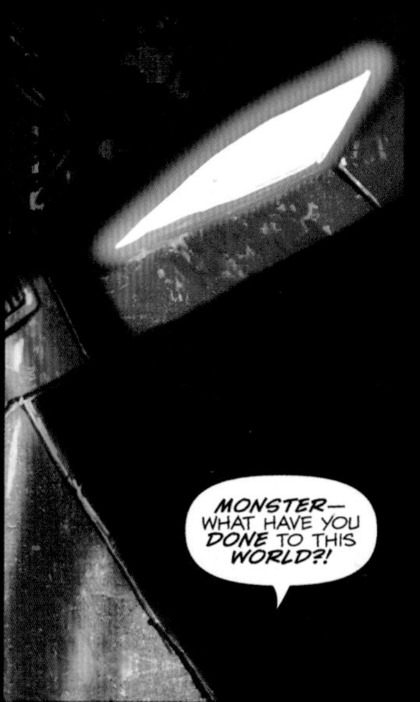
MONSTER— WHAT HAVE YOU DONE TO THIS WORLD?!

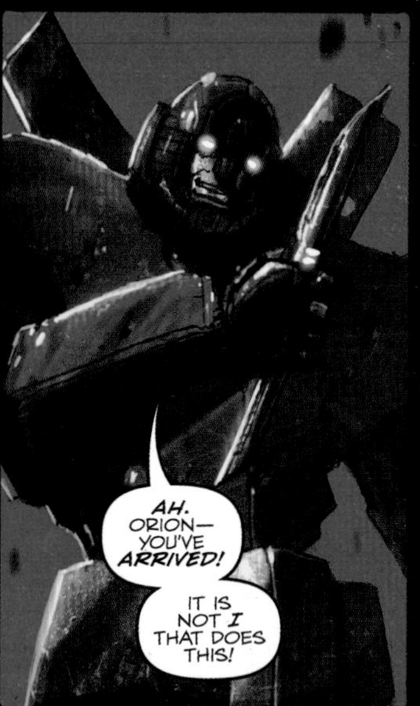
AH. ORION— YOU'VE ARRIVED!
IT IS NOT I THAT DOES THIS!

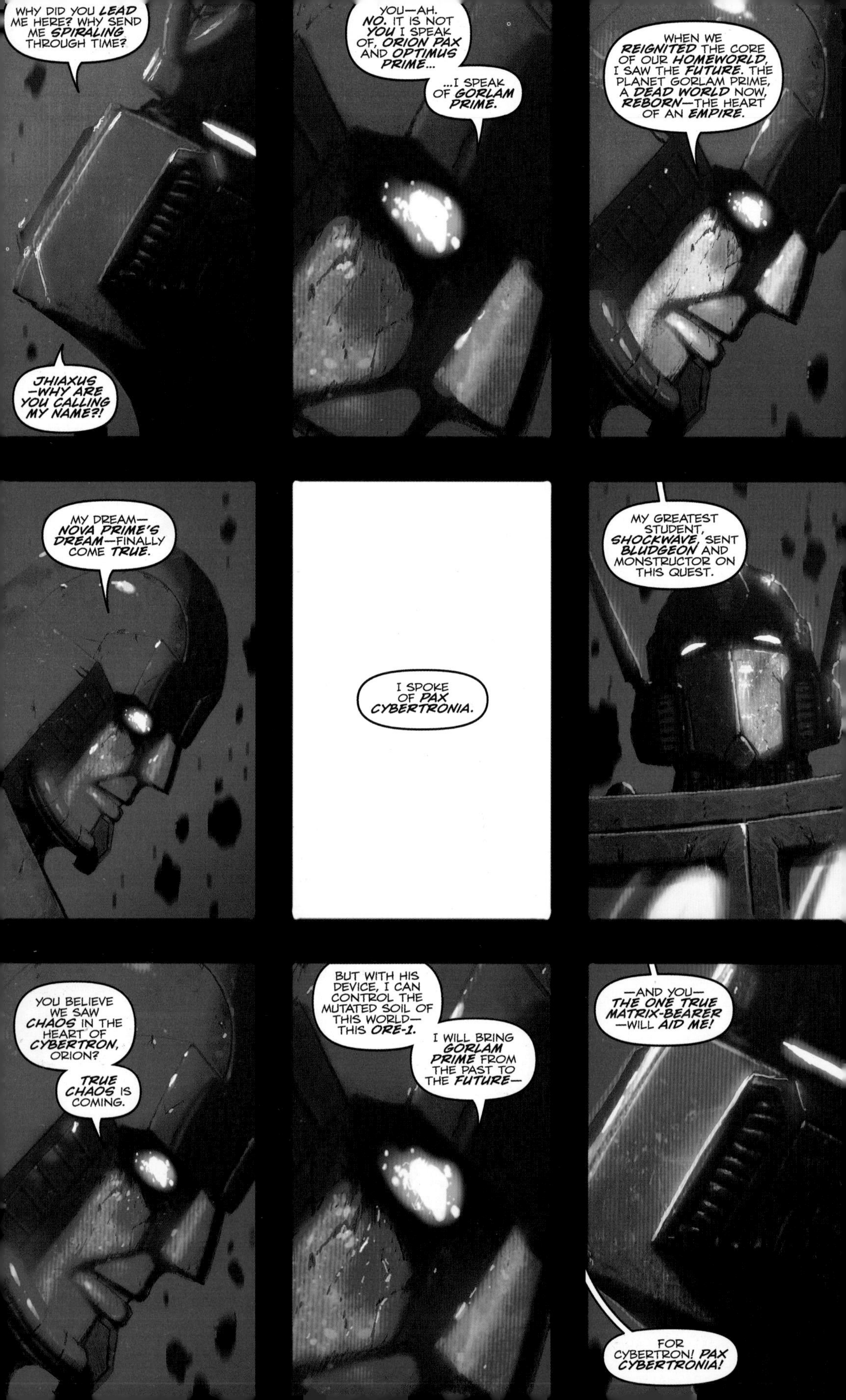
WHY DID YOU LEAD ME HERE? WHY SEND ME SPIRALING THROUGH TIME?
JHIAXUS—WHY ARE YOU CALLING MY NAME?!
YOU—AH. NO. IT IS NOT YOU I SPEAK OF, ORION PAX AND OPTIMUS PRIME...
...I SPEAK OF GORLAM PRIME.
WHEN WE REIGNITED THE CORE OF OUR HOMEWORLD, I SAW THE FUTURE. THE PLANET GORLAM PRIME, A DEAD WORLD NOW, REBORN—THE HEART OF AN EMPIRE.
MY DREAM—NOVA PRIME'S DREAM—FINALLY COME TRUE.
I SPOKE OF PAX CYBERTRONIA.
MY GREATEST STUDENT, SHOCKWAVE, SENT BLUDGEON AND MONSTRUCTOR ON THIS QUEST.
YOU BELIEVE WE SAW CHAOS IN THE HEART OF CYBERTRON, ORION?
TRUE CHAOS IS COMING.
BUT WITH HIS DEVICE, I CAN CONTROL THE MUTATED SOIL OF THIS WORLD—THIS ORE-1.
I WILL BRING GORLAM PRIME FROM THE PAST TO THE FUTURE—
—AND YOU—THE ONE TRUE MATRIX-BEARER—WILL AID ME!
FOR CYBERTRON! PAX CYBERTRONIA!

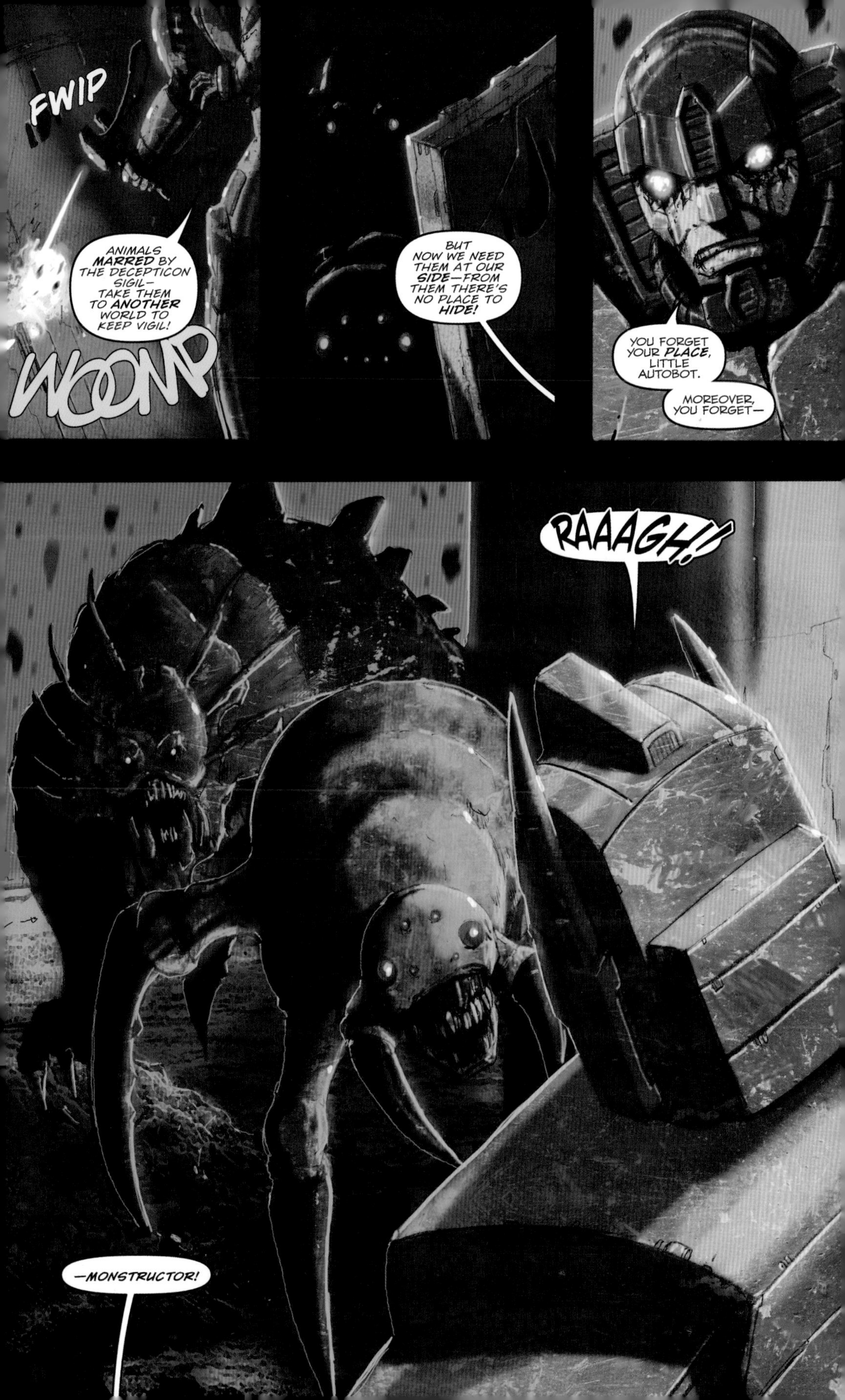
FWIP
ANIMALS MARRED BY THE DECEPTICON SIGIL— TAKE THEM TO ANOTHER WORLD TO KEEP VIGIL!
WOOMP
BUT NOW WE NEED THEM AT OUR SIDE—FROM THEM THERE'S NO PLACE TO HIDE!
YOU FORGET YOUR PLACE, LITTLE AUTOBOT.
MOREOVER, YOU FORGET—
RAAAGH!!
—MONSTRUCTOR!

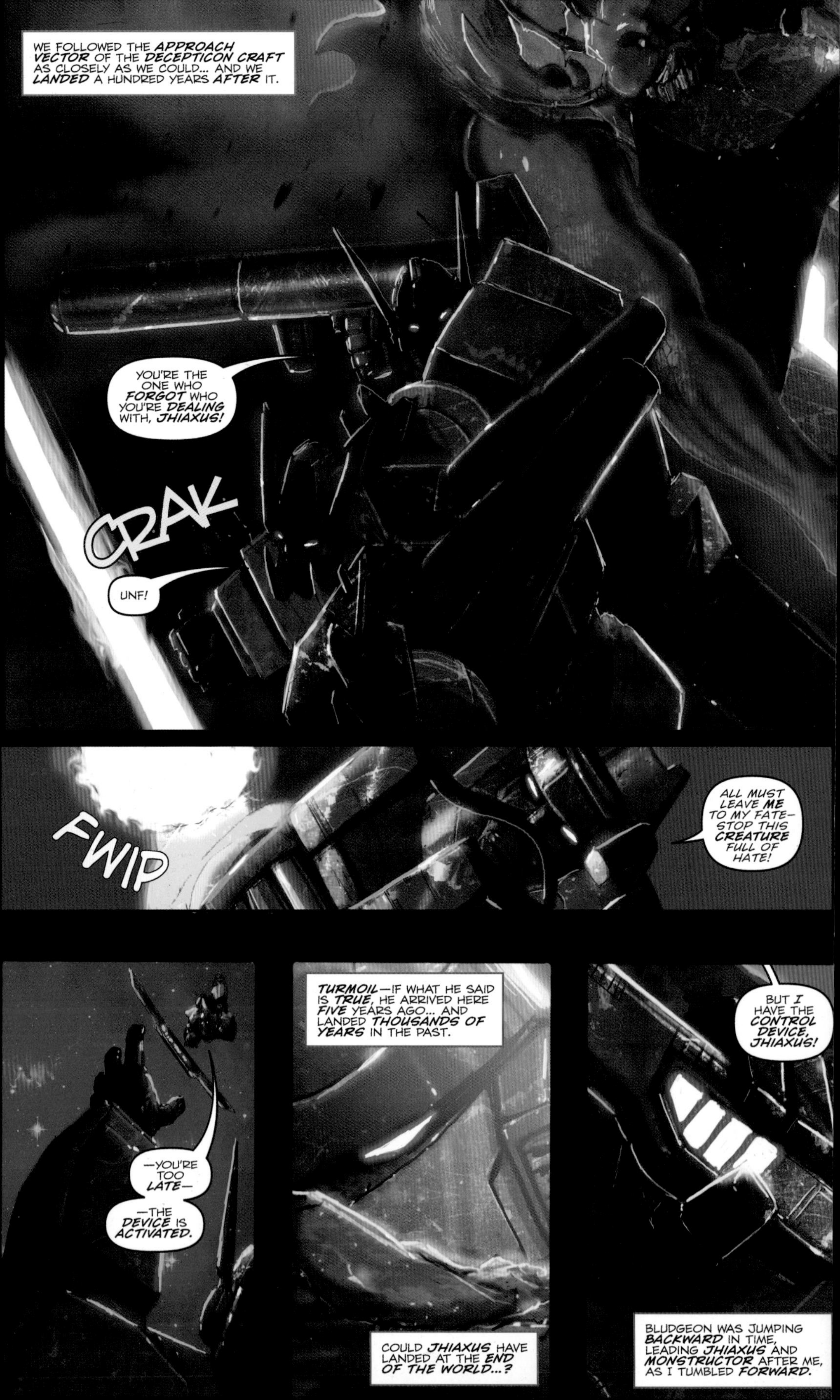

WE FOLLOWED THE APPROACH VECTOR OF THE DECEPTICON CRAFT AS CLOSELY AS WE COULD... AND WE LANDED A HUNDRED YEARS AFTER IT.
YOU'RE THE ONE WHO FORGOT WHO YOU'RE DEALING WITH, JHIAXUS!
CRAK
UNF!
FWIP
ALL MUST LEAVE ME TO MY FATE—STOP THIS CREATURE FULL OF HATE!
—YOU'RE TOO LATE—
—THE DEVICE IS ACTIVATED.
TURMOIL—IF WHAT HE SAID IS TRUE, HE ARRIVED HERE FIVE YEARS AGO... AND LANDED THOUSANDS OF YEARS IN THE PAST.
COULD JHIAXUS HAVE LANDED AT THE END OF THE WORLD...?
BUT I HAVE THE CONTROL DEVICE, JHIAXUS!
BLUDGEON WAS JUMPING BACKWARD IN TIME, LEADING JHIAXUS AND MONSTRUCTOR AFTER ME, AS I TUMBLED FORWARD.

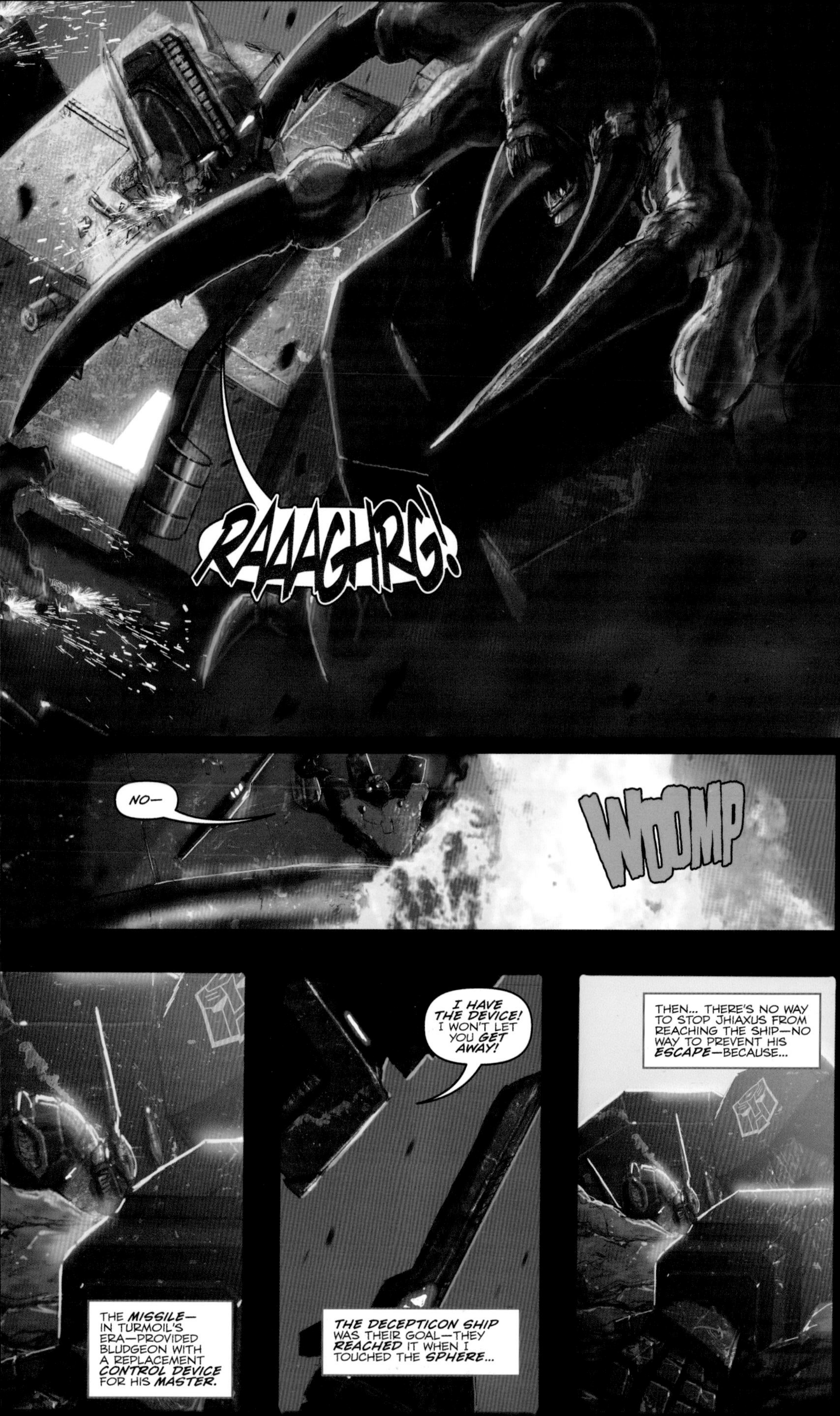
RAAAGHRG!
NO—
WOOMP
THE MISSILE— IN TURMOIL'S ERA—PROVIDED BLUDGEON WITH A REPLACEMENT CONTROL DEVICE FOR HIS MASTER.
I HAVE THE DEVICE! I WON'T LET YOU GET AWAY!
THE DECEPTICON SHIP WAS THEIR GOAL—THEY REACHED IT WHEN I TOUCHED THE SPHERE...
THEN... THERE'S NO WAY TO STOP JHIAXUS FROM REACHING THE SHIP—NO WAY TO PREVENT HIS ESCAPE—BECAUSE...

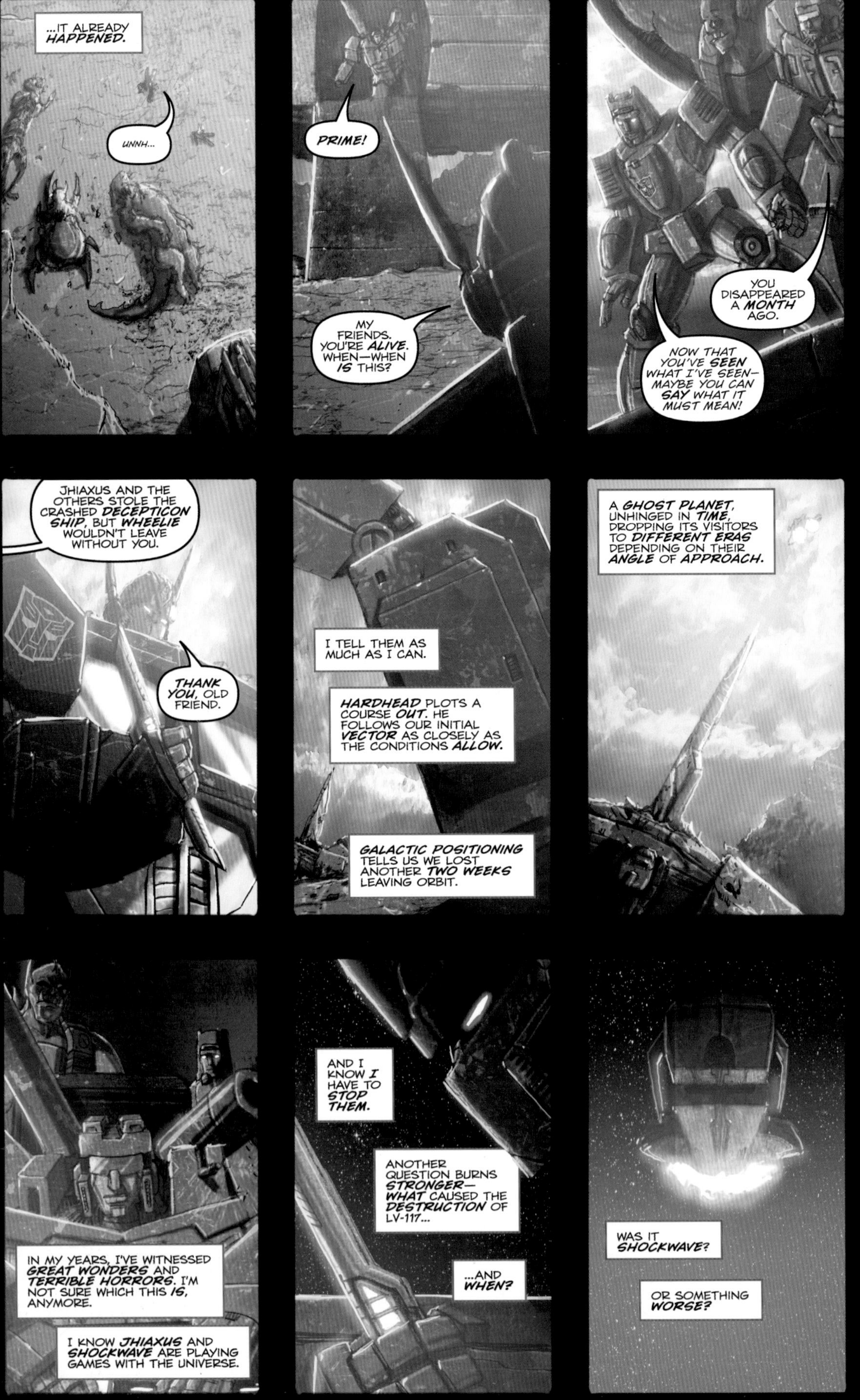
...IT ALREADY HAPPENED.
UNNH...
PRIME!
MY FRIENDS. YOU'RE ALIVE. WHEN—WHEN IS THIS?
YOU DISAPPEARED A MONTH AGO.
NOW THAT YOU'VE SEEN WHAT I'VE SEEN—MAYBE YOU CAN SAY WHAT IT MUST MEAN!
JHIAXUS AND THE OTHERS STOLE THE CRASHED DECEPTICON SHIP, BUT WHEELIE WOULDN'T LEAVE WITHOUT YOU.
THANK YOU, OLD FRIEND.
I TELL THEM AS MUCH AS I CAN.
HARDHEAD PLOTS A COURSE OUT. HE FOLLOWS OUR INITIAL VECTOR AS CLOSELY AS THE CONDITIONS ALLOW.
GALACTIC POSITIONING TELLS US WE LOST ANOTHER TWO WEEKS LEAVING ORBIT.
A GHOST PLANET, UNHINGED IN TIME, DROPPING ITS VISITORS TO DIFFERENT ERAS DEPENDING ON THEIR ANGLE OF APPROACH.
IN MY YEARS, I'VE WITNESSED GREAT WONDERS AND TERRIBLE HORRORS. I'M NOT SURE WHICH THIS IS, ANYMORE.
I KNOW JHIAXUS AND SHOCKWAVE ARE PLAYING GAMES WITH THE UNIVERSE.
AND I KNOW I HAVE TO STOP THEM.
ANOTHER QUESTION BURNS STRONGER—WHAT CAUSED THE DESTRUCTION OF LV-117...
...AND WHEN?
WAS IT SHOCKWAVE?
OR SOMETHING WORSE?

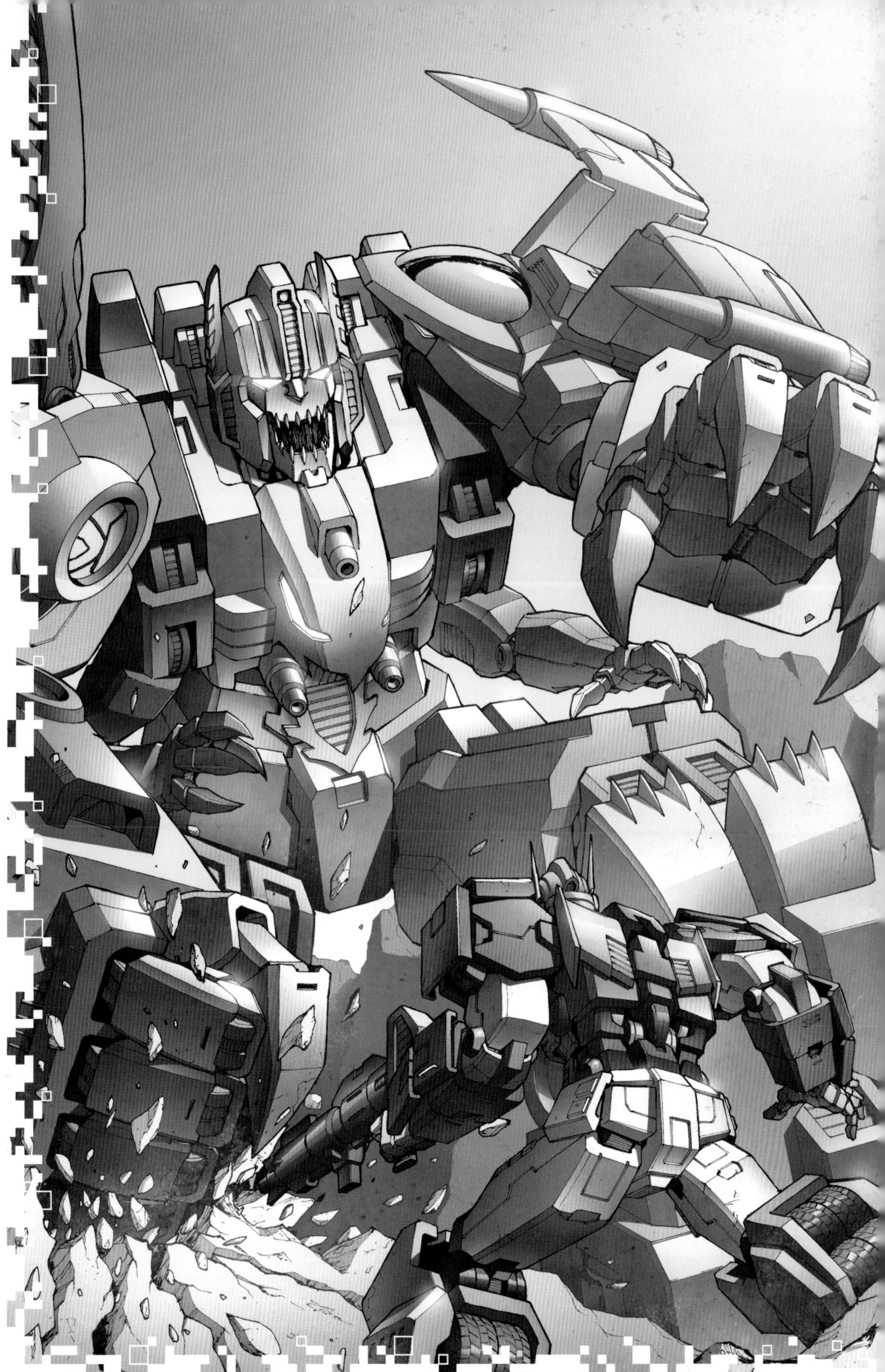

ROBOTS IN DISGUISE #10 COVER B

by **CASEY W. COLLER** Colors by **JOANA LAFUENTE**

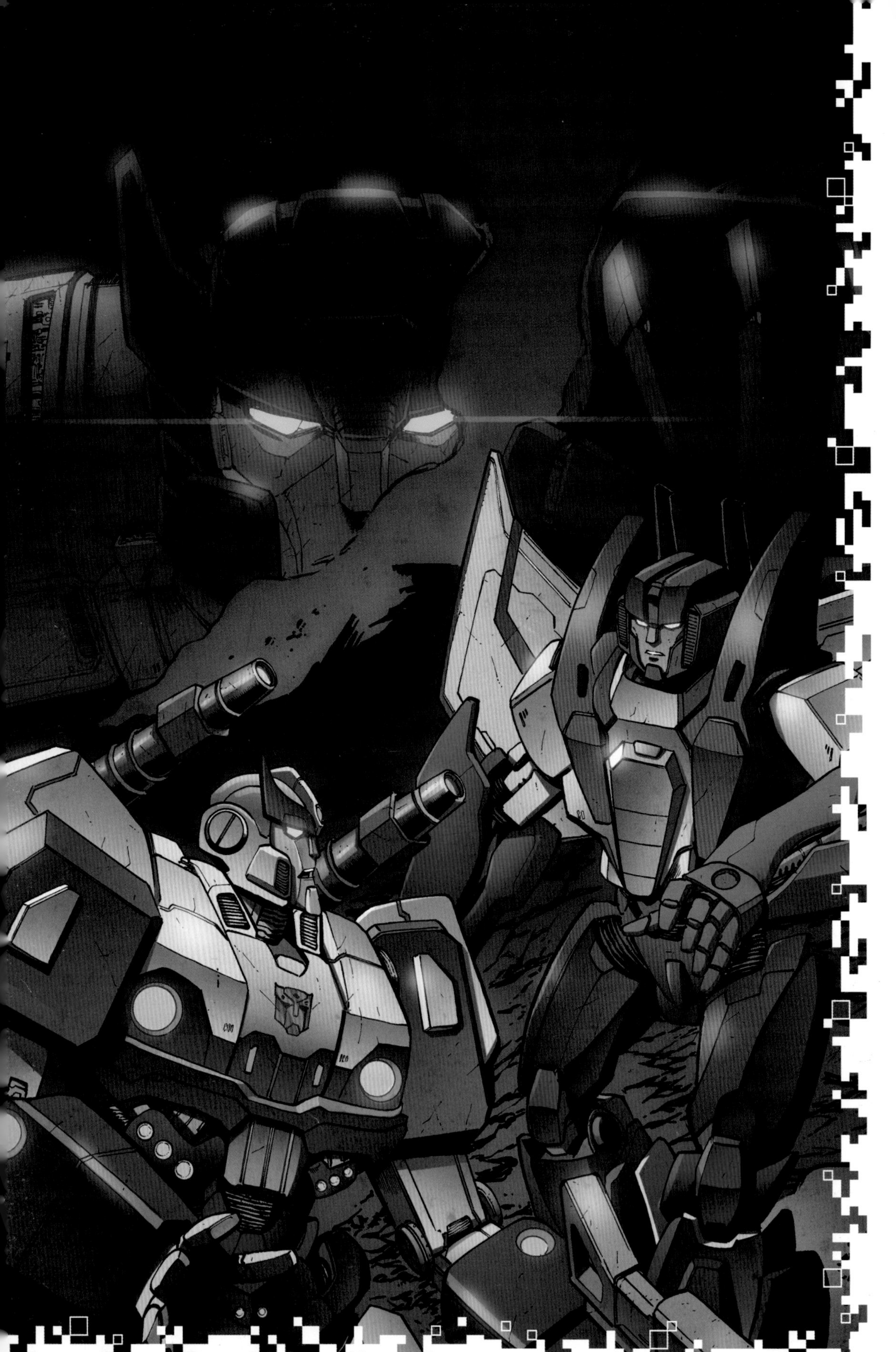

ROBOTS IN DISGUISE ANNUAL COVER A

by **TIM SEELEY** Colors by **JOANA LAFUENTE**

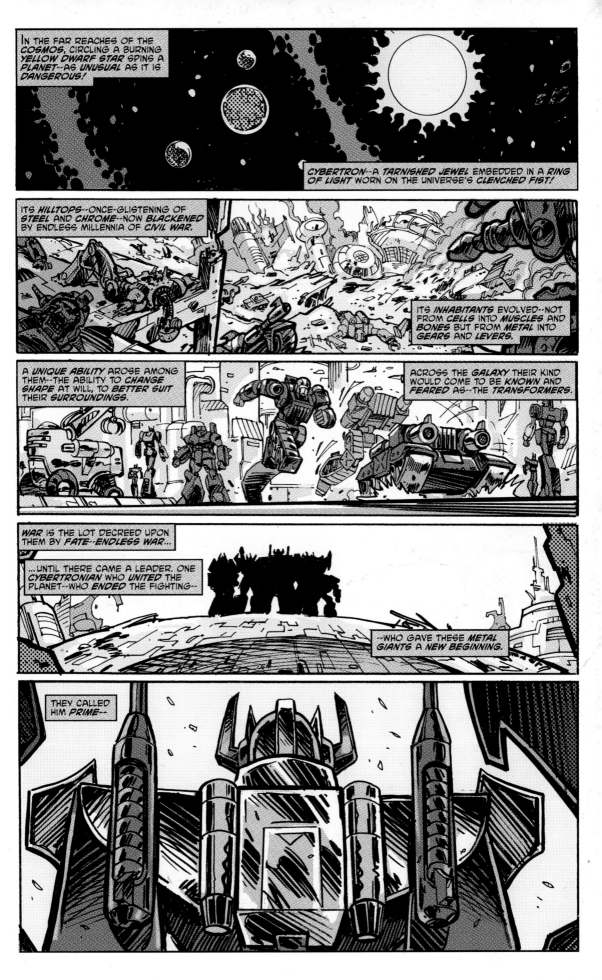

IN THE FAR REACHES OF THE *COSMOS*, CIRCLING A BURNING *YELLOW DWARF STAR* SPINS A *PLANET*—AS *UNUSUAL* AS IT IS *DANGEROUS!*

*CYBERTRON*—A *TARNISHED JEWEL* EMBEDDED IN A *RING OF LIGHT* WORN ON THE UNIVERSE'S *CLENCHED FIST!*

ITS *HILLTOPS*—ONCE-GLISTENING OF *STEEL* AND *CHROME*—NOW *BLACKENED* BY ENDLESS MILLENNIA OF *CIVIL WAR.*

ITS *INHABITANTS* EVOLVED—NOT FROM *CELLS* INTO *MUSCLES* AND *BONES* BUT FROM *METAL* INTO *GEARS* AND *LEVERS.*

A *UNIQUE ABILITY* AROSE AMONG THEM—THE ABILITY TO *CHANGE SHAPE* AT WILL, TO *BETTER SUIT* THEIR *SURROUNDINGS*

ACROSS THE *GALAXY* THEIR KIND WOULD COME TO BE *KNOWN* AND *FEARED* AS—THE *TRANSFORMERS.*

*WAR* IS THE LOT DECREED UPON THEM BY *FATE*—ENDLESS WAR...

...UNTIL THERE CAME A LEADER. ONE *CYBERTRONIAN* WHO *UNITED* THE PLANET—WHO *ENDED* THE FIGHTING—

—WHO GAVE THESE *METAL GIANTS* A *NEW BEGINNING.*

THEY CALLED HIM *PRIME*—

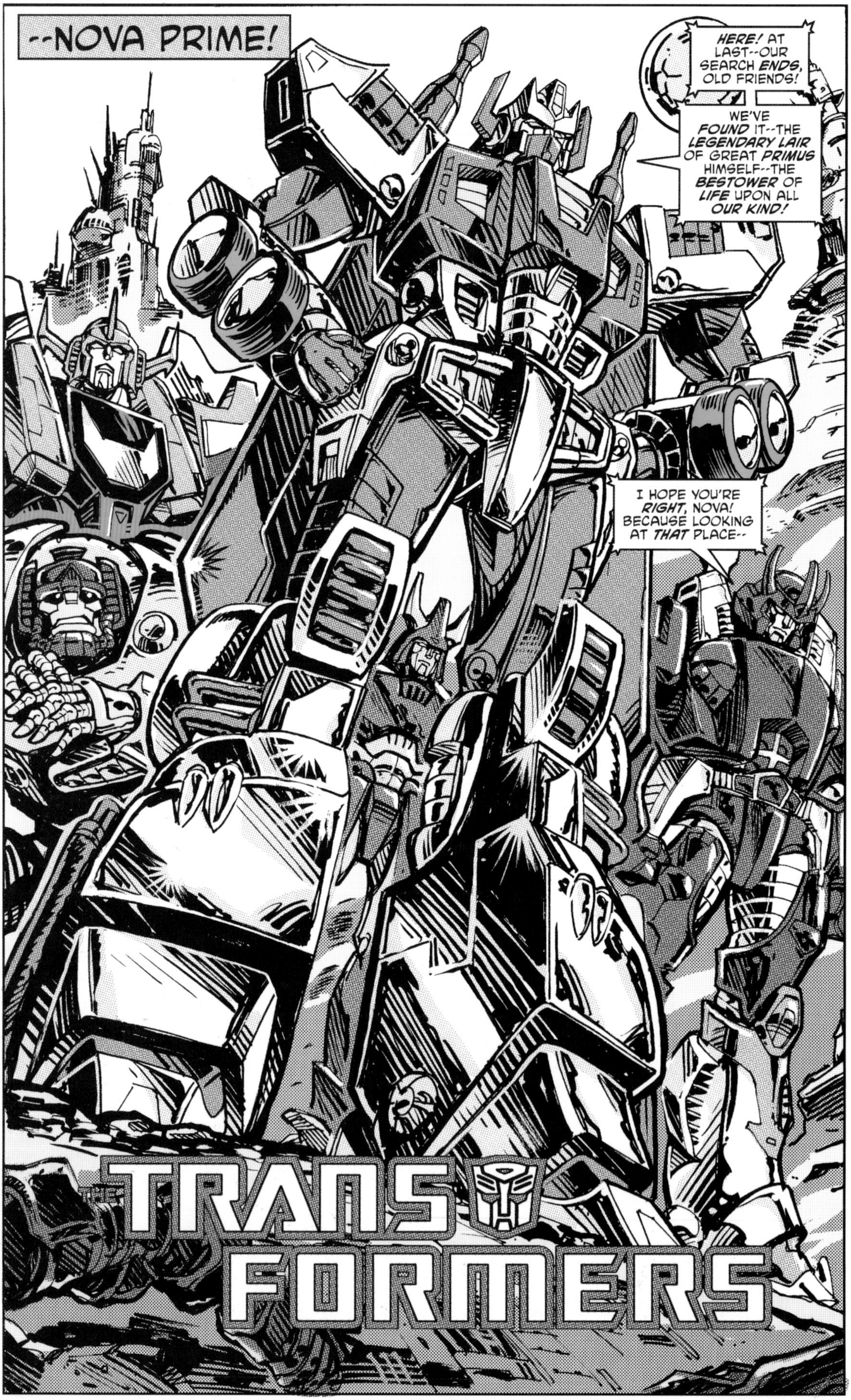
--NOVA PRIME!
HERE! AT LAST--OUR SEARCH ENDS, OLD FRIENDS!
WE'VE FOUND IT--THE LEGENDARY LAIR OF GREAT PRIMUS HIMSELF--THE BESTOWER OF LIFE UPON ALL OUR KIND!
I HOPE YOU'RE RIGHT, NOVA! BECAUSE LOOKING AT THAT PLACE--
THE TRANSFORMERS

--I'M *WORRIED* THAT IT ISN'T THE *HOME* OF HIS *OPPOSITE!*

NO MATTER, VALIANT *GALVATRON*--WE FACE WHAT *DANGERS* WE *MUST!*

SO WE *EXPLORE,* SIRE...?

*HA!*--I'VE ASKED YOU NOT TO *CALL* ME THAT, *JHIAXUS!*

BUT YOU'RE *RIGHT!* REGARDLESS OF THE *RISK* TO *OURSELVES,* WE PUT OUR FEARS *ASIDE!*

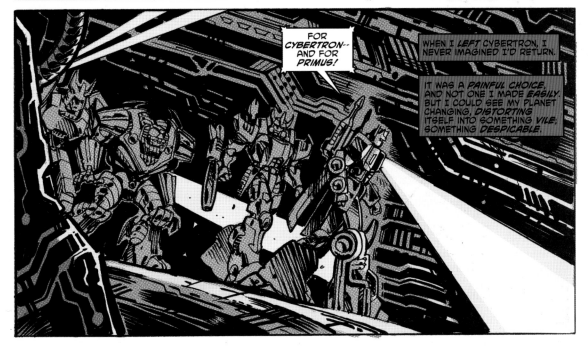

FOR *CYBERTRON*-- AND FOR *PRIMUS!*

WHEN I *LEFT* CYBERTRON, I NEVER IMAGINED I'D RETURN.

IT WAS A *PAINFUL CHOICE,* AND NOT ONE I MADE *EASILY.* BUT I COULD SEE MY PLANET CHANGING, *DISTORTING* ITSELF INTO SOMETHING *VILE,* SOMETHING *DESPICABLE.*

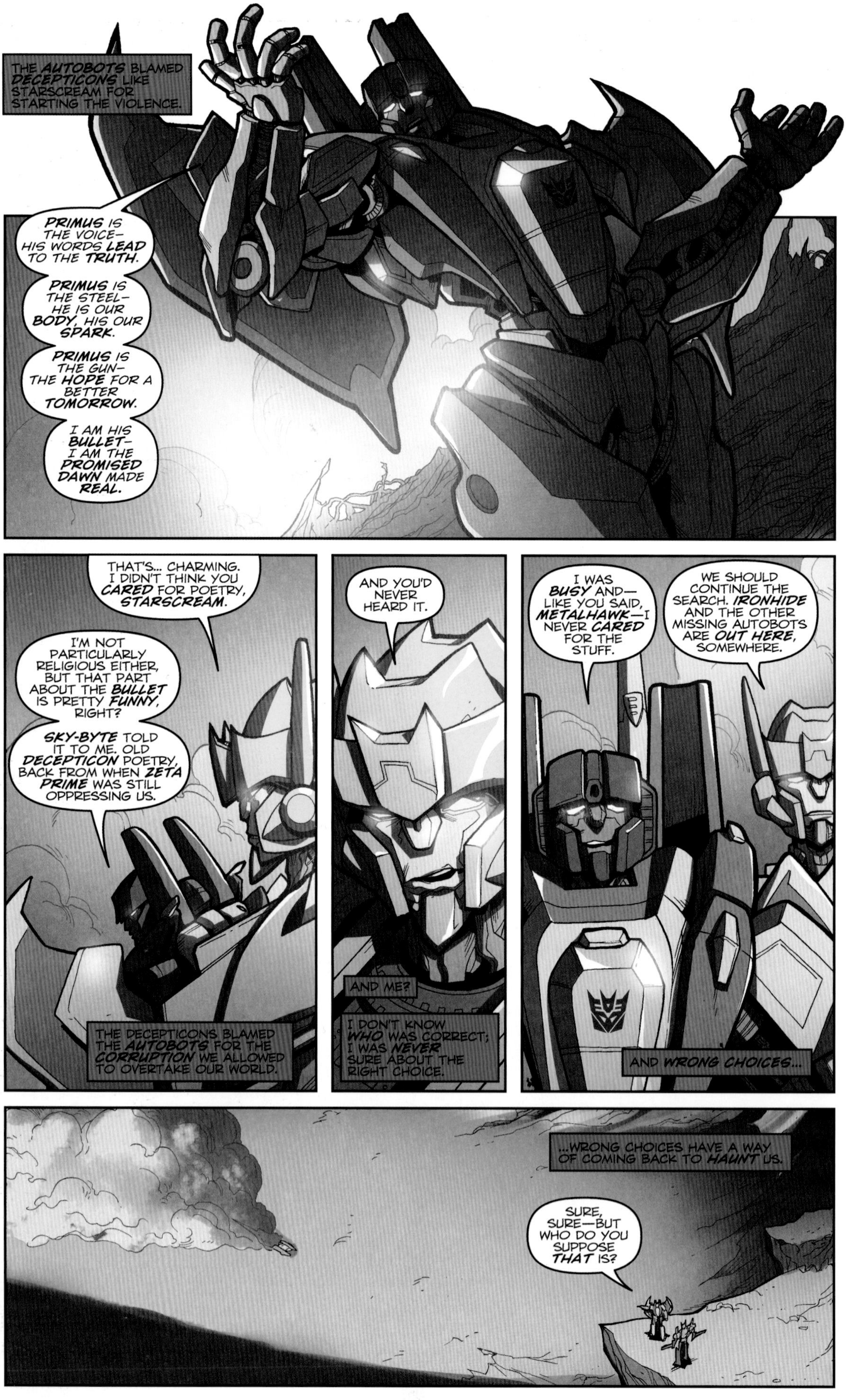

THE AUTOBOTS BLAMED DECEPTICONS LIKE STARSCREAM FOR STARTING THE VIOLENCE.
PRIMUS IS THE VOICE– HIS WORDS LEAD TO THE TRUTH.
PRIMUS IS THE STEEL– HE IS OUR BODY, HIS OUR SPARK.
PRIMUS IS THE GUN– THE HOPE FOR A BETTER TOMORROW.
I AM HIS BULLET– I AM THE PROMISED DAWN MADE REAL.
THAT'S... CHARMING. I DIDN'T THINK YOU CARED FOR POETRY, STARSCREAM.
I'M NOT PARTICULARLY RELIGIOUS EITHER, BUT THAT PART ABOUT THE BULLET IS PRETTY FUNNY, RIGHT?
SKY-BYTE TOLD IT TO ME. OLD DECEPTICON POETRY, BACK FROM WHEN ZETA PRIME WAS STILL OPPRESSING US.
THE DECEPTICONS BLAMED THE AUTOBOTS FOR THE CORRUPTION WE ALLOWED TO OVERTAKE OUR WORLD.
AND YOU'D NEVER HEARD IT.
AND ME?
I DON'T KNOW WHO WAS CORRECT; I WAS NEVER SURE ABOUT THE RIGHT CHOICE.
I WAS BUSY AND— LIKE YOU SAID, METALHAWK—I NEVER CARED FOR THE STUFF.
WE SHOULD CONTINUE THE SEARCH. IRONHIDE AND THE OTHER MISSING AUTOBOTS ARE OUT HERE, SOMEWHERE.
AND WRONG CHOICES...
...WRONG CHOICES HAVE A WAY OF COMING BACK TO HAUNT US.
SURE, SURE—BUT WHO DO YOU SUPPOSE THAT IS?

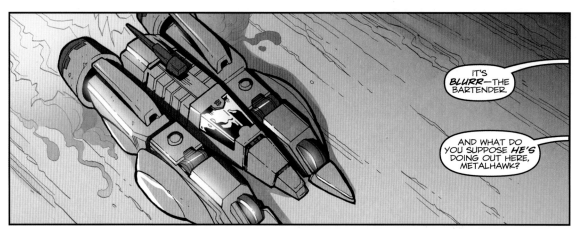

IT'S *BLURR*—THE BARTENDER.

AND WHAT DO YOU SUPPOSE *HE'S* DOING OUT HERE, METALHAWK?

YOU... YOU *WERE* RIGHT ABOUT HIM. I SUPPOSE BUMBLEBEE *DOES* BELIEVE THAT IF *YOU* FIND THE *MISSING* AUTOBOTS—

IT'LL FORCE HIM TO CALL FOR ELECTIONS, WHICH HE'S WORRIED *YOU* AND I CAN *WIN*.

I DIDN'T *IMAGINE* HE WAS SO...

CYNICAL. YEAH. IT SEEMS TO BE GOING AROUND *AUTOBOT HIGH COMMAND* THESE DAYS...

...BUT WHY DID THEY SEND *BLURR?* HE'S GOT *NO LOVE* FOR THOSE GUYS, NOT AFTER WHAT *PROWL* DID. AND *ANYWAY*—

"—WHAT DOES HE *SEE* THERE...?"

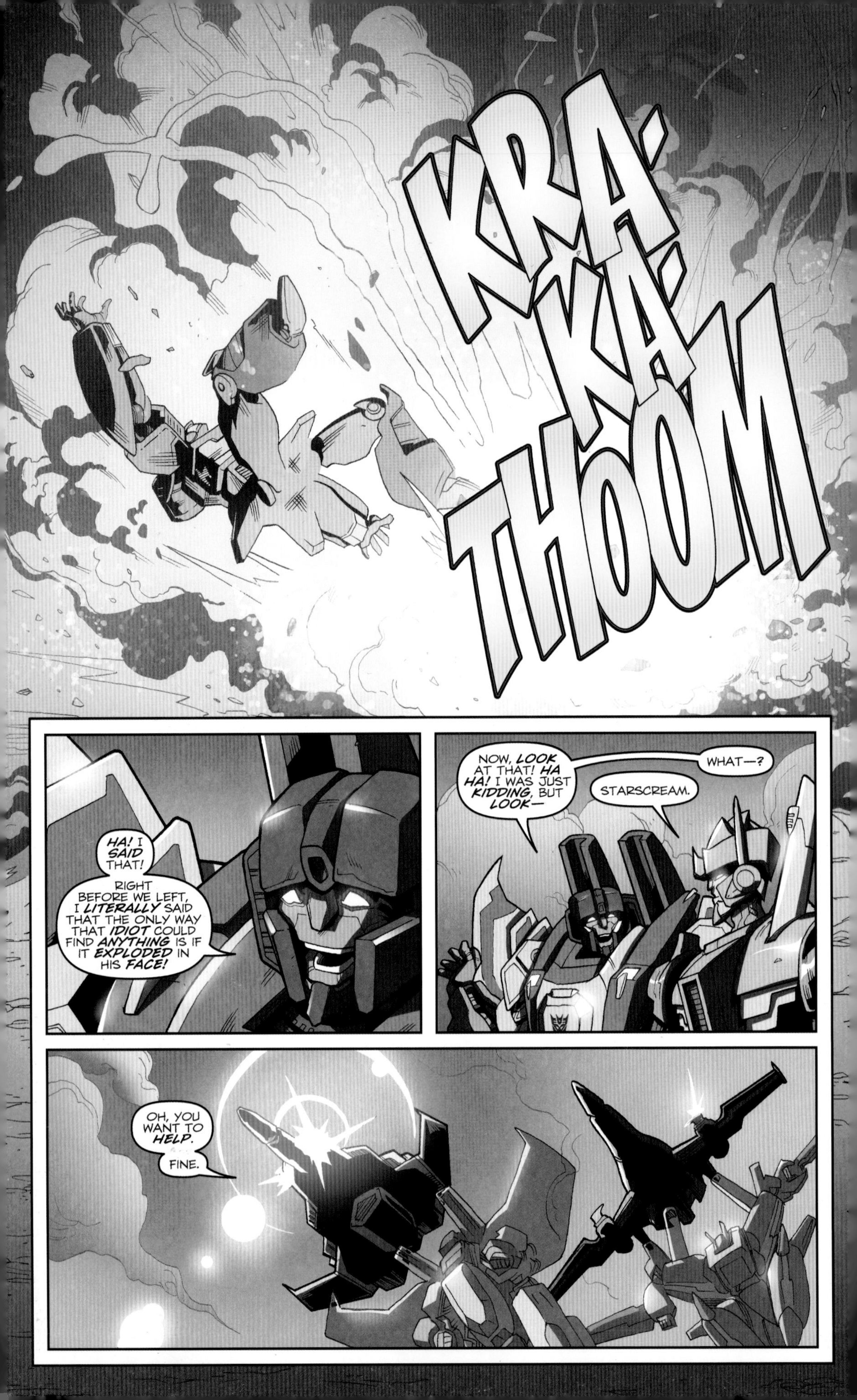
KRA-KA-THOOM
HA! I SAID THAT!
RIGHT BEFORE WE LEFT, I LITERALLY SAID THAT THE ONLY WAY THAT IDIOT COULD FIND ANYTHING IS IF IT EXPLODED IN HIS FACE!
NOW, LOOK AT THAT! HA HA! I WAS JUST KIDDING, BUT LOOK—
WHAT—?
STARSCREAM.
OH, YOU WANT TO HELP.
FINE.

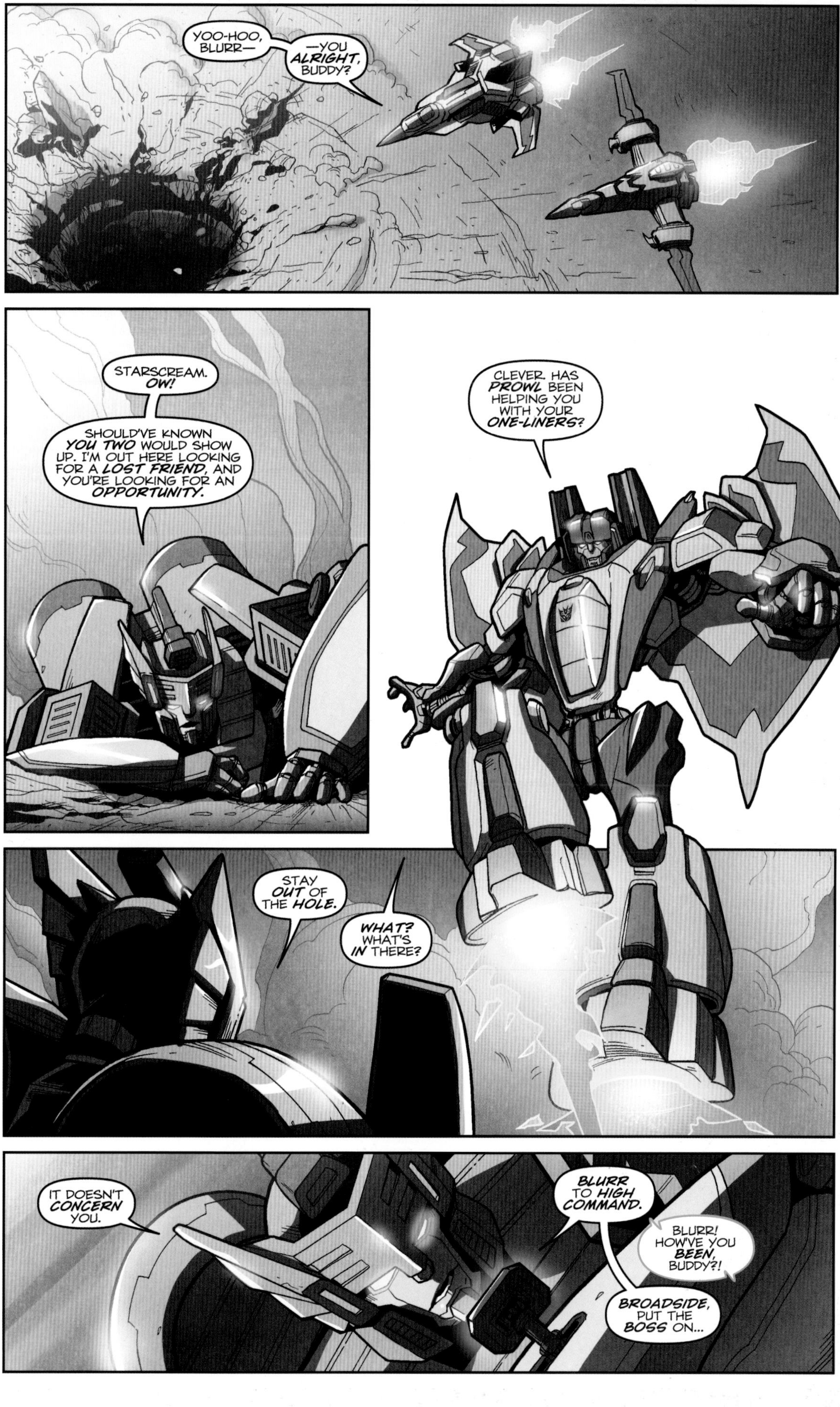
YOO-HOO, BLURR—
—YOU ALRIGHT, BUDDY?
STARSCREAM. OW!
SHOULD'VE KNOWN YOU TWO WOULD SHOW UP. I'M OUT HERE LOOKING FOR A LOST FRIEND, AND YOU'RE LOOKING FOR AN OPPORTUNITY.
CLEVER. HAS PROWL BEEN HELPING YOU WITH YOUR ONE-LINERS?
STAY OUT OF THE HOLE.
WHAT? WHAT'S IN THERE?
IT DOESN'T CONCERN YOU.
BLURR TO HIGH COMMAND.
BLURR! HOW'VE YOU BEEN, BUDDY?!
BROADSIDE, PUT THE BOSS ON...

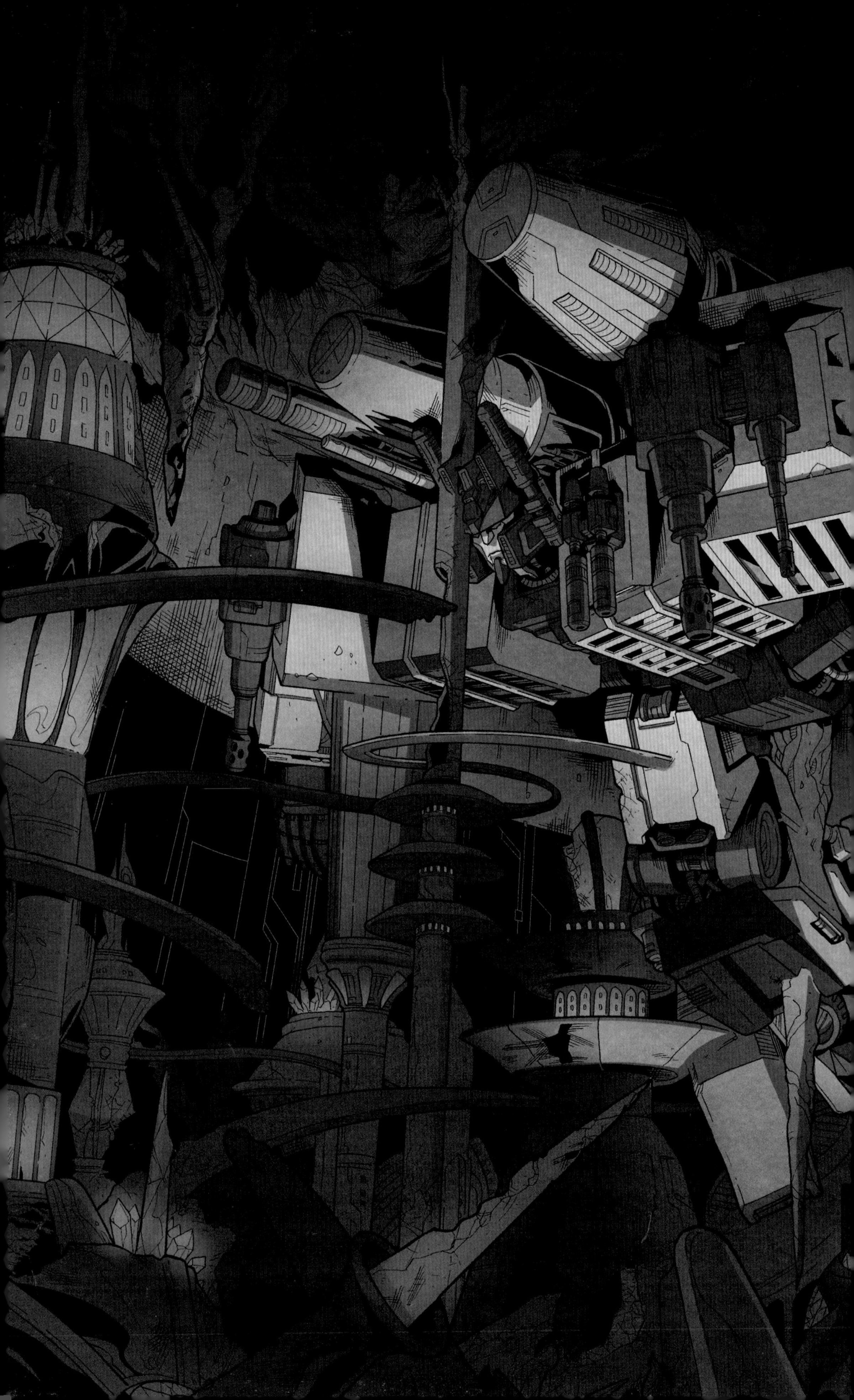

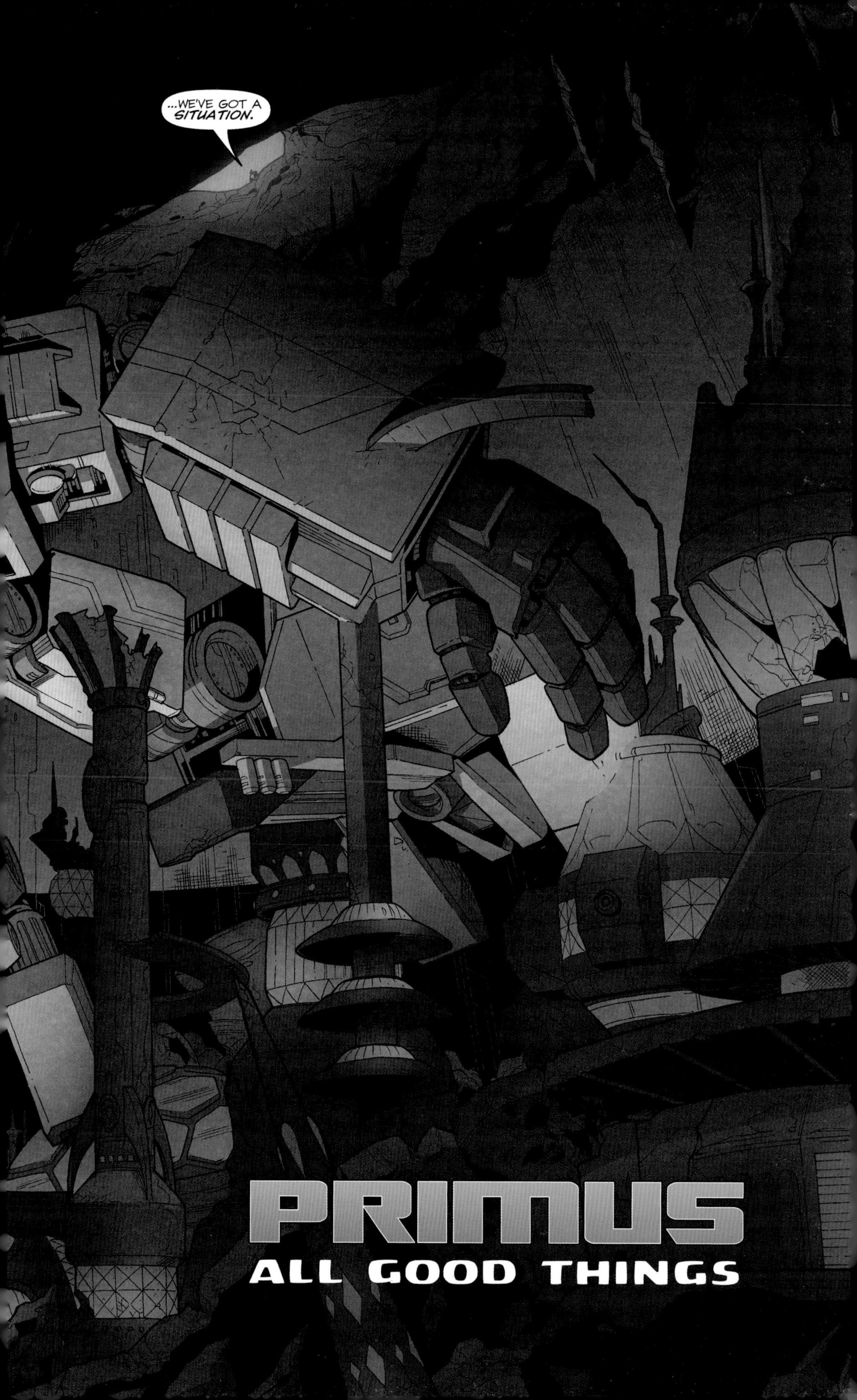
...WE'VE GOT A SITUATION.
PRIMUS
ALL GOOD THINGS

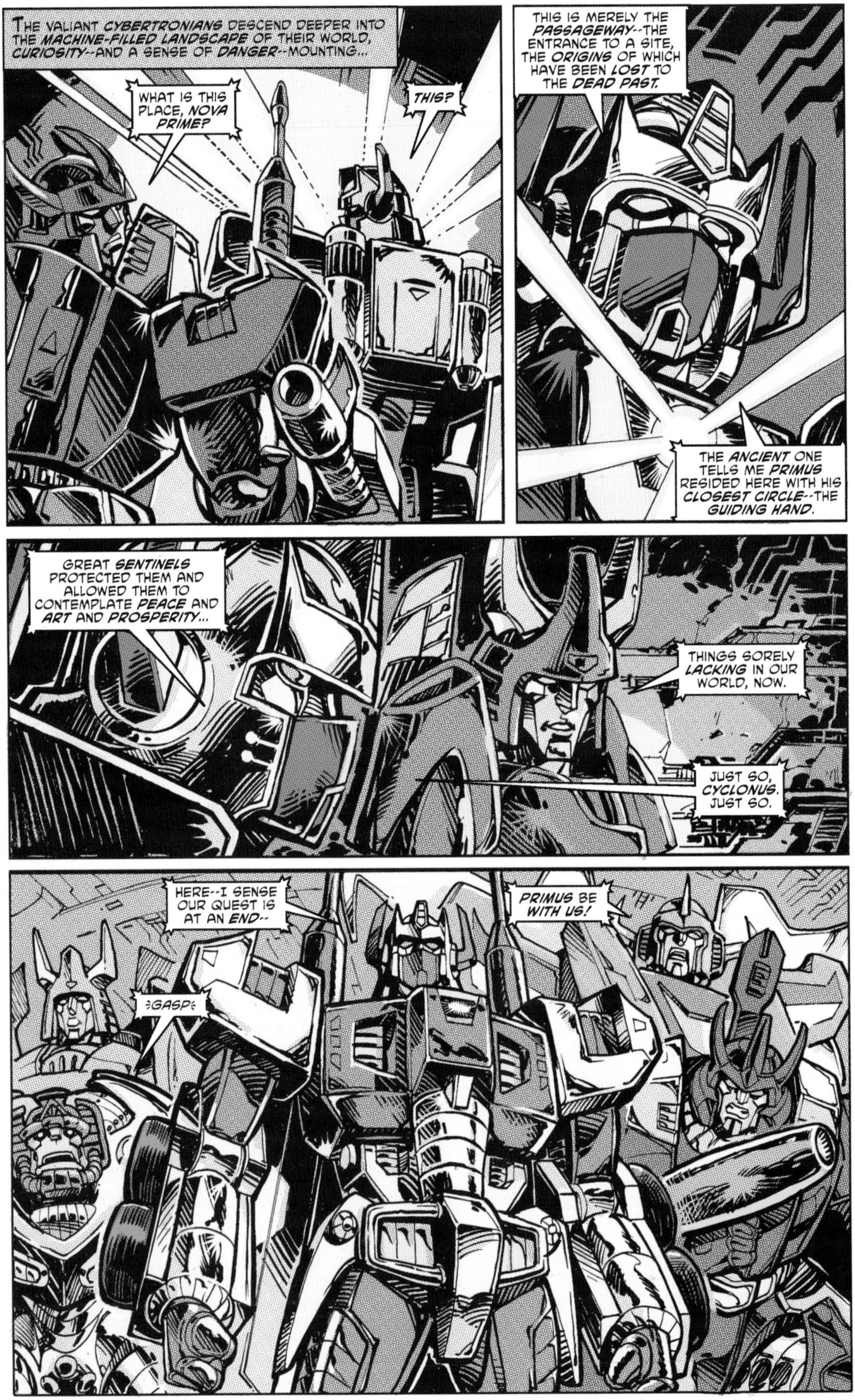
THE VALIANT CYBERTRONIANS DESCEND DEEPER INTO THE MACHINE-FILLED LANDSCAPE OF THEIR WORLD, CURIOSITY--AND A SENSE OF DANGER--MOUNTING...
WHAT IS THIS PLACE, NOVA PRIME?
THIS?
THIS IS MERELY THE PASSAGEWAY--THE ENTRANCE TO A SITE, THE ORIGINS OF WHICH HAVE BEEN LOST TO THE DEAD PAST.
THE ANCIENT ONE TELLS ME PRIMUS RESIDED HERE WITH HIS CLOSEST CIRCLE--THE GUIDING HAND.
GREAT SENTINELS PROTECTED THEM AND ALLOWED THEM TO CONTEMPLATE PEACE AND ART AND PROSPERITY...
THINGS SORELY LACKING IN OUR WORLD, NOW.
JUST SO, CYCLONUS. JUST SO.
HERE--I SENSE OUR QUEST IS AT AN END--
PRIMUS BE WITH US!
GASP

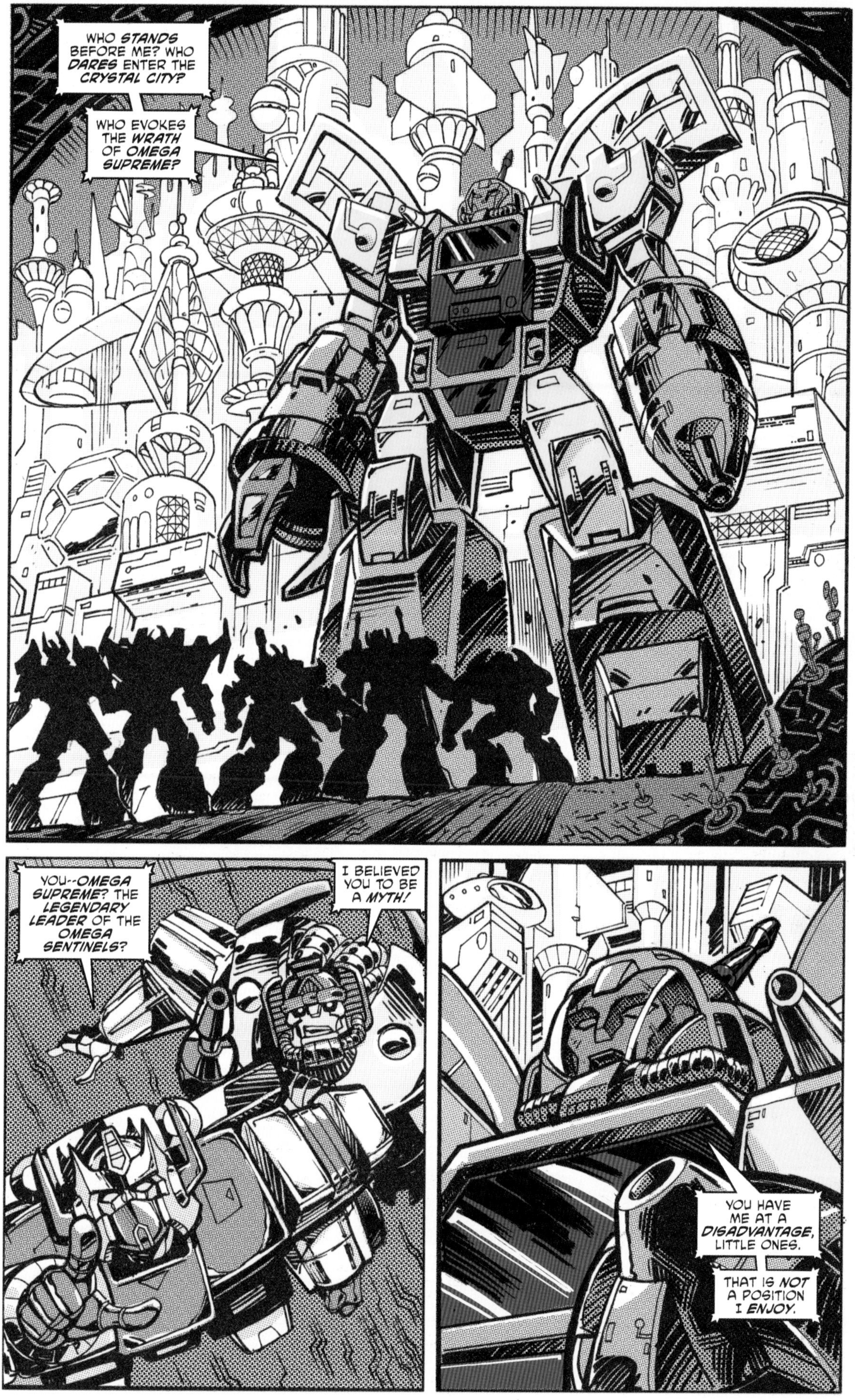
WHO STANDS BEFORE ME? WHO DARES ENTER THE CRYSTAL CITY?
WHO EVOKES THE WRATH OF OMEGA SUPREME?
YOU--OMEGA SUPREME? THE LEGENDARY LEADER OF THE OMEGA SENTINELS?
I BELIEVED YOU TO BE A MYTH!
YOU HAVE ME AT A DISADVANTAGE, LITTLE ONES.
THAT IS NOT A POSITION I ENJOY.

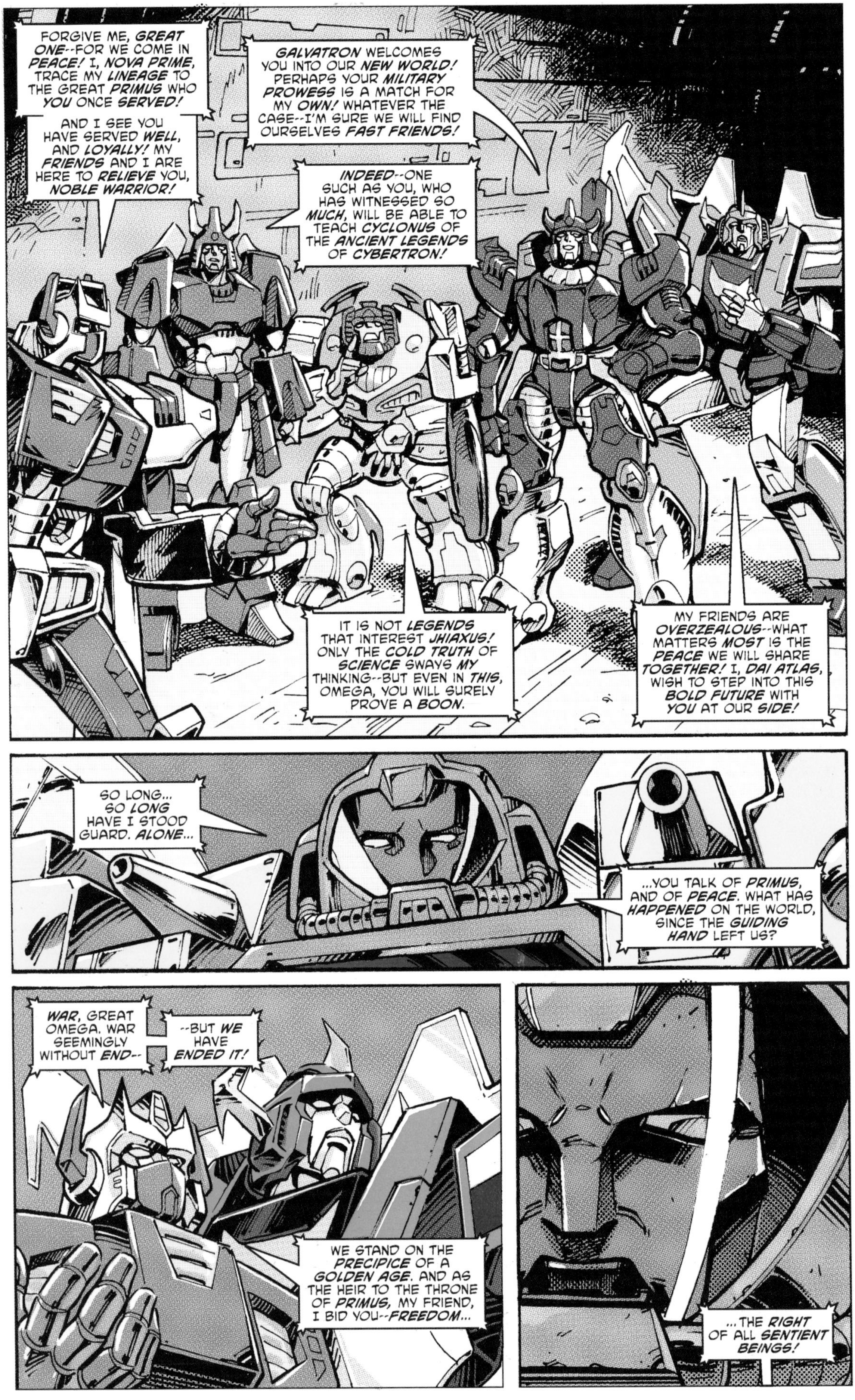
FORGIVE ME, GREAT ONE--FOR WE COME IN PEACE! I, NOVA PRIME, TRACE MY LINEAGE TO THE GREAT PRIMUS WHO YOU ONCE SERVED!
AND I SEE YOU HAVE SERVED WELL, AND LOYALLY! MY FRIENDS AND I ARE HERE TO RELIEVE YOU, NOBLE WARRIOR!
GALVATRON WELCOMES YOU INTO OUR NEW WORLD! PERHAPS YOUR MILITARY PROWESS IS A MATCH FOR MY OWN! WHATEVER THE CASE--I'M SURE WE WILL FIND OURSELVES FAST FRIENDS!
INDEED--ONE SUCH AS YOU, WHO HAS WITNESSED SO MUCH, WILL BE ABLE TO TEACH CYCLONUS OF THE ANCIENT LEGENDS OF CYBERTRON!
IT IS NOT LEGENDS THAT INTEREST JHIAXUS! ONLY THE COLD TRUTH OF SCIENCE SWAYS MY THINKING--BUT EVEN IN THIS, OMEGA, YOU WILL SURELY PROVE A BOON.
MY FRIENDS ARE OVERZEALOUS--WHAT MATTERS MOST IS THE PEACE WE WILL SHARE TOGETHER! I, DAI ATLAS, WISH TO STEP INTO THIS BOLD FUTURE WITH YOU AT OUR SIDE!
SO LONG... SO LONG HAVE I STOOD GUARD. ALONE...
...YOU TALK OF PRIMUS, AND OF PEACE. WHAT HAS HAPPENED ON THE WORLD, SINCE THE GUIDING HAND LEFT US?
WAR, GREAT OMEGA. WAR SEEMINGLY WITHOUT END--
--BUT WE HAVE ENDED IT!
WE STAND ON THE PRECIPICE OF A GOLDEN AGE. AND AS THE HEIR TO THE THRONE OF PRIMUS, MY FRIEND, I BID YOU--FREEDOM...
...THE RIGHT OF ALL SENTIENT BEINGS!

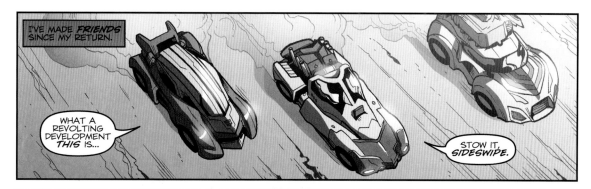

I'VE MADE *FRIENDS* SINCE MY RETURN.

WHAT A *REVOLTING* DEVELOPMENT *THIS* IS...

STOW IT, *SIDESWIPE.*

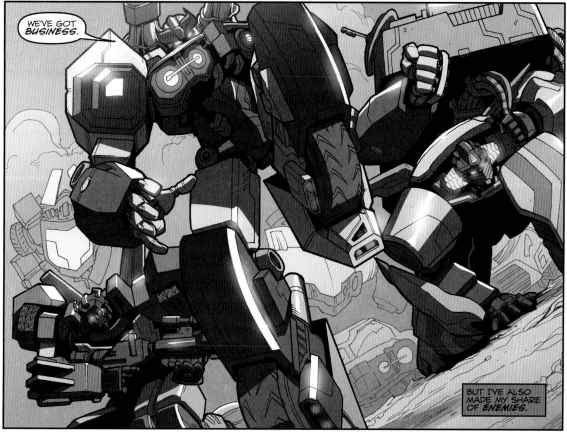

WE'VE GOT *BUSINESS.*

BUT I'VE ALSO MADE MY SHARE OF *ENEMIES.*

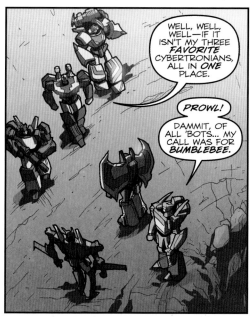

WELL, WELL, WELL—IF IT ISN'T MY THREE *FAVORITE* CYBERTRONIANS, ALL IN *ONE* PLACE.

PROWL!

DAMMIT, OF ALL 'BOTS... MY CALL WAS FOR *BUMBLEBEE.*

BUMBLEBEE'S *BUSY.* MAYBE YOU HEARD ABOUT A MISSING *DECEPTICON STARSHIP?*

*WASN'T ME.* IN FACT, I THINK THAT *THEFT* IS A *PERFECT* EXAMPLE OF WHAT HAPPENS WHEN YOU SQUEEZE A PEOPLE *PAST* THE POINT OF *BREAKING.*

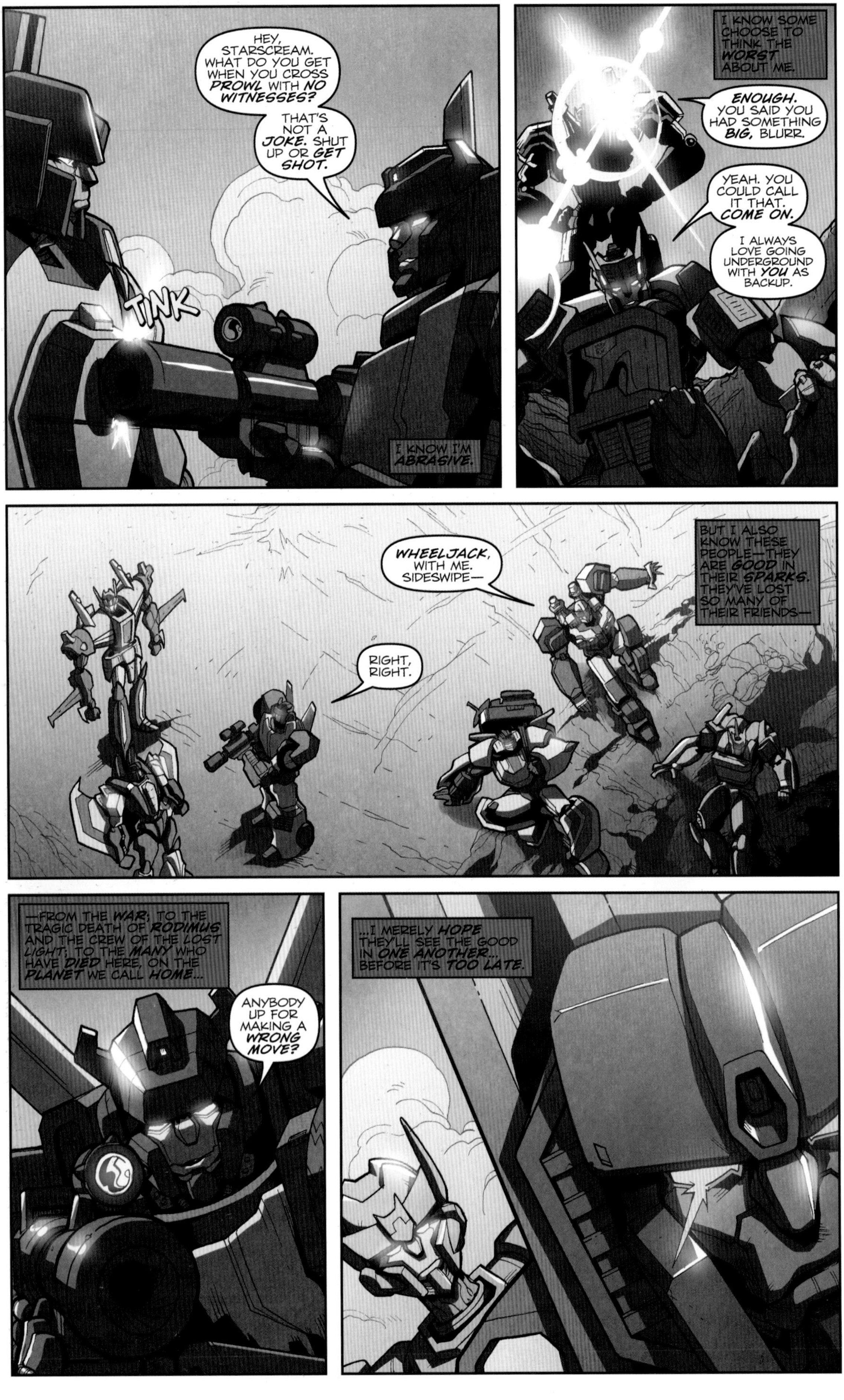
HEY, STARSCREAM. WHAT DO YOU GET WHEN YOU CROSS *PROWL* WITH *NO WITNESSES?*
THAT'S NOT A *JOKE.* SHUT UP OR *GET SHOT.*
TINK
I KNOW I'M *ABRASIVE.*
I KNOW SOME CHOOSE TO THINK THE *WORST* ABOUT ME.
*ENOUGH.* YOU SAID YOU HAD SOMETHING *BIG,* BLURR.
YEAH. YOU COULD CALL IT THAT. *COME ON.*
I ALWAYS LOVE GOING UNDERGROUND WITH *YOU* AS BACKUP.
BUT I ALSO KNOW THESE PEOPLE—THEY ARE *GOOD* IN THEIR *SPARKS.* THEY'VE LOST SO MANY OF THEIR FRIENDS—
*WHEELJACK,* WITH ME. SIDESWIPE—
RIGHT, RIGHT.
—FROM THE *WAR;* TO THE TRAGIC DEATH OF *RODIMUS* AND THE CREW OF THE *LOST LIGHT;* TO THE *MANY* WHO HAVE *DIED* HERE, ON THE *PLANET* WE CALL *HOME*...
ANYBODY UP FOR MAKING A *WRONG MOVE?*
...I MERELY *HOPE* THEY'LL SEE THE GOOD IN *ONE ANOTHER*... BEFORE IT'S *TOO LATE.*

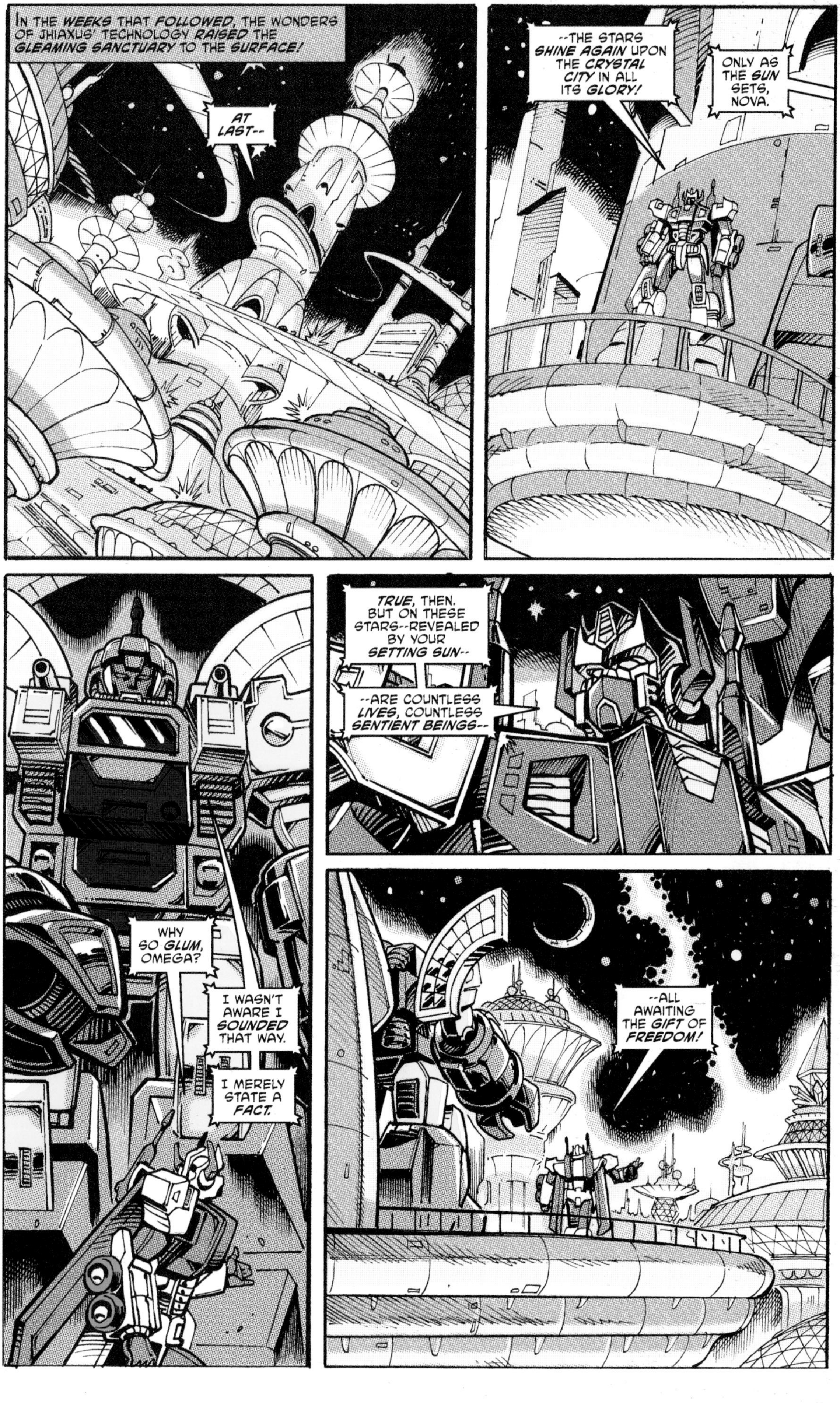
In the weeks that followed, the wonders of Jhiaxus' technology raised the gleaming sanctuary to the surface!
At last--
--The stars shine again upon the crystal city in all its glory!
Only as the sun sets, Nova.
Why so glum, Omega?
I wasn't aware I sounded that way.
I merely state a fact.
True, then. But on these stars--revealed by your setting sun--
--are countless lives, countless sentient beings--
--All awaiting the gift of freedom!

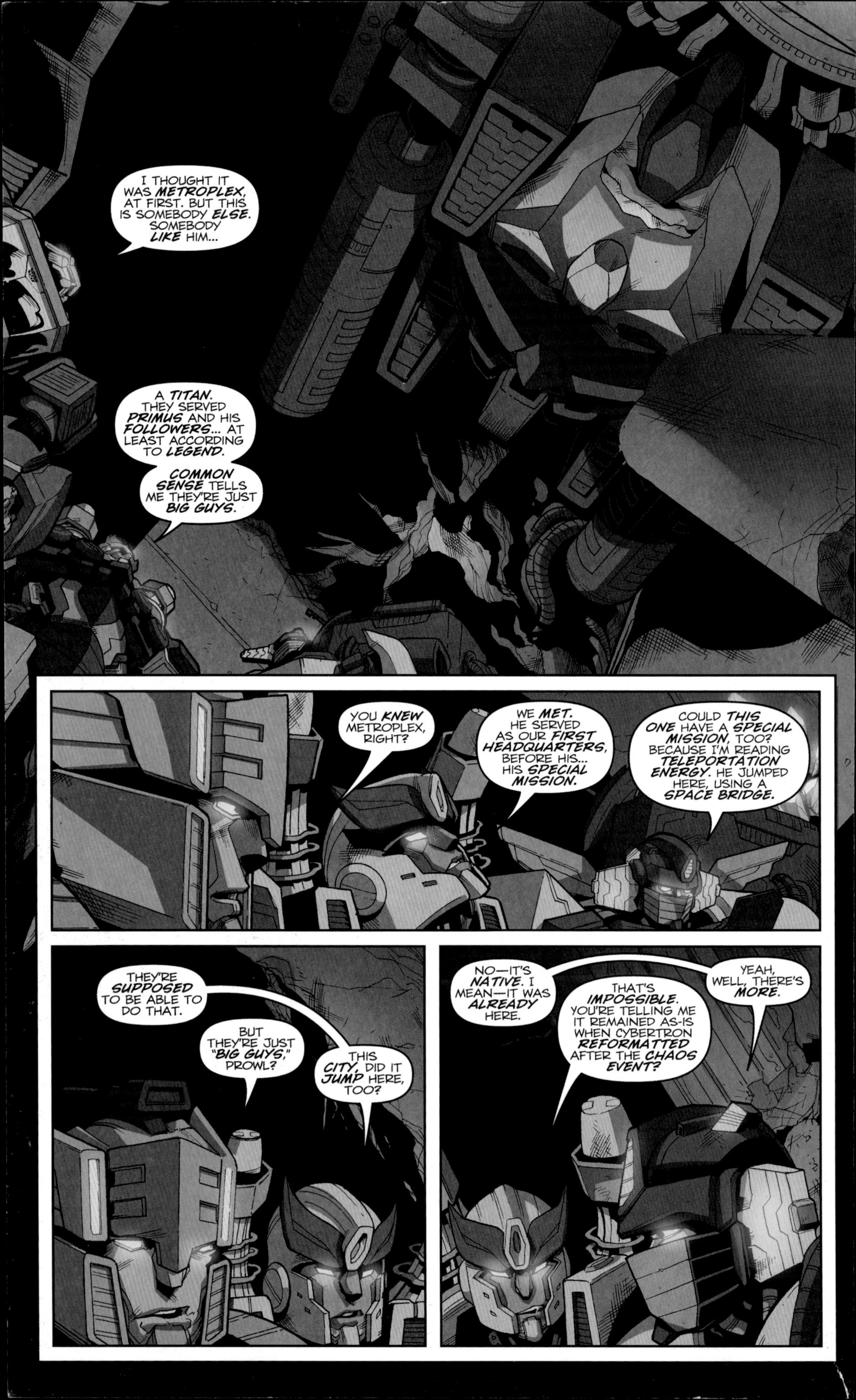
I THOUGHT IT WAS METROPLEX, AT FIRST. BUT THIS IS SOMEBODY ELSE. SOMEBODY LIKE HIM...
A TITAN. THEY SERVED PRIMUS AND HIS FOLLOWERS... AT LEAST ACCORDING TO LEGEND.
COMMON SENSE TELLS ME THEY'RE JUST BIG GUYS.
YOU KNEW METROPLEX, RIGHT?
WE MET. HE SERVED AS OUR FIRST HEADQUARTERS, BEFORE HIS... HIS SPECIAL MISSION.
COULD THIS ONE HAVE A SPECIAL MISSION, TOO? BECAUSE I'M READING TELEPORTATION ENERGY. HE JUMPED HERE, USING A SPACE BRIDGE.
THEY'RE SUPPOSED TO BE ABLE TO DO THAT.
BUT THEY'RE JUST "BIG GUYS," PROWL?
THIS CITY, DID IT JUMP HERE, TOO?
NO—IT'S NATIVE. I MEAN—IT WAS ALREADY HERE.
THAT'S IMPOSSIBLE. YOU'RE TELLING ME IT REMAINED AS-IS WHEN CYBERTRON REFORMATTED AFTER THE CHAOS EVENT?
YEAH, WELL, THERE'S MORE.

THE CHARGED **ANTI-PROTONS** FROM THE—THE **TITAN**... THEY'RE INTERACTING, UM, ODDLY WITH THE REGULAR PROTONS OF THE CITY.

"ODDLY."

YEAH, THIS, WELL—THIS SHOULDN'T BE **POSSIBLE**. AND, I MEAN, THIS IS JUST MY **INITIAL READING**, BUT, UM, **VECTOR SPACE** SEEMS TO BE **DECAYING**.

"VECTOR SPACE."

HE MEANS "**REALITY ITSELF**," PROWL. HE'S JUST TRYING TO SOUND **CLEVER**.

I **KNOW** WHAT HE MEANS—

BREEP BRAAP

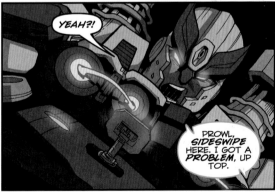

YEAH?!

PROWL, **SIDESWIPE** HERE. I GOT A **PROBLEM**, UP TOP.

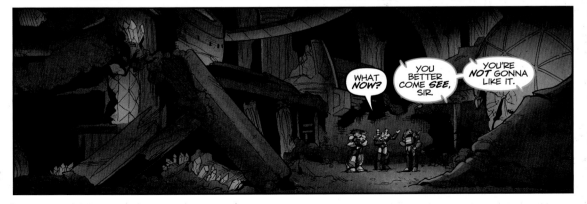

WHAT **NOW?**

YOU BETTER COME **SEE**, SIR.

YOU'RE **NOT** GONNA LIKE IT.

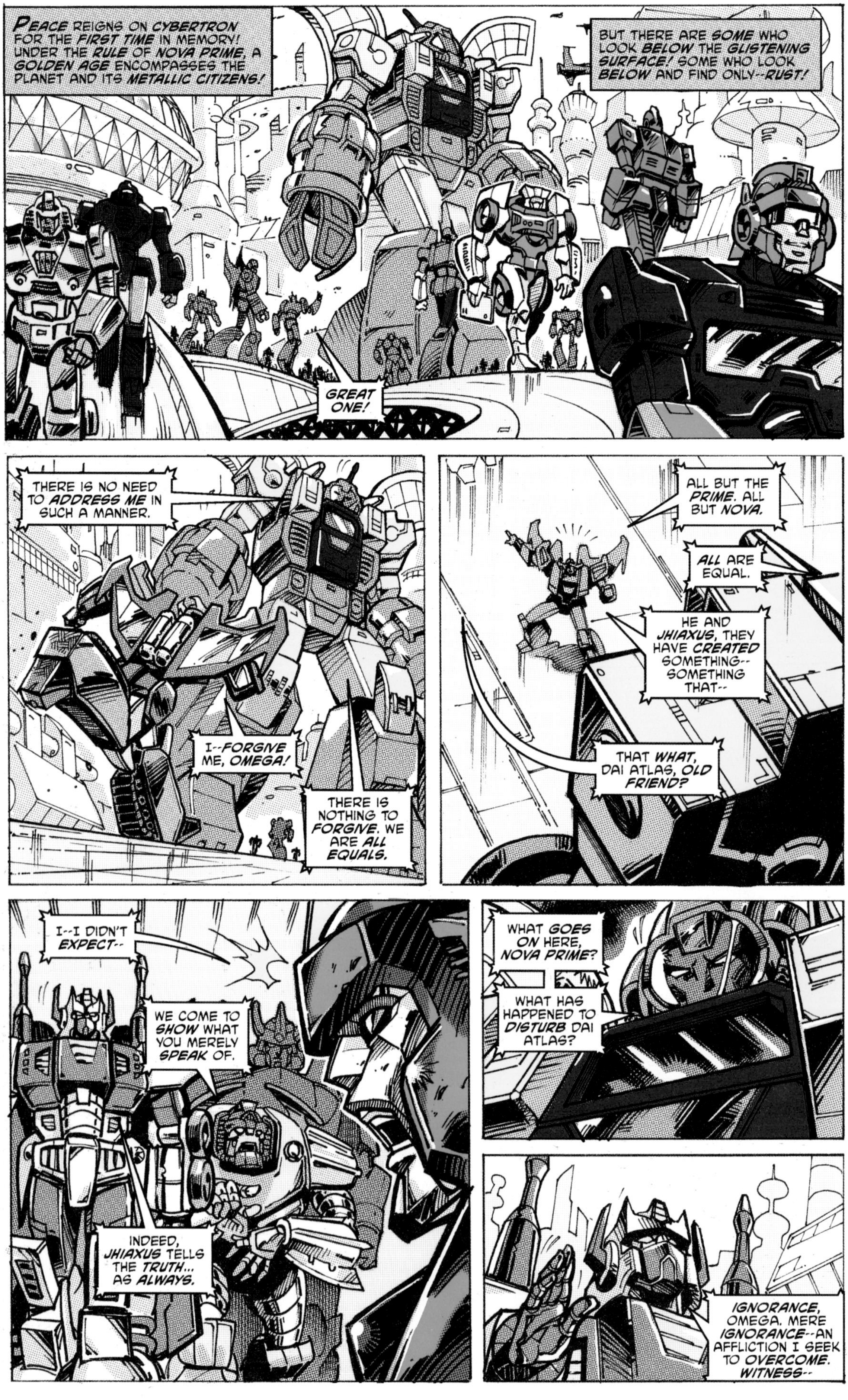
PEACE REIGNS ON CYBERTRON FOR THE FIRST TIME IN MEMORY! UNDER THE RULE OF NOVA PRIME, A GOLDEN AGE ENCOMPASSES THE PLANET AND ITS METALLIC CITIZENS!
BUT THERE ARE SOME WHO LOOK BELOW THE GLISTENING SURFACE! SOME WHO LOOK BELOW AND FIND ONLY--RUST!
GREAT ONE!
THERE IS NO NEED TO ADDRESS ME IN SUCH A MANNER.
I--FORGIVE ME, OMEGA!
THERE IS NOTHING TO FORGIVE. WE ARE ALL EQUALS.
ALL BUT THE PRIME. ALL BUT NOVA.
ALL ARE EQUAL.
HE AND JHIAXUS, THEY HAVE CREATED SOMETHING-- SOMETHING THAT--
THAT WHAT, DAI ATLAS, OLD FRIEND?
I--I DIDN'T EXPECT--
WE COME TO SHOW WHAT YOU MERELY SPEAK OF.
INDEED, JHIAXUS TELLS THE TRUTH... AS ALWAYS.
WHAT GOES ON HERE, NOVA PRIME?
WHAT HAS HAPPENED TO DISTURB DAI ATLAS?
IGNORANCE, OMEGA. MERE IGNORANCE--AN AFFLICTION I SEEK TO OVERCOME. WITNESS--

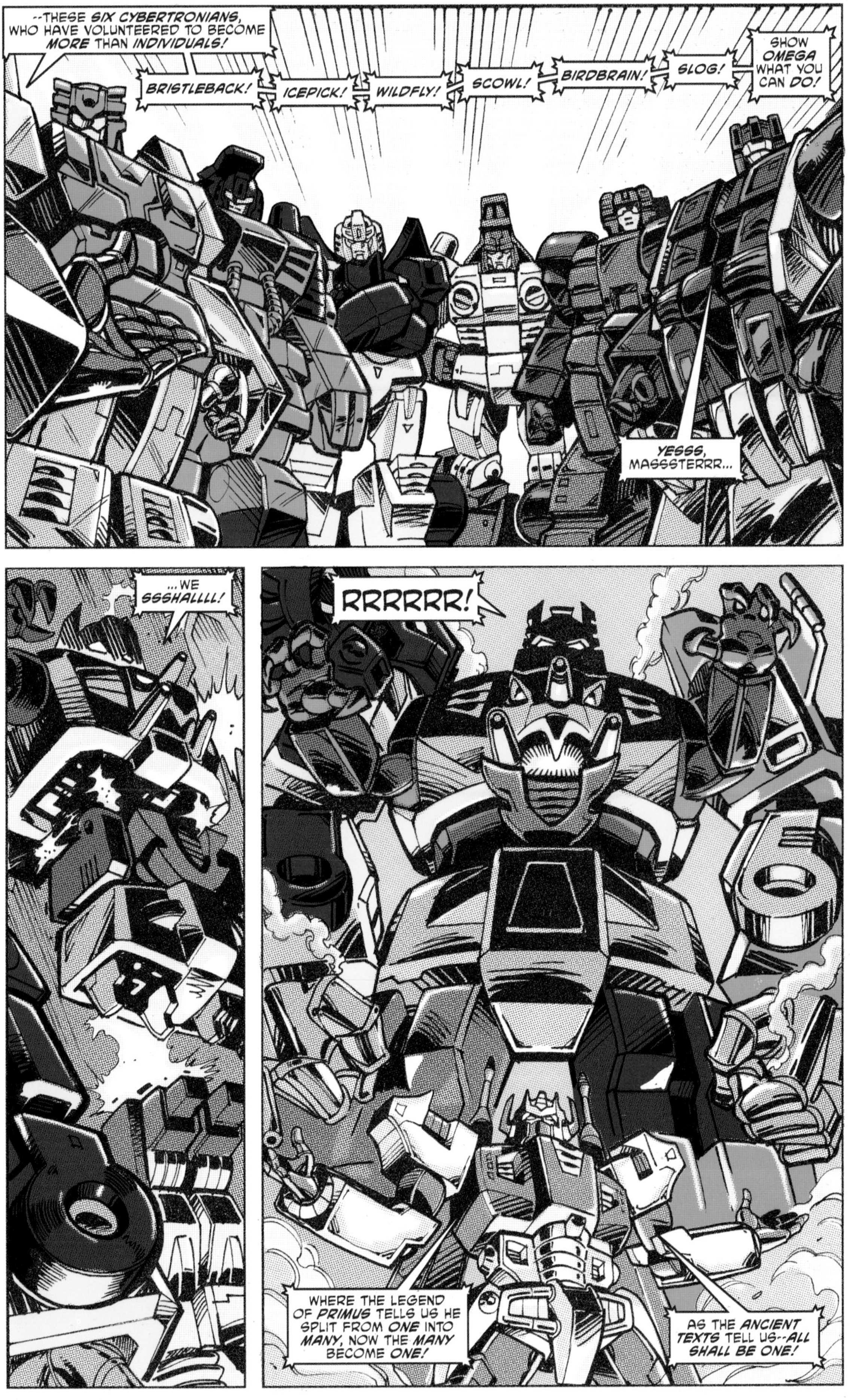
--THESE SIX CYBERTRONIANS, WHO HAVE VOLUNTEERED TO BECOME MORE THAN INDIVIDUALS!
BRISTLEBACK!
ICEPICK!
WILDFLY!
SCOWL!
BIRDBRAIN!
SLOG!
SHOW OMEGA WHAT YOU CAN DO!
YESSS, MASSSTERRR...
...WE SSSHALLLL!
RRRRRR!
WHERE THE LEGEND OF PRIMUS TELLS US HE SPLIT FROM ONE INTO MANY, NOW THE MANY BECOME ONE!
AS THE ANCIENT TEXTS TELL US--ALL SHALL BE ONE!

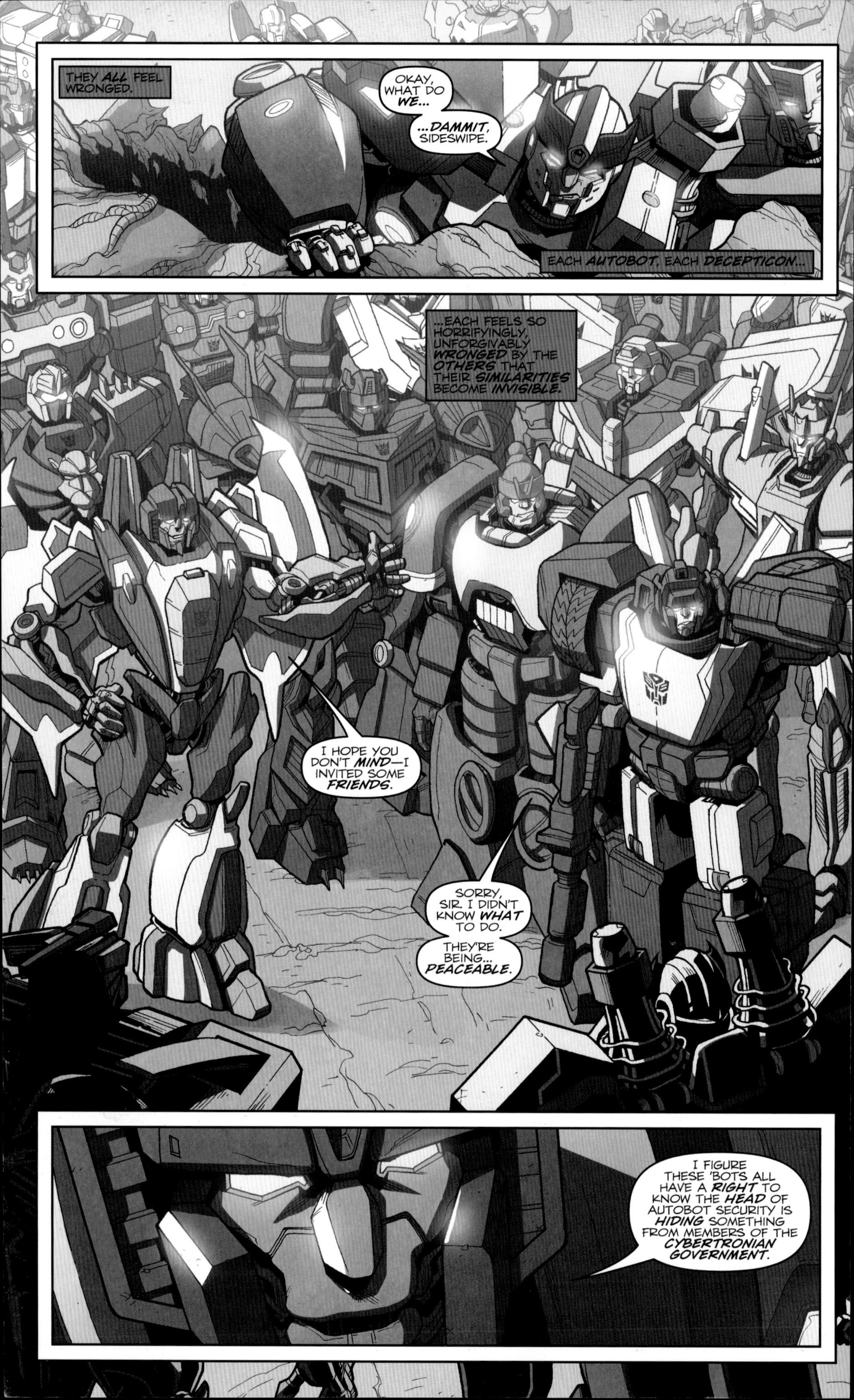
THEY ALL FEEL WRONGED.
OKAY, WHAT DO WE...
...DAMMIT, SIDESWIPE.
EACH AUTOBOT, EACH DECEPTICON...
...EACH FEELS SO HORRIFYINGLY, UNFORGIVABLY WRONGED BY THE OTHERS THAT THEIR SIMILARITIES BECOME INVISIBLE.
I HOPE YOU DON'T MIND—I INVITED SOME FRIENDS.
SORRY, SIR. I DIDN'T KNOW WHAT TO DO.
THEY'RE BEING... PEACEABLE.
I FIGURE THESE 'BOTS ALL HAVE A RIGHT TO KNOW THE HEAD OF AUTOBOT SECURITY IS HIDING SOMETHING FROM MEMBERS OF THE CYBERTRONIAN GOVERNMENT.

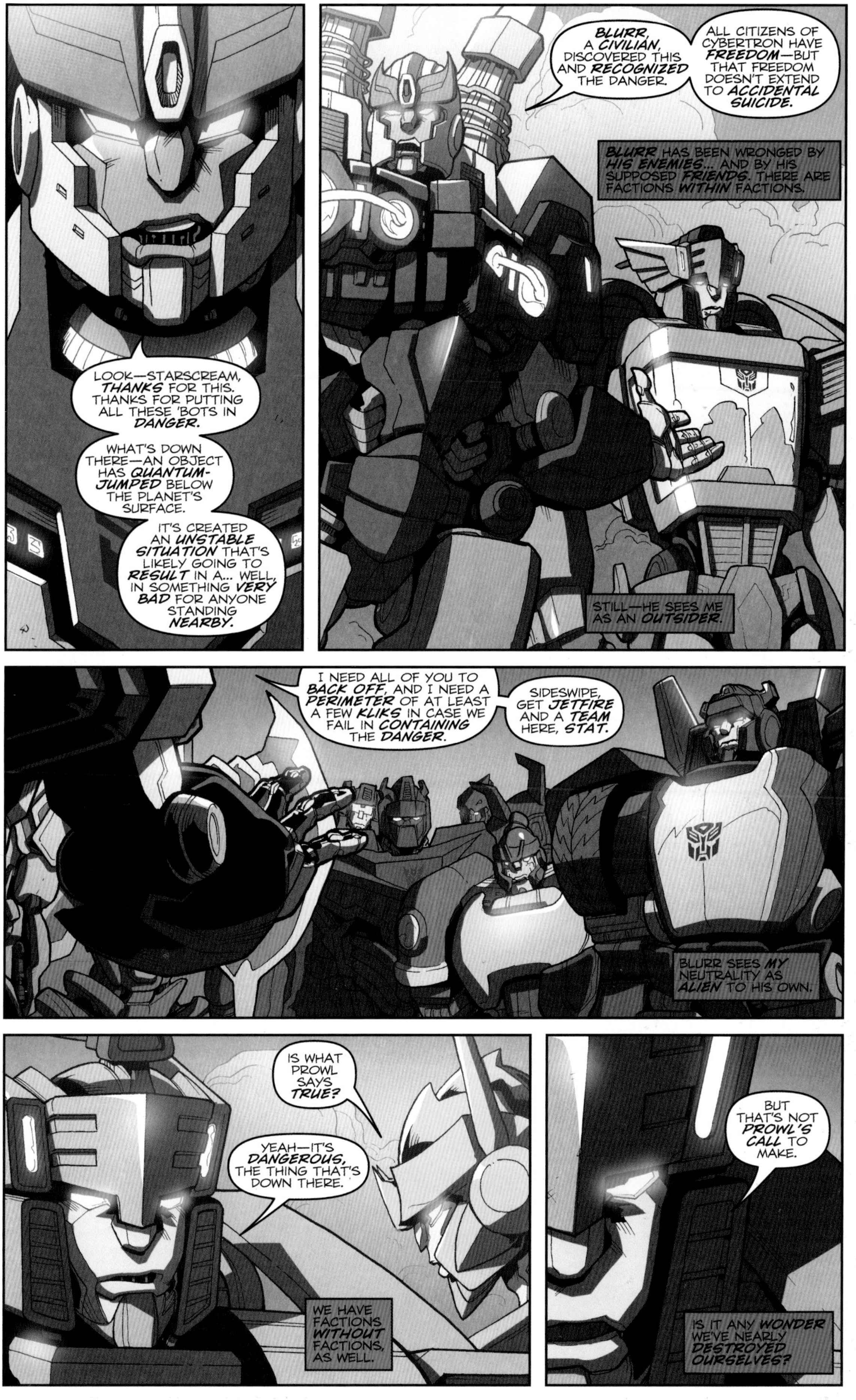
LOOK—STARSCREAM, THANKS FOR THIS. THANKS FOR PUTTING ALL THESE 'BOTS IN DANGER.
WHAT'S DOWN THERE—AN OBJECT HAS QUANTUM-JUMPED BELOW THE PLANET'S SURFACE.
IT'S CREATED AN UNSTABLE SITUATION THAT'S LIKELY GOING TO RESULT IN A... WELL, IN SOMETHING VERY BAD FOR ANYONE STANDING NEARBY.
BLURR, A CIVILIAN, DISCOVERED THIS AND RECOGNIZED THE DANGER.
ALL CITIZENS OF CYBERTRON HAVE FREEDOM—BUT THAT FREEDOM DOESN'T EXTEND TO ACCIDENTAL SUICIDE.
BLURR HAS BEEN WRONGED BY HIS ENEMIES... AND BY HIS SUPPOSED FRIENDS. THERE ARE FACTIONS WITHIN FACTIONS.
STILL—HE SEES ME AS AN OUTSIDER.
I NEED ALL OF YOU TO BACK OFF, AND I NEED A PERIMETER OF AT LEAST A FEW KLIKS IN CASE WE FAIL IN CONTAINING THE DANGER.
SIDESWIPE, GET JETFIRE AND A TEAM HERE, STAT.
BLURR SEES MY NEUTRALITY AS ALIEN TO HIS OWN.
IS WHAT PROWL SAYS TRUE?
YEAH—IT'S DANGEROUS, THE THING THAT'S DOWN THERE.
WE HAVE FACTIONS WITHOUT FACTIONS, AS WELL.
BUT THAT'S NOT PROWL'S CALL TO MAKE.
IS IT ANY WONDER WE'VE NEARLY DESTROYED OURSELVES?

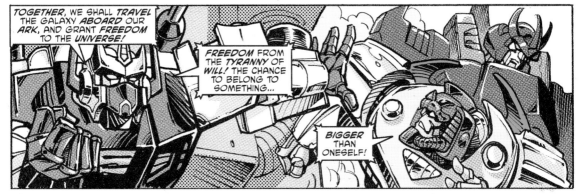

TOGETHER, WE SHALL *TRAVEL* THE GALAXY *ABOARD* OUR *ARK*, AND GRANT *FREEDOM* TO THE *UNIVERSE!*

*FREEDOM* FROM THE *TYRANNY OF WILL!* THE CHANCE TO BELONG TO SOMETHING...

...*BIGGER* THAN ONESELF!

THIS IS *NOT* WHEN *ALL* ARE *ONE.*

THIS IS *NOT* WHAT THE *ANCIENTS MEAN.*

RRR--MEAN-- RR--MON--RR

MONSTRUCTOR!

TAKE HIM *AWAY* FROM HERE. WE WILL BROOK NO *DISSENT,* DAI ATLAS.

IT'S THE *END* OF FREEDOM, OMEGA!

THE *DESTRUCTION* OF THE *INDIVIDUAL* FOR THE *EXPANSION* OF THE *STATE!*

I *KNOW* WHAT IT IS...

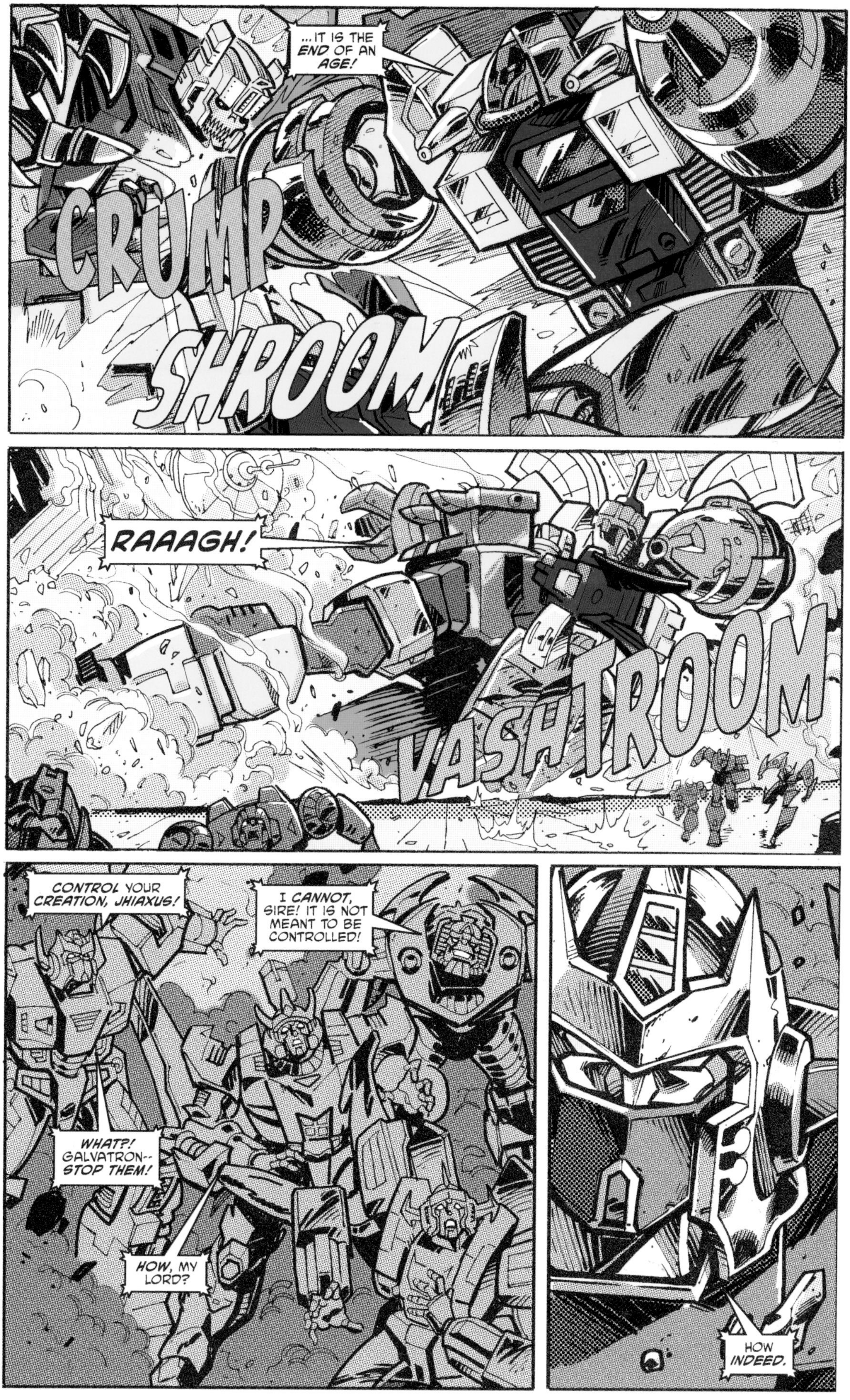
...IT IS THE END OF AN AGE!
CRUMP
SHROOM
RAAAGH!
VASHTROOM
CONTROL YOUR CREATION, JHIAXUS!
I CANNOT, SIRE! IT IS NOT MEANT TO BE CONTROLLED!
WHAT?! GALVATRON-- STOP THEM!
HOW, MY LORD?
HOW INDEED.

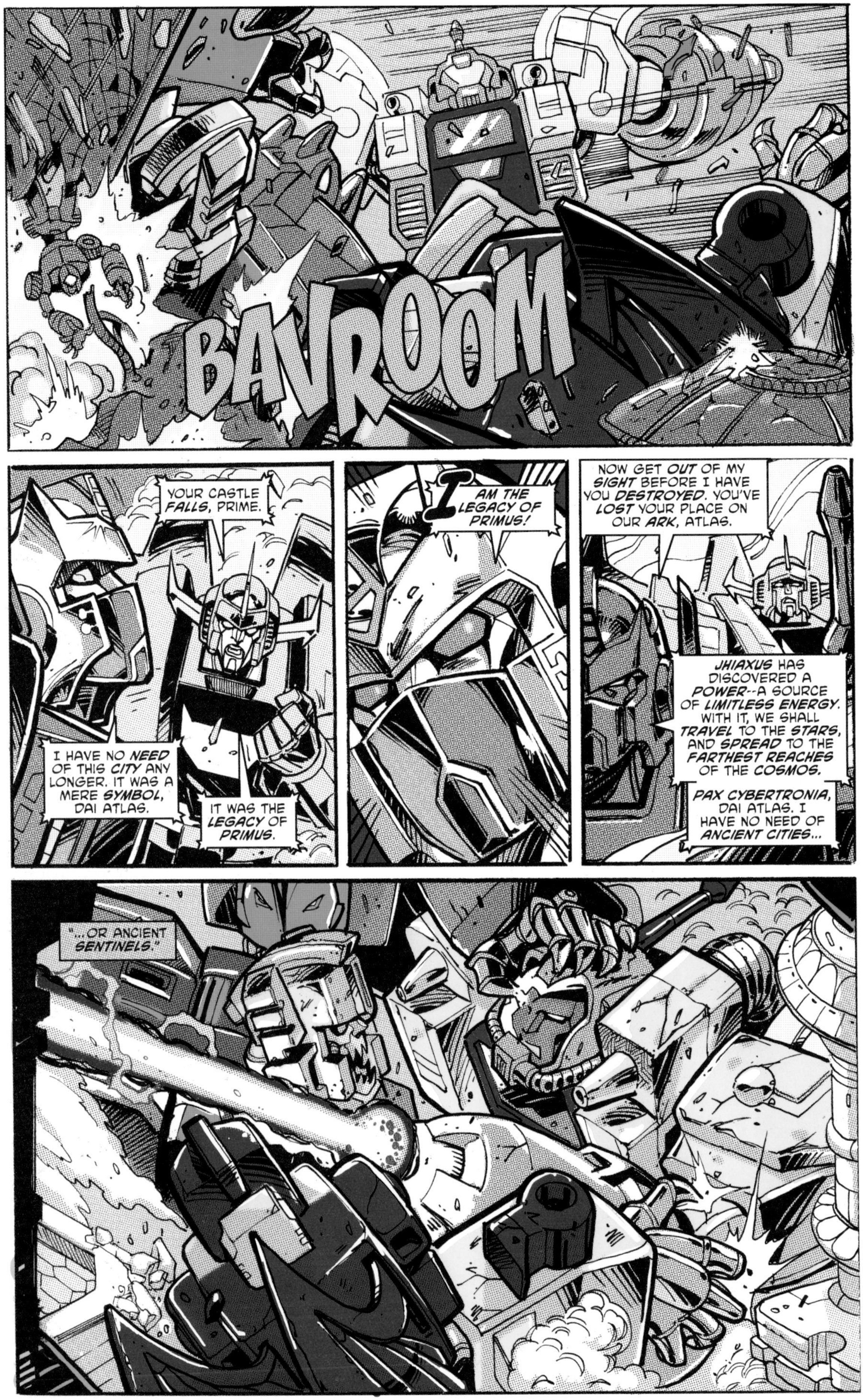
BAVROOM
YOUR CASTLE FALLS, PRIME.
I HAVE NO NEED OF THIS CITY ANY LONGER. IT WAS A MERE SYMBOL, DAI ATLAS.
IT WAS THE LEGACY OF PRIMUS.
I AM THE LEGACY OF PRIMUS!
NOW GET OUT OF MY SIGHT BEFORE I HAVE YOU DESTROYED. YOU'VE LOST YOUR PLACE ON OUR ARK, ATLAS.
JHIAXUS HAS DISCOVERED A POWER--A SOURCE OF LIMITLESS ENERGY. WITH IT, WE SHALL TRAVEL TO THE STARS, AND SPREAD TO THE FARTHEST REACHES OF THE COSMOS.
PAX CYBERTRONIA, DAI ATLAS. I HAVE NO NEED OF ANCIENT CITIES...
"...OR ANCIENT SENTINELS."

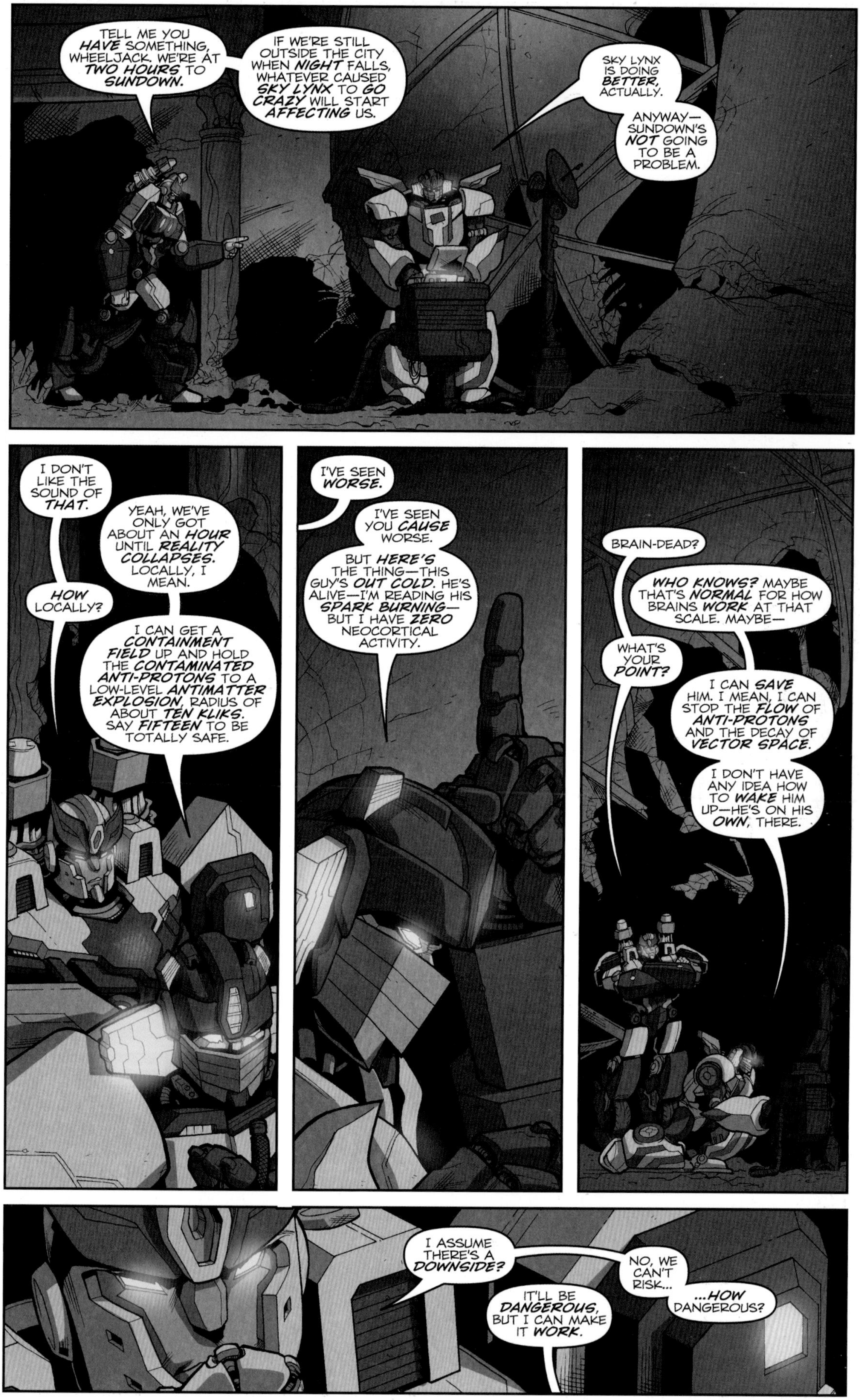

TELL ME YOU HAVE SOMETHING, WHEELJACK. WE'RE AT TWO HOURS TO SUNDOWN.
IF WE'RE STILL OUTSIDE THE CITY WHEN NIGHT FALLS, WHATEVER CAUSED SKY LYNX TO GO CRAZY WILL START AFFECTING US.
SKY LYNX IS DOING BETTER, ACTUALLY.
ANYWAY— SUNDOWN'S NOT GOING TO BE A PROBLEM.
I DON'T LIKE THE SOUND OF THAT.
YEAH, WE'VE ONLY GOT ABOUT AN HOUR UNTIL REALITY COLLAPSES. LOCALLY, I MEAN.
HOW LOCALLY?
I CAN GET A CONTAINMENT FIELD UP AND HOLD THE CONTAMINATED ANTI-PROTONS TO A LOW-LEVEL ANTIMATTER EXPLOSION, RADIUS OF ABOUT TEN KLIKS. SAY FIFTEEN TO BE TOTALLY SAFE.
I'VE SEEN WORSE.
I'VE SEEN YOU CAUSE WORSE.
BUT HERE'S THE THING—THIS GUY'S OUT COLD. HE'S ALIVE—I'M READING HIS SPARK BURNING—BUT I HAVE ZERO NEOCORTICAL ACTIVITY.
BRAIN-DEAD?
WHO KNOWS? MAYBE THAT'S NORMAL FOR HOW BRAINS WORK AT THAT SCALE. MAYBE—
WHAT'S YOUR POINT?
I CAN SAVE HIM. I MEAN, I CAN STOP THE FLOW OF ANTI-PROTONS AND THE DECAY OF VECTOR SPACE.
I DON'T HAVE ANY IDEA HOW TO WAKE HIM UP—HE'S ON HIS OWN, THERE.
I ASSUME THERE'S A DOWNSIDE?
IT'LL BE DANGEROUS, BUT I CAN MAKE IT WORK.
NO, WE CAN'T RISK...
...HOW DANGEROUS?

IT'S, ON A SCALE FROM *REASONABLE* TO SOMETHING *BRAINSTORM* WOULD COME UP WITH... ABOUT 0.6, 0.7 *BRAINSTORMS.*

MEANING...?

IF I START THIS *GOING* AND THE *ANTI-PROTONS* KEEP *ACCUMULATING,* WE'LL GET AN *UNCONTROLLED ANTIMATTER REACTION* AND A CASCADING EFFECT OF PROTONS FALLING TO A *POINT,* PROBABLY CREATING A *SINGULARITY.*

MEANING...?

*PLANET-SIZED FIREBALL* AND OUR *ENTIRE STAR SYSTEM* TURNING INTO A *SUPERMASSIVE BLACK HOLE.*

THAT'S 0.6 *BRAINSTORMS?*

YOU, UH, YOU *DO* KNOW WHAT HE GETS UP TO, RIGHT?

I MEAN, *GOT* UP TO, BEFORE THE *LOST LIGHT* BLEW UP.

WE CAN'T RISK IT. WE'LL *CLEAR* THE AREA.

CHUFF

WHAT THE—?

DAMMIT— *WHEELJACK,* KEEP THE OTHERS OUT...

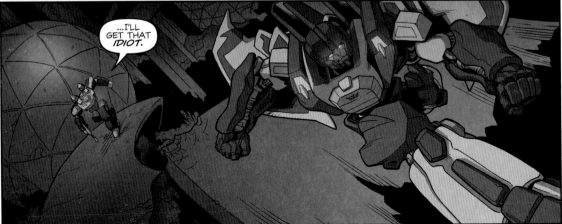

...I'LL GET THAT *IDIOT.*

THE FORCES *UNLEASHED* IN THE *BATTLE* OF THE *METAL GIANTS* WERE *STAGGERING*--INCONCEIVABLE.

WHEN IT WAS *OVER*, PRIMUS' SANCTUARY WAS LAID TO *WASTE*... AND *ONE* CYBERTONIAN REIGNED--*SUPREME!*

YOU... YOU TOOK *CARE* OF IT.

OF *THEM*. THEY... ARE *NOT* ONE.

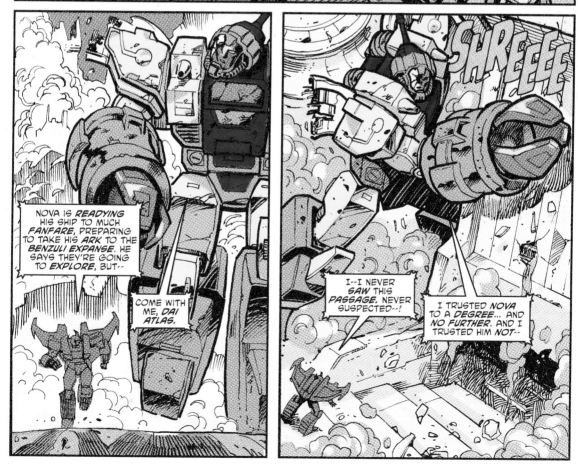

NOVA IS *READYING* HIS SHIP TO MUCH *FANFARE*, PREPARING TO TAKE HIS *ARK* TO THE *BENZULI EXPANSE*. HE SAYS THEY'RE GOING TO *EXPLORE*, BUT--

COME WITH ME, *DAI ATLAS*.

SHREEE

I--I NEVER *SAW* THIS *PASSAGE*. NEVER SUSPECTED--!

I TRUSTED *NOVA* TO A *DEGREE*... AND *NO FURTHER*. AND I TRUSTED HIM *NOT*--

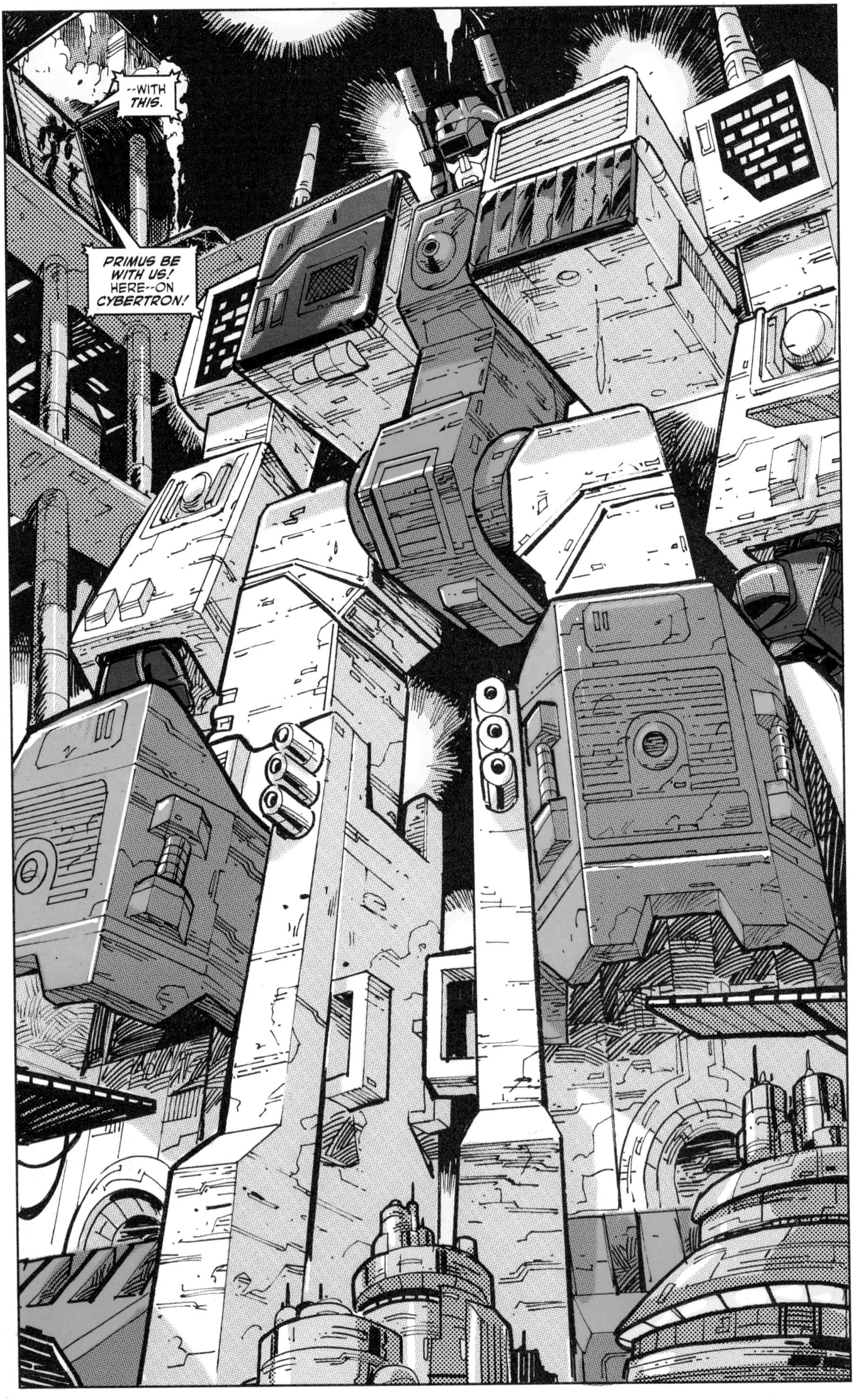
--WITH THIS.
PRIMUS BE WITH US! HERE--ON CYBERTRON!

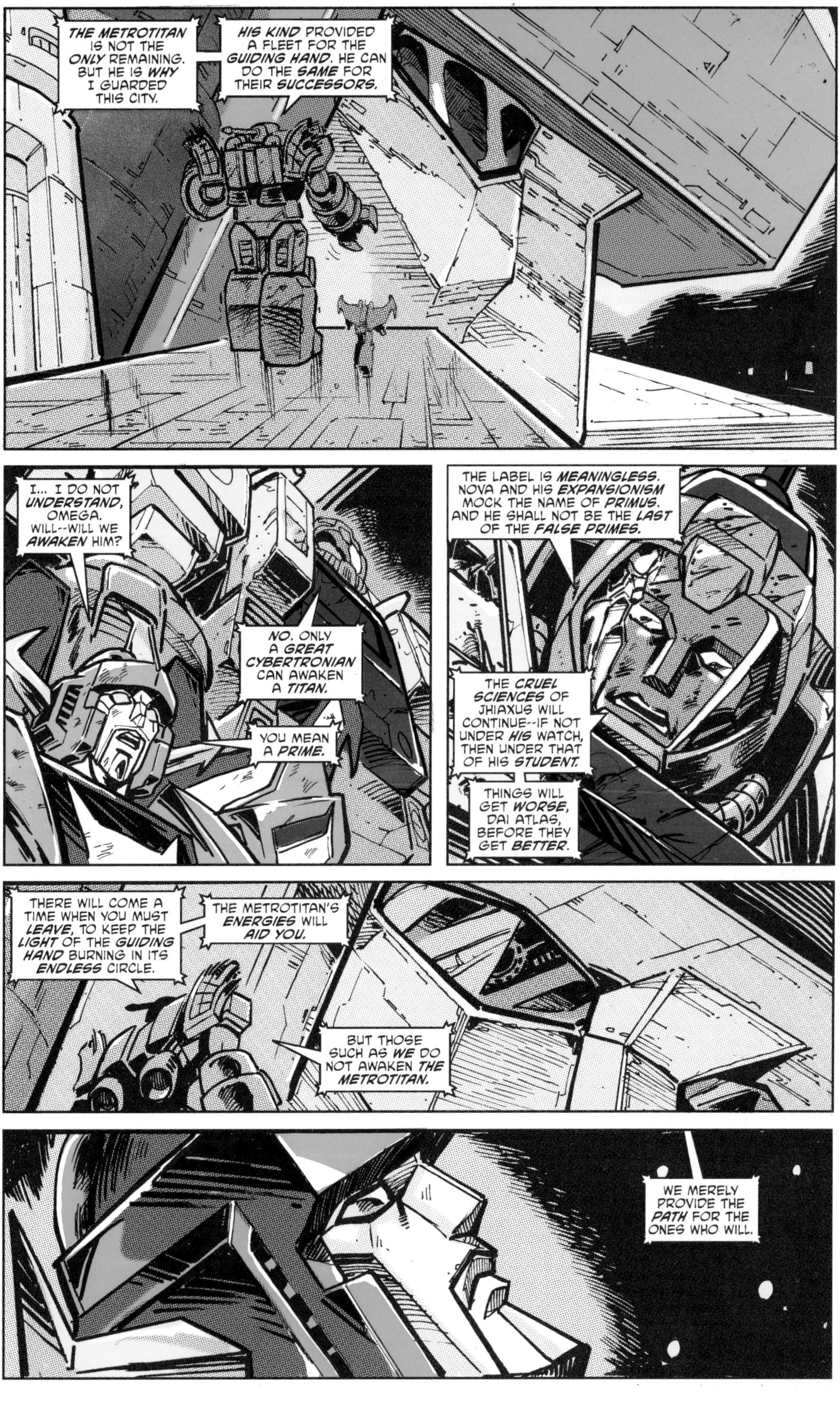
THE METROTITAN IS NOT THE ONLY REMAINING. BUT HE IS WHY I GUARDED THIS CITY.
HIS KIND PROVIDED A FLEET FOR THE GUIDING HAND. HE CAN DO THE SAME FOR THEIR SUCCESSORS.
I... I DO NOT UNDERSTAND, OMEGA. WILL--WILL WE AWAKEN HIM?
NO. ONLY A GREAT CYBERTRONIAN CAN AWAKEN A TITAN.
YOU MEAN A PRIME.
THE LABEL IS MEANINGLESS. NOVA AND HIS EXPANSIONISM MOCK THE NAME OF PRIMUS. AND HE SHALL NOT BE THE LAST OF THE FALSE PRIMES.
THE CRUEL SCIENCES OF JHIAXUS WILL CONTINUE--IF NOT UNDER HIS WATCH, THEN UNDER THAT OF HIS STUDENT.
THINGS WILL GET WORSE, DAI ATLAS, BEFORE THEY GET BETTER.
THERE WILL COME A TIME WHEN YOU MUST LEAVE, TO KEEP THE LIGHT OF THE GUIDING HAND BURNING IN ITS ENDLESS CIRCLE.
THE METROTITAN'S ENERGIES WILL AID YOU.
BUT THOSE SUCH AS WE DO NOT AWAKEN THE METROTITAN.
WE MERELY PROVIDE THE PATH FOR THE ONES WHO WILL.

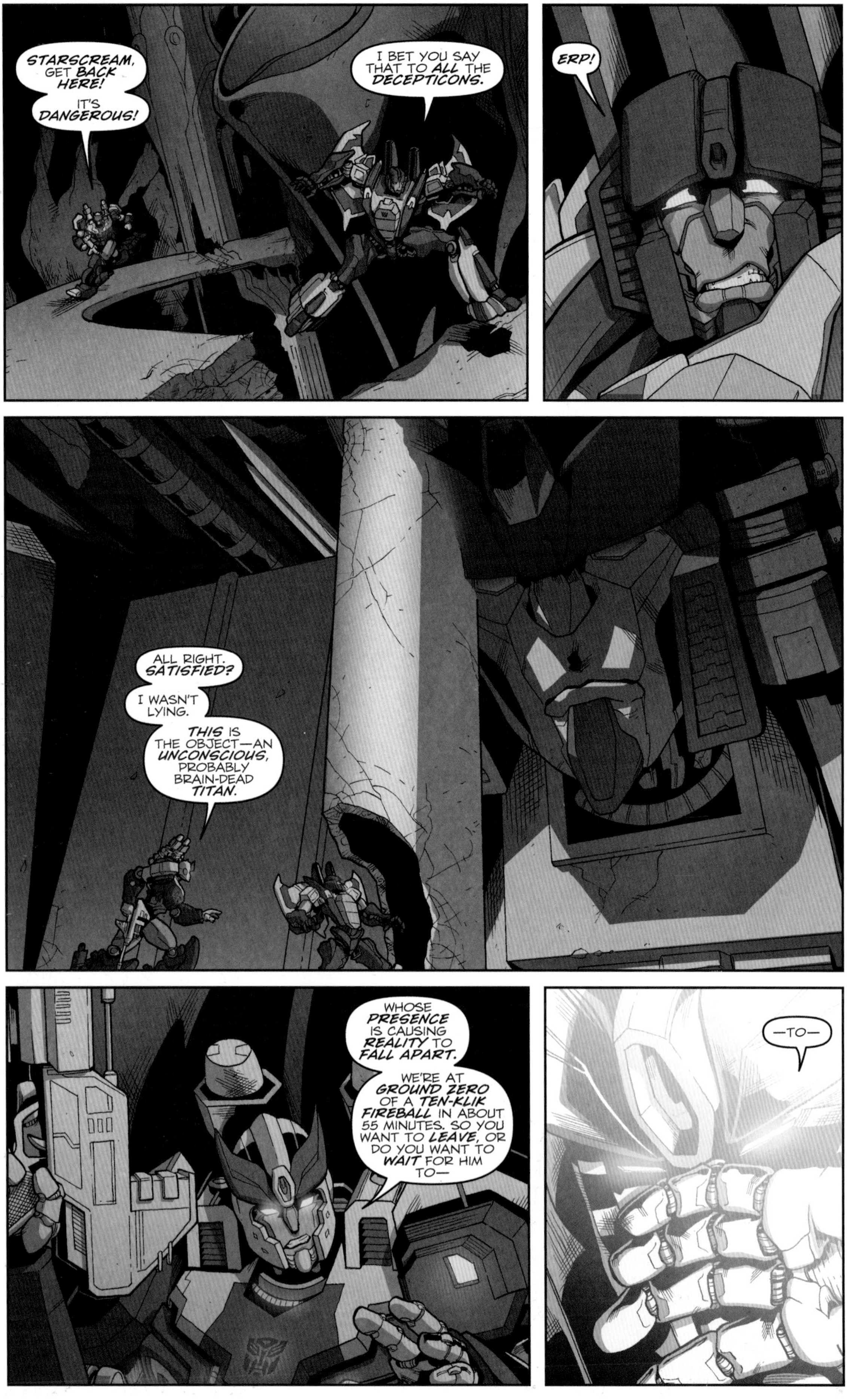
STARSCREAM, GET BACK HERE!
IT'S DANGEROUS!
I BET YOU SAY THAT TO ALL THE DECEPTICONS.
ERP!
ALL RIGHT. SATISFIED?
I WASN'T LYING.
THIS IS THE OBJECT—AN UNCONSCIOUS, PROBABLY BRAIN-DEAD TITAN.
WHOSE PRESENCE IS CAUSING REALITY TO FALL APART.
WE'RE AT GROUND ZERO OF A TEN-KLIK FIREBALL IN ABOUT 55 MINUTES. SO YOU WANT TO LEAVE, OR DO YOU WANT TO WAIT FOR HIM TO—
—TO—

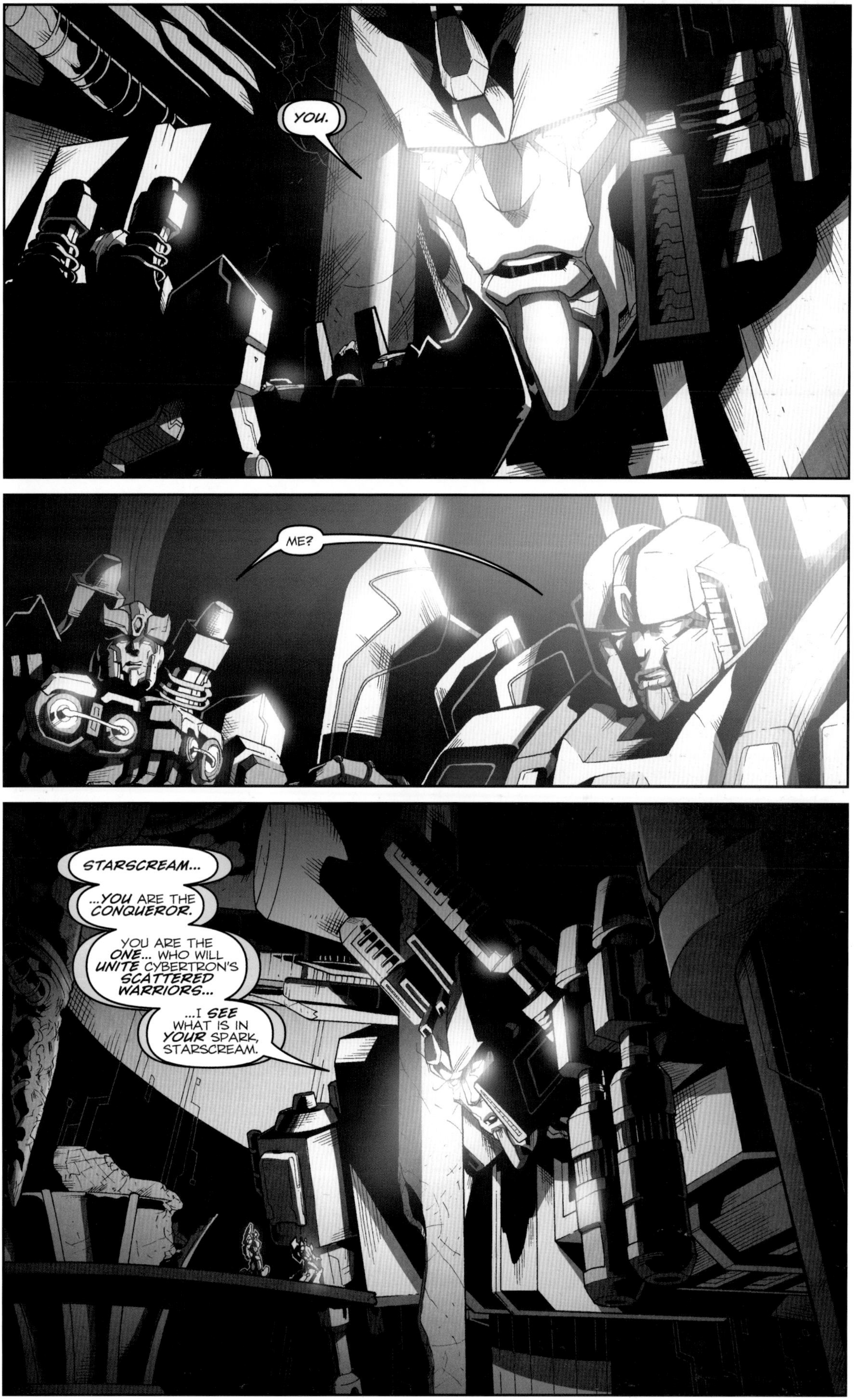
YOU.
ME?
STARSCREAM...
...YOU ARE THE CONQUEROR.
YOU ARE THE ONE... WHO WILL UNITE CYBERTRON'S SCATTERED WARRIORS...
...I SEE WHAT IS IN YOUR SPARK, STARSCREAM.

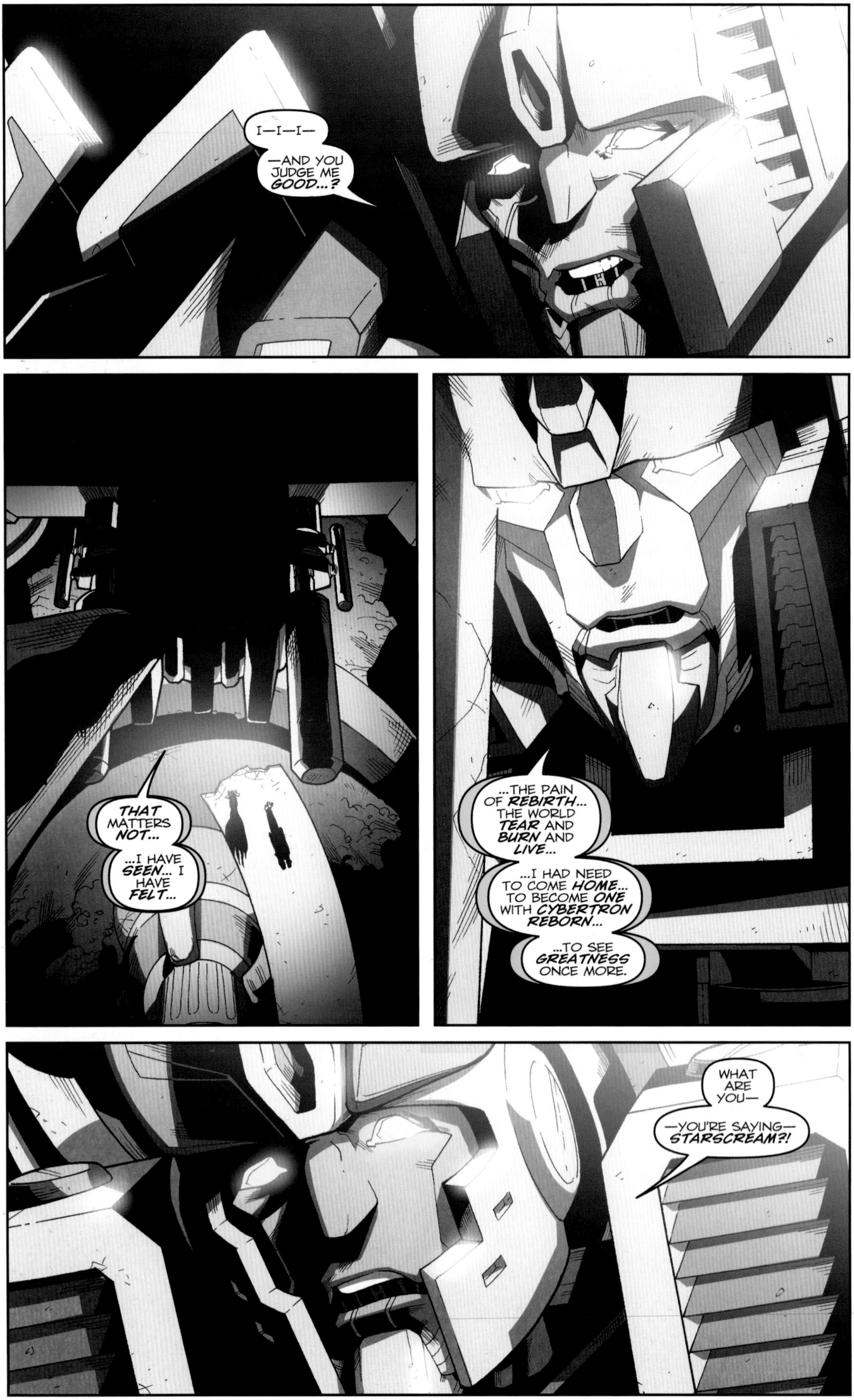

I—I—I—
—AND YOU JUDGE ME GOOD...?
THAT MATTERS NOT...
...I HAVE SEEN... I HAVE FELT...
...THE PAIN OF REBIRTH... THE WORLD TEAR AND BURN AND LIVE...
...I HAD NEED TO COME HOME... TO BECOME ONE WITH CYBERTRON REBORN...
...TO SEE GREATNESS ONCE MORE.
WHAT ARE YOU—
—YOU'RE SAYING— STARSCREAM?!

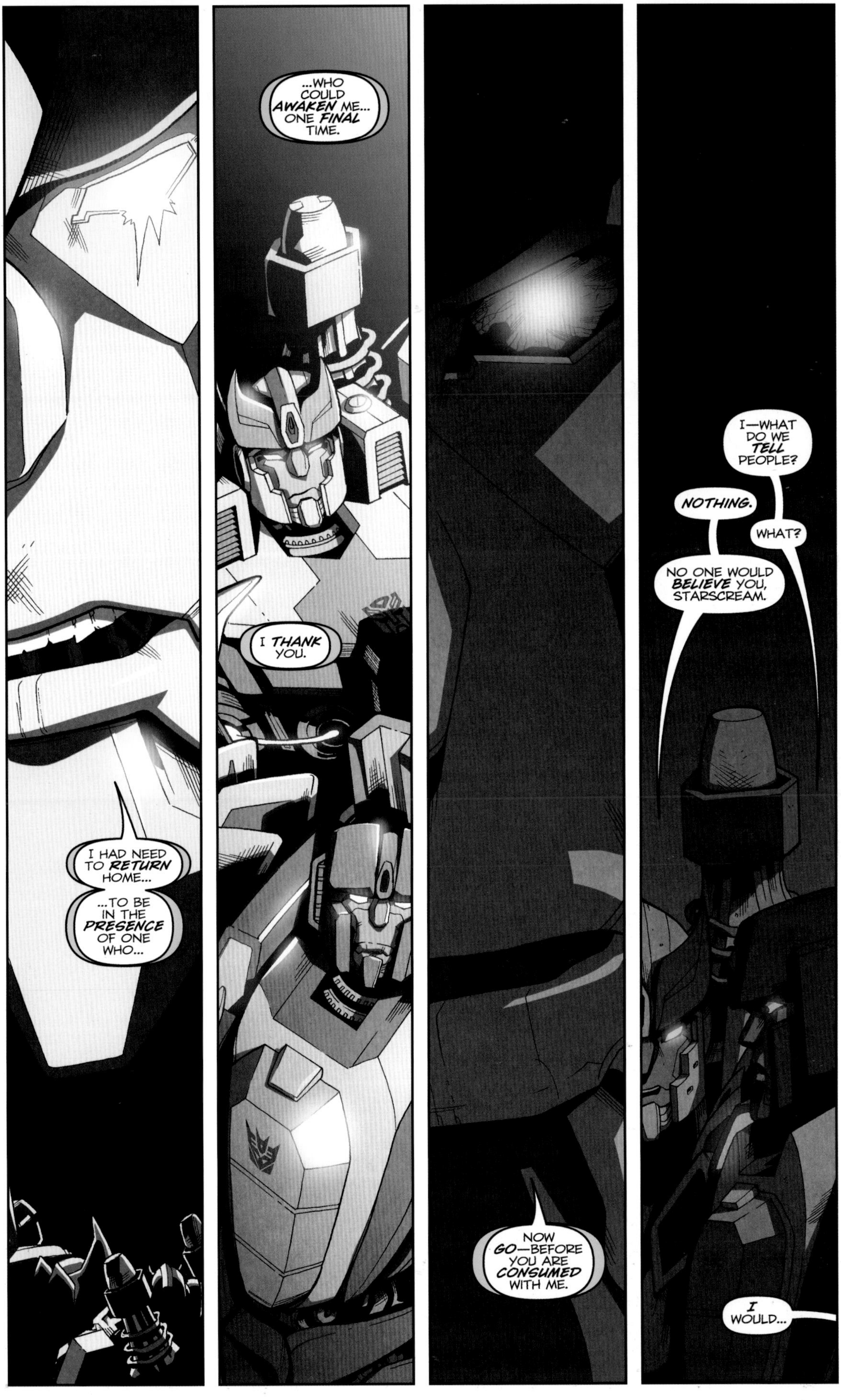
I HAD NEED TO RETURN HOME...
...TO BE IN THE PRESENCE OF ONE WHO...
...WHO COULD AWAKEN ME... ONE FINAL TIME.
I THANK YOU.
NOW GO—BEFORE YOU ARE CONSUMED WITH ME.
I—WHAT DO WE TELL PEOPLE?
NOTHING.
WHAT?
NO ONE WOULD BELIEVE YOU, STARSCREAM.
I WOULD...

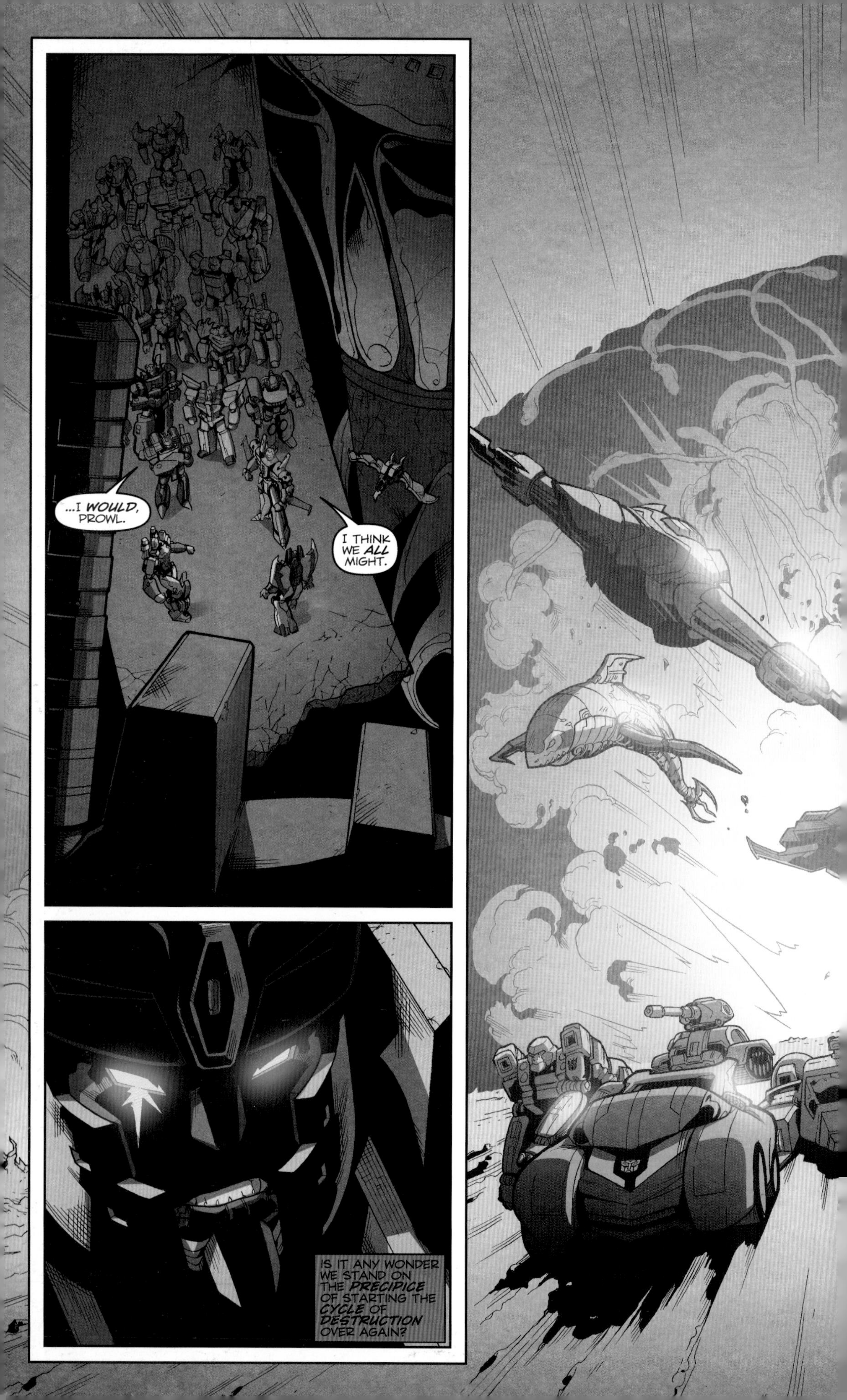
...I WOULD, PROWL.
I THINK WE ALL MIGHT.
IS IT ANY WONDER WE STAND ON THE PRECIPICE OF STARTING THE CYCLE OF DESTRUCTION OVER AGAIN?

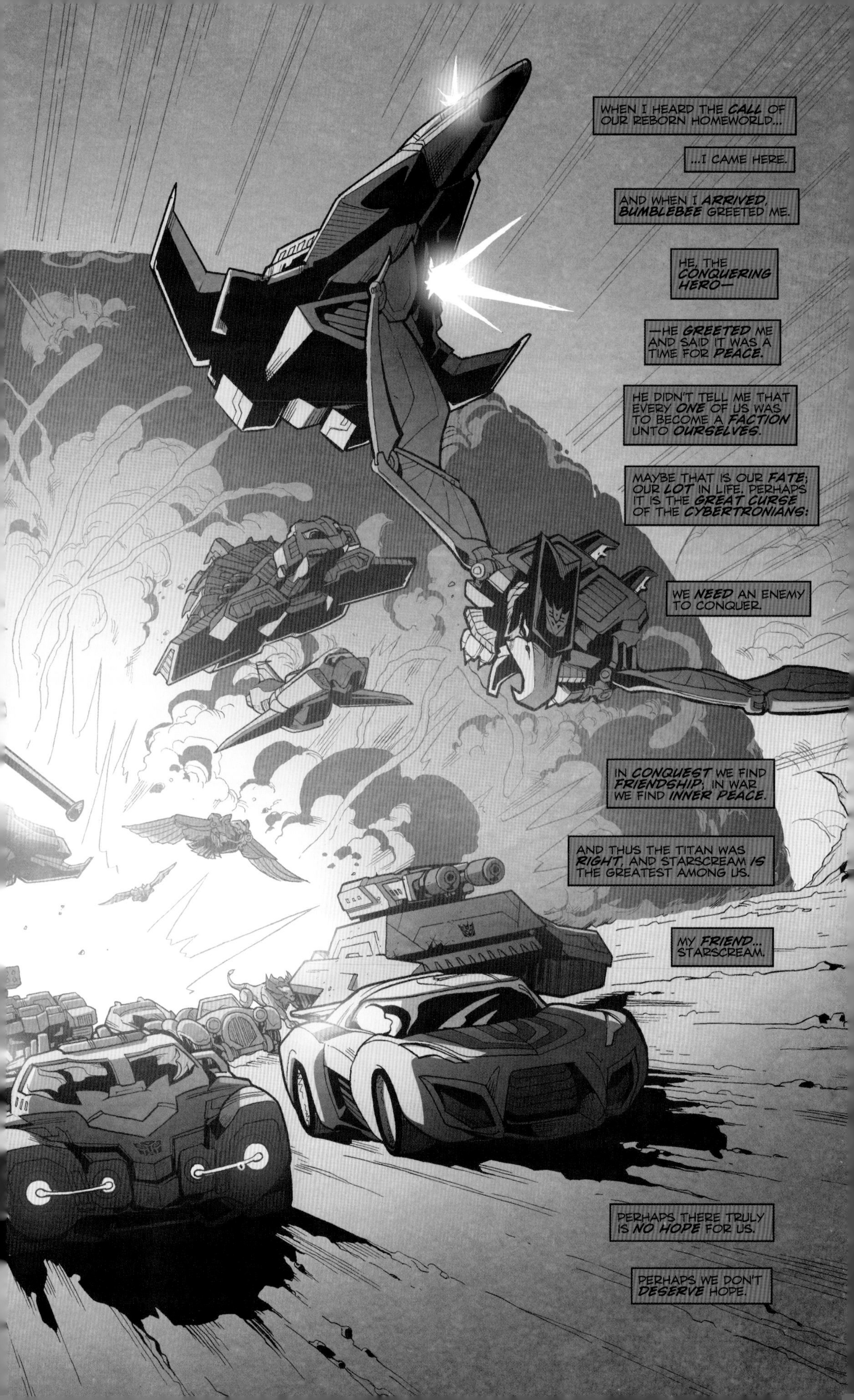
WHEN I HEARD THE CALL OF OUR REBORN HOMEWORLD...
...I CAME HERE.
AND WHEN I ARRIVED, BUMBLEBEE GREETED ME.
HE, THE CONQUERING HERO—
—HE GREETED ME AND SAID IT WAS A TIME FOR PEACE.
HE DIDN'T TELL ME THAT EVERY ONE OF US WAS TO BECOME A FACTION UNTO OURSELVES.
MAYBE THAT IS OUR FATE; OUR LOT IN LIFE. PERHAPS IT IS THE GREAT CURSE OF THE CYBERTRONIANS:
WE NEED AN ENEMY TO CONQUER.
IN CONQUEST WE FIND FRIENDSHIP; IN WAR WE FIND INNER PEACE.
AND THUS THE TITAN WAS RIGHT, AND STARSCREAM IS THE GREATEST AMONG US.
MY FRIEND... STARSCREAM.
PERHAPS THERE TRULY IS NO HOPE FOR US.
PERHAPS WE DON'T DESERVE HOPE.

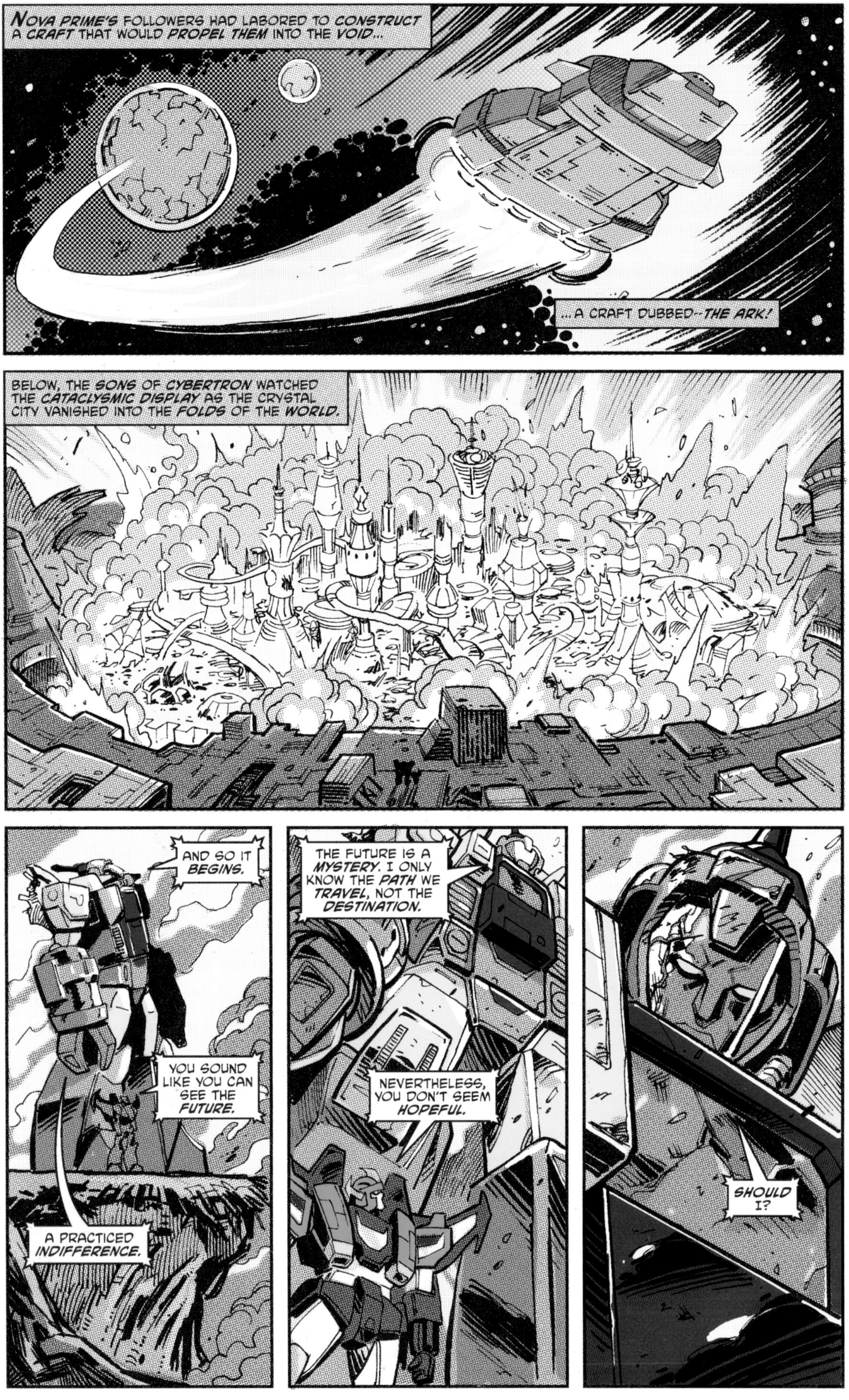
NOVA PRIME'S FOLLOWERS HAD LABORED TO CONSTRUCT A CRAFT THAT WOULD PROPEL THEM INTO THE VOID...
...A CRAFT DUBBED--THE ARK!
BELOW, THE SONS OF CYBERTRON WATCHED THE CATACLYSMIC DISPLAY AS THE CRYSTAL CITY VANISHED INTO THE FOLDS OF THE WORLD.
AND SO IT BEGINS.
YOU SOUND LIKE YOU CAN SEE THE FUTURE.
A PRACTICED INDIFFERENCE.
THE FUTURE IS A MYSTERY. I ONLY KNOW THE PATH WE TRAVEL, NOT THE DESTINATION.
NEVERTHELESS, YOU DON'T SEEM HOPEFUL.
SHOULD I?

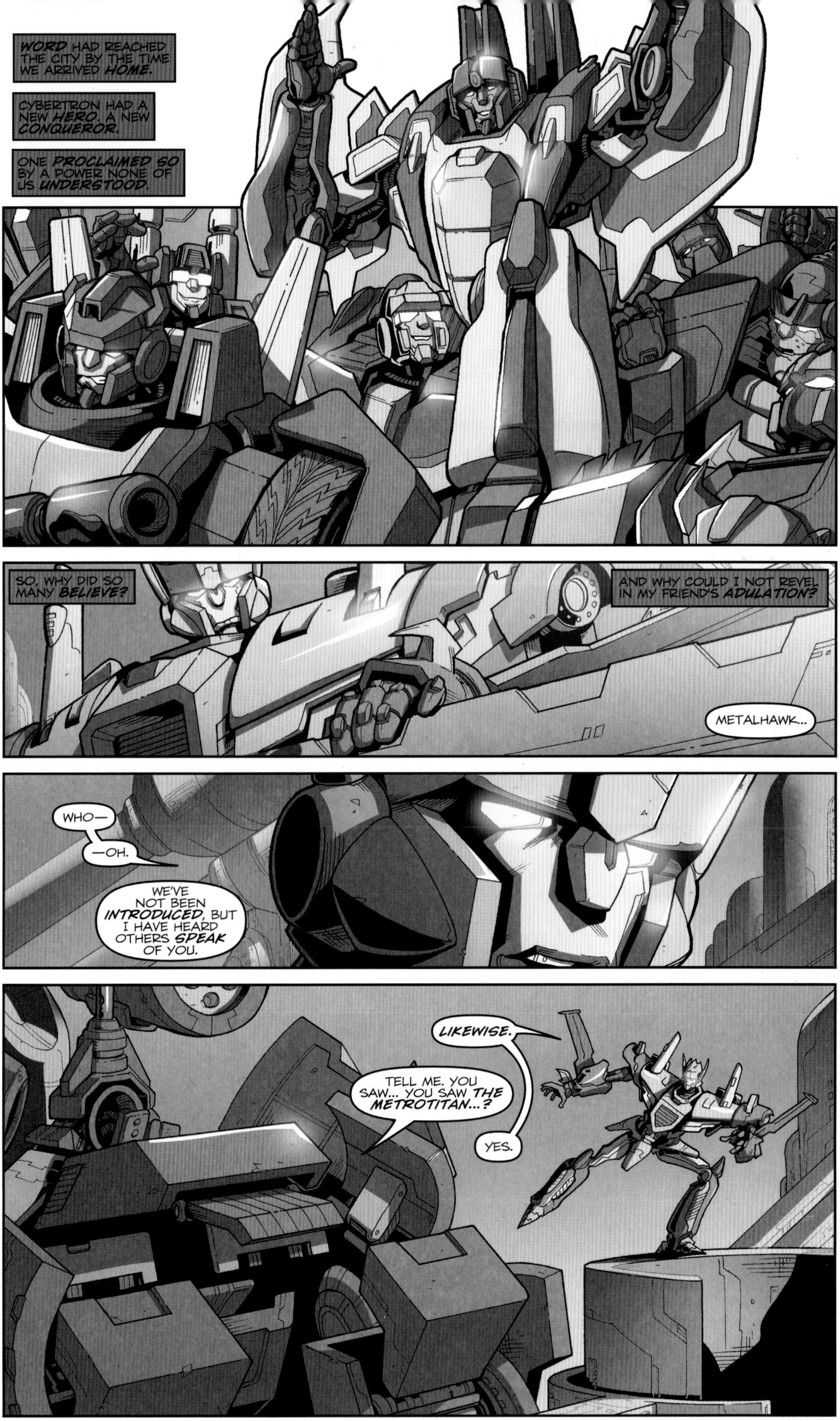
WORD HAD REACHED THE CITY BY THE TIME WE ARRIVED HOME.
CYBERTRON HAD A NEW HERO. A NEW CONQUEROR.
ONE PROCLAIMED SO BY A POWER NONE OF US UNDERSTOOD.
SO, WHY DID SO MANY BELIEVE?
AND WHY COULD I NOT REVEL IN MY FRIEND'S ADULATION?
METALHAWK...
WHO—
—OH.
WE'VE NOT BEEN INTRODUCED, BUT I HAVE HEARD OTHERS SPEAK OF YOU.
LIKEWISE.
TELL ME. YOU SAW... YOU SAW THE METROTITAN...?
YES.

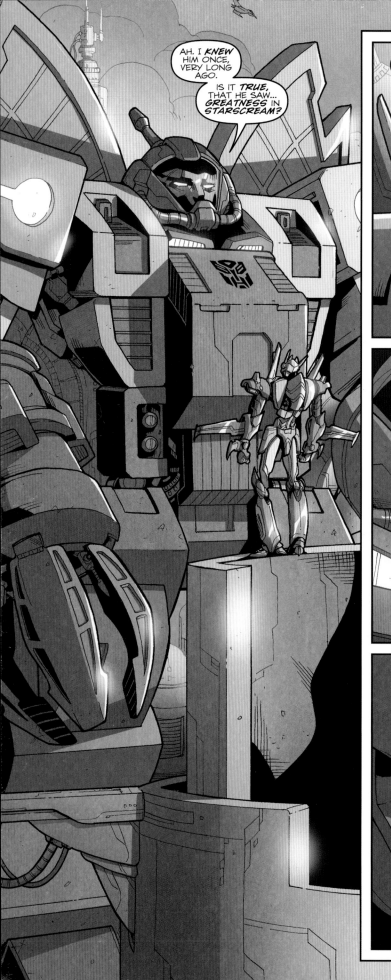

AH. I *KNEW* HIM ONCE, VERY LONG AGO.

IS IT *TRUE*, THAT HE SAW... *GREATNESS* IN STARSCREAM?

HE SAW A *CONQUEROR.* THAT'S WHAT THIS... METROTITAN *SAID.*

HM.

THAT'S *IT?*

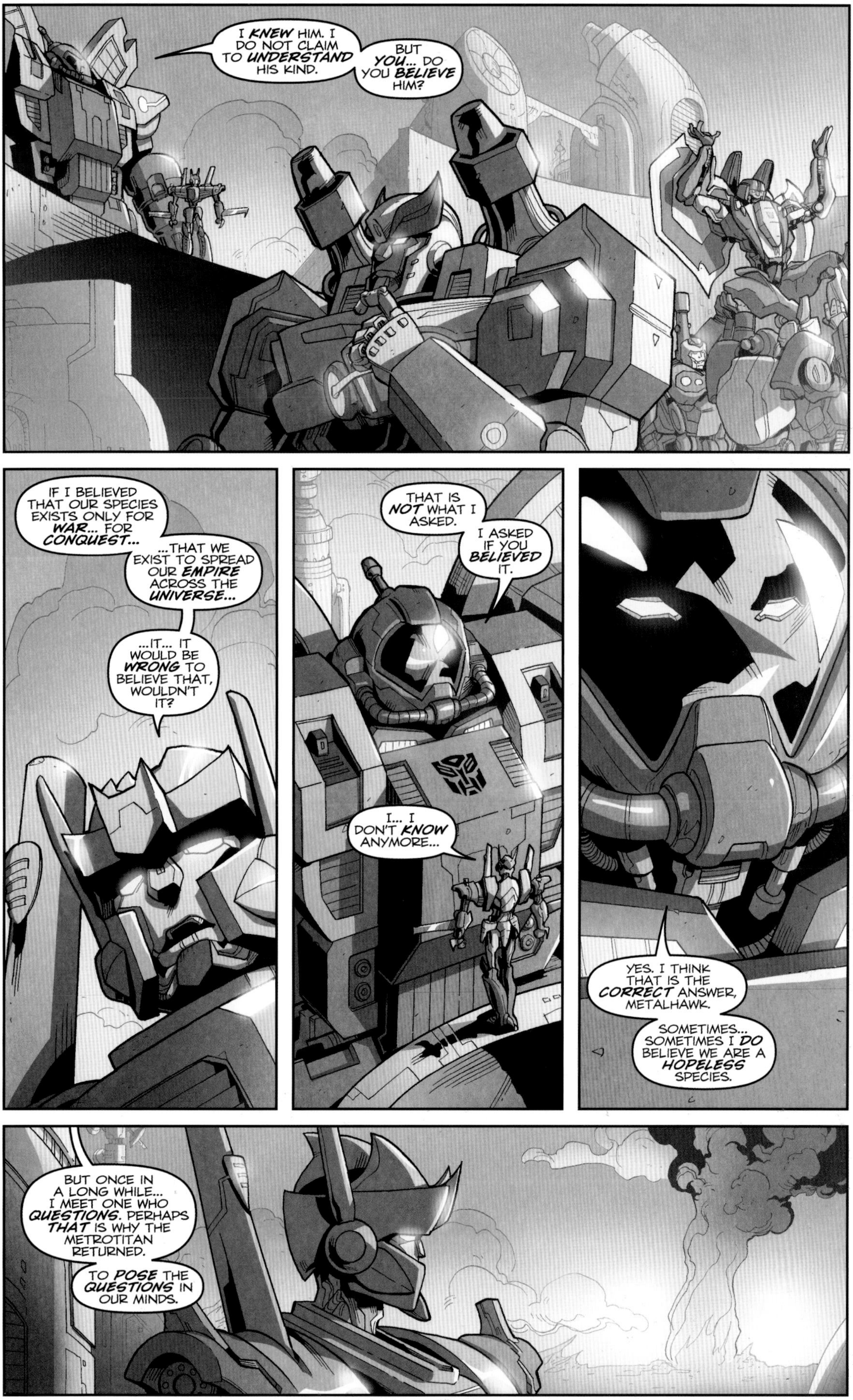
I KNEW HIM. I DO NOT CLAIM TO UNDERSTAND HIS KIND.
BUT YOU... DO YOU BELIEVE HIM?
IF I BELIEVED THAT OUR SPECIES EXISTS ONLY FOR WAR... FOR CONQUEST...
...THAT WE EXIST TO SPREAD OUR EMPIRE ACROSS THE UNIVERSE...
...IT... IT WOULD BE WRONG TO BELIEVE THAT, WOULDN'T IT?
THAT IS NOT WHAT I ASKED.
I ASKED IF YOU BELIEVED IT.
I... I DON'T KNOW ANYMORE...
YES. I THINK THAT IS THE CORRECT ANSWER, METALHAWK.
SOMETIMES... SOMETIMES I DO BELIEVE WE ARE A HOPELESS SPECIES.
BUT ONCE IN A LONG WHILE... I MEET ONE WHO QUESTIONS. PERHAPS THAT IS WHY THE METROTITAN RETURNED.
TO POSE THE QUESTIONS IN OUR MINDS.

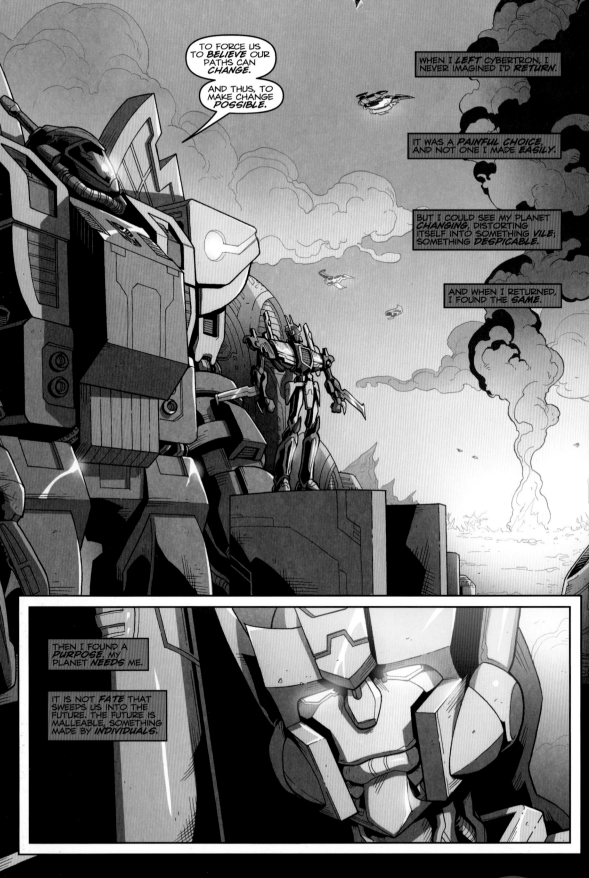

TO FORCE US TO *BELIEVE* OUR PATHS CAN *CHANGE*.

AND THUS, TO MAKE CHANGE *POSSIBLE*.

WHEN I *LEFT* CYBERTRON, I NEVER IMAGINED I'D *RETURN*.

IT WAS A *PAINFUL CHOICE*, AND NOT ONE I MADE *EASILY*.

BUT I COULD SEE MY PLANET *CHANGING*, DISTORTING ITSELF INTO SOMETHING *VILE*; SOMETHING *DESPICABLE*.

AND WHEN I RETURNED, I FOUND THE *SAME*.

THEN I FOUND A *PURPOSE*. MY PLANET *NEEDS* ME.

IT IS NOT *FATE* THAT SWEEPS US INTO THE FUTURE. THE FUTURE IS MALLEABLE, SOMETHING MADE BY *INDIVIDUALS*.

AND MY PLANET NEEDS *ME*.

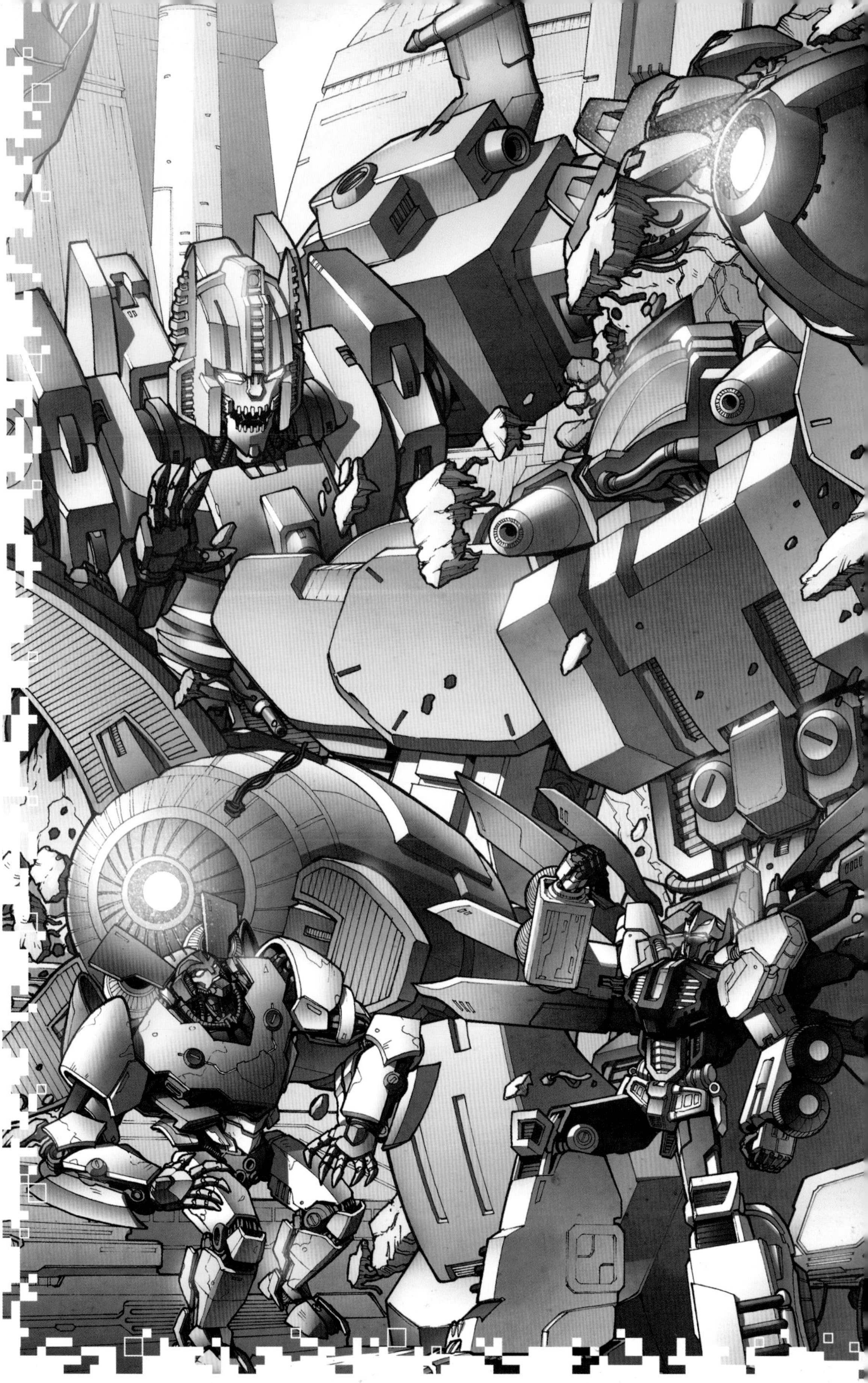

ROBOTS IN DISGUISE ANNUAL COVER B
by **ANDREW GRIFFITH** Colors by **JOANA LAFUENTE**

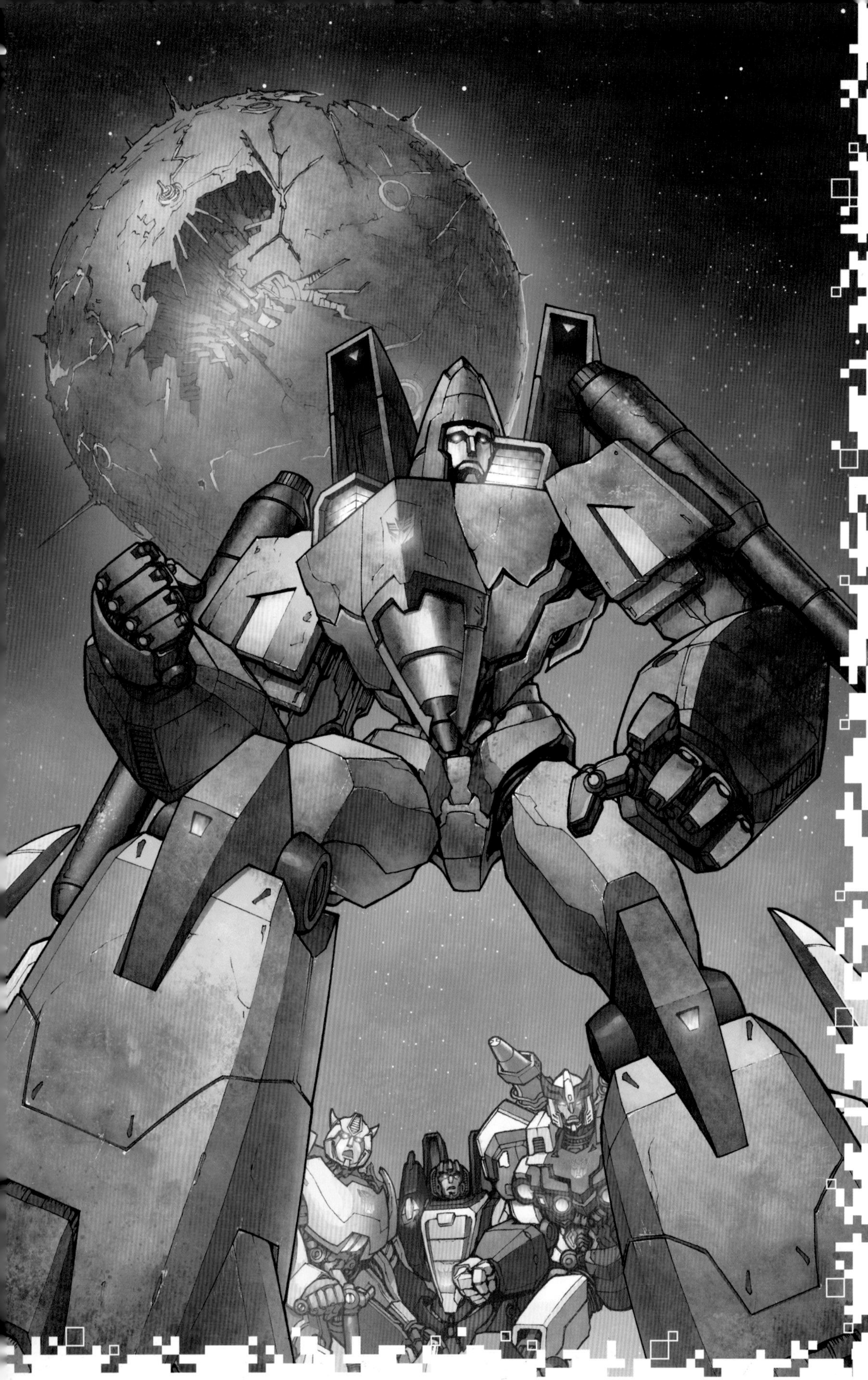

ROBOTS IN DISGUISE #11 COVER A

by **ANDREW GRIFFITH** Colors by **JOSH PEREZ**

WHAT IS IT YOU **WANT** FROM ME?

COME ON, HURRY UP—

—GET ME IN THE **FRAME** AND GET US BROADCASTING.

I **KNOW** MY JOB.

WHY, GREAT **OMEGA SUPREME**—I WANT NOTHING MORE THAN TO **THANK YOU** FOR YOUR LONG SERVICE TO THE **CYBERTRONIAN CAUSE!**

THOUGH WE FOUND OURSELVES ON **OPPOSITE** SIDES OF OUR... **LONG CONFLICT,** IT WAS ALWAYS WITH THE UTMOST OF **RESPECT** THAT—

I ASKED WHAT YOU **WANT,** STARSCREAM.

AH, SO YOU **DO** REMEMBER ME. AS YOU KNOW, I MET A, **UH, COLLEAGUE** OF YOURS—THE **METROTITAN,** WHO SUGGESTED THERE MIGHT BE SOMETHING **SPECIAL** ABOUT ME.

I WAS **CURIOUS**—THE **PUBLIC** WAS CURIOUS— IF YOU HAD ANYTHING YOU WANTED TO **ADD** TO HIS... **ENDORSEMENT?**

THERE IS NOTHING TO **ADD.** NOW LEAVE ME. I HAVE MATTERS TO **PONDER.**

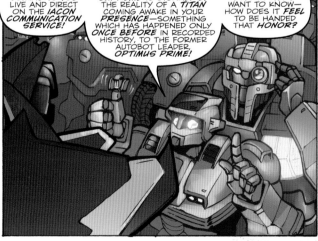

THIS IS **CIRCUIT,** COMING TO YOU LIVE AND DIRECT ON THE **IACON COMMUNICATION SERVICE!**

EVEN THE GREAT **OMEGA SUPREME** IS STUNNED BY THE REALITY OF A **TITAN** COMING AWAKE IN YOUR **PRESENCE**—SOMETHING WHICH HAS HAPPENED ONLY **ONCE BEFORE** IN RECORDED HISTORY, TO THE FORMER AUTOBOT LEADER, **OPTIMUS PRIME!**

CYBERTRONIANS **EVERYWHERE** WANT TO KNOW— HOW DOES IT **FEEL** TO BE HANDED THAT **HONOR?**

WELL, **OPTIMUS** AND I HAD OUR **DIFFERENCES.** BUT CLEARLY HE WAS THE **RIGHT LEADER** FOR **HIS** TIME—A TIME OF **WAR.**

**NOW** IS A TIME OF PEACE, AND THE FACTS ARE **CLEAR.** POOR, FALLEN **METROTITAN,** WHOSE LIFE MY **OPPONENTS** FAILED TO SAVE—

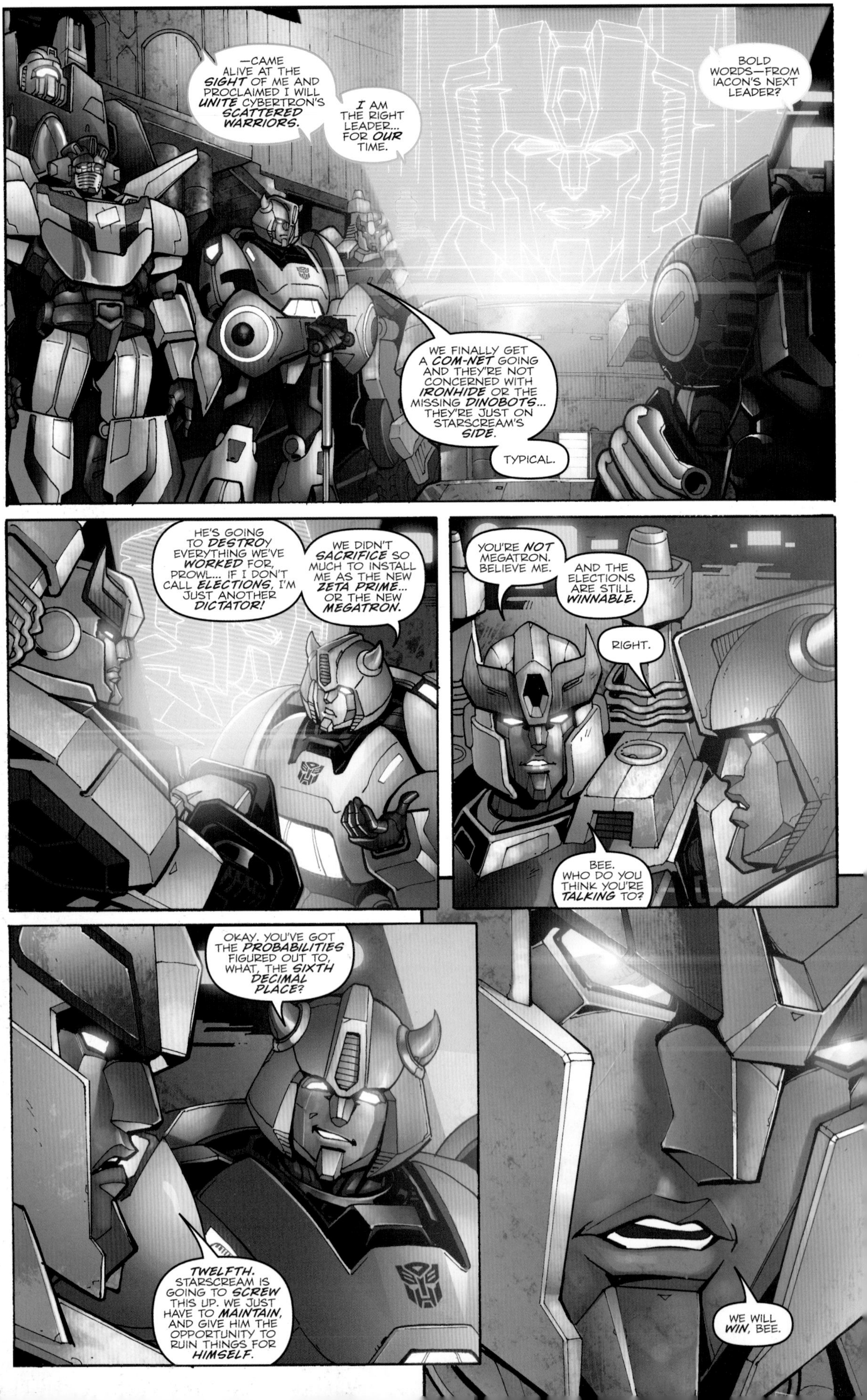

—CAME ALIVE AT THE SIGHT OF ME AND PROCLAIMED I WILL UNITE CYBERTRON'S SCATTERED WARRIORS.
I AM THE RIGHT LEADER... FOR OUR TIME.
BOLD WORDS—FROM IACON'S NEXT LEADER?
WE FINALLY GET A COM-NET GOING AND THEY'RE NOT CONCERNED WITH IRONHIDE OR THE MISSING DINOBOTS... THEY'RE JUST ON STARSCREAM'S SIDE.
TYPICAL.
HE'S GOING TO DESTROY EVERYTHING WE'VE WORKED FOR, PROWL... IF I DON'T CALL ELECTIONS, I'M JUST ANOTHER DICTATOR!
WE DIDN'T SACRIFICE SO MUCH TO INSTALL ME AS THE NEW ZETA PRIME... OR THE NEW MEGATRON.
YOU'RE NOT MEGATRON. BELIEVE ME.
AND THE ELECTIONS ARE STILL WINNABLE.
RIGHT.
BEE. WHO DO YOU THINK YOU'RE TALKING TO?
OKAY. YOU'VE GOT THE PROBABILITIES FIGURED OUT TO, WHAT, THE SIXTH DECIMAL PLACE?
TWELFTH. STARSCREAM IS GOING TO SCREW THIS UP. WE JUST HAVE TO MAINTAIN, AND GIVE HIM THE OPPORTUNITY TO RUIN THINGS FOR HIMSELF.
WE WILL WIN, BEE.

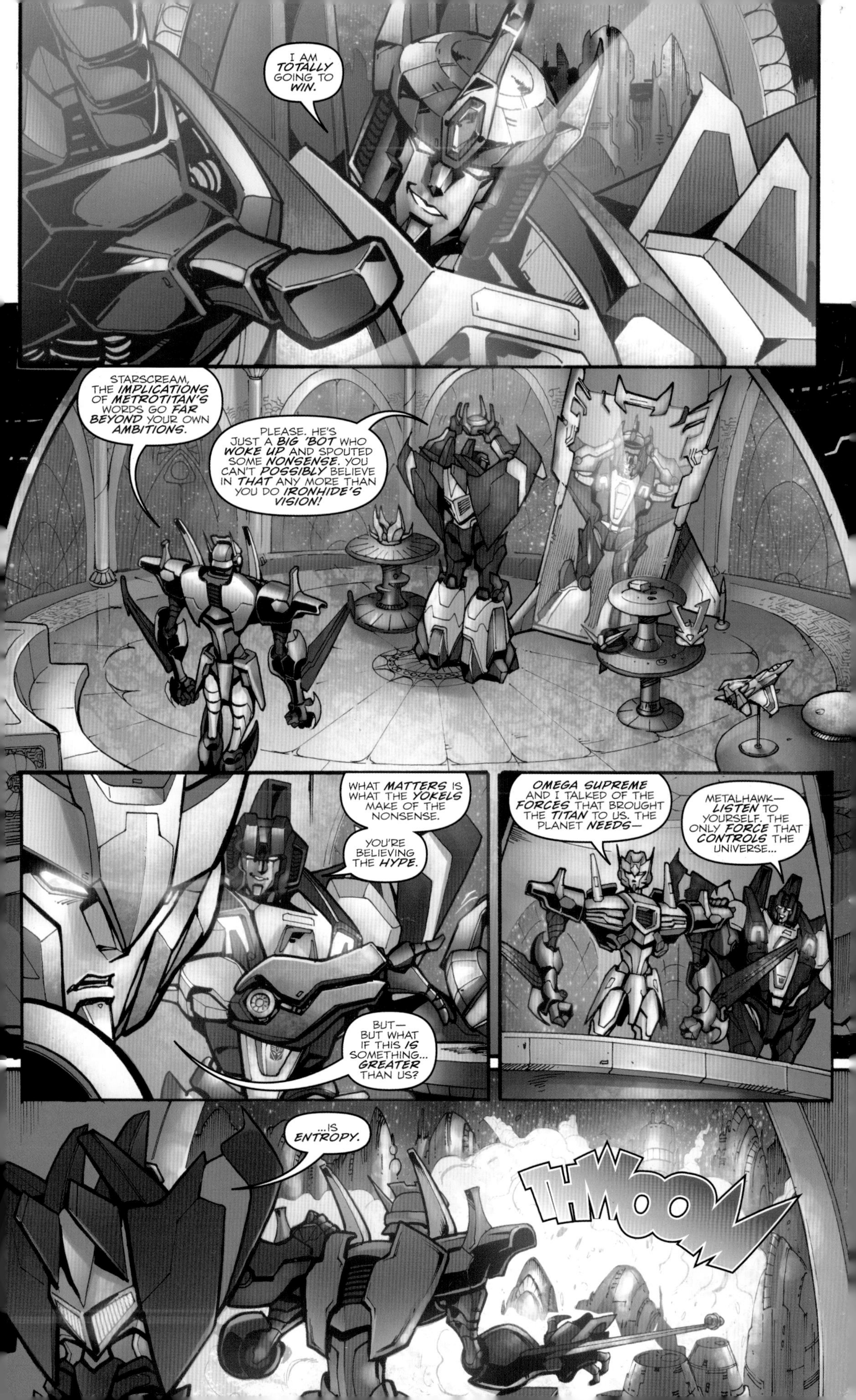
I AM *TOTALLY* GOING TO *WIN*.
STARSCREAM, THE *IMPLICATIONS* OF *METROTITAN'S* WORDS GO *FAR BEYOND* YOUR OWN *AMBITIONS*.
PLEASE. HE'S JUST A *BIG 'BOT* WHO *WOKE UP* AND SPOUTED SOME *NONSENSE*. YOU CAN'T *POSSIBLY* BELIEVE IN *THAT* ANY MORE THAN YOU DO *IRONHIDE'S VISION!*
WHAT *MATTERS* IS WHAT THE *YOKELS* MAKE OF THE NONSENSE.
YOU'RE BELIEVING THE *HYPE*.
BUT— BUT WHAT IF THIS *IS* SOMETHING... *GREATER* THAN US?
*OMEGA SUPREME* AND I TALKED OF THE *FORCES* THAT BROUGHT THE *TITAN* TO US. THE PLANET *NEEDS*—
METALHAWK— *LISTEN* TO YOURSELF. THE ONLY *FORCE* THAT *CONTROLS* THE UNIVERSE...
...IS *ENTROPY*.
THWOOM

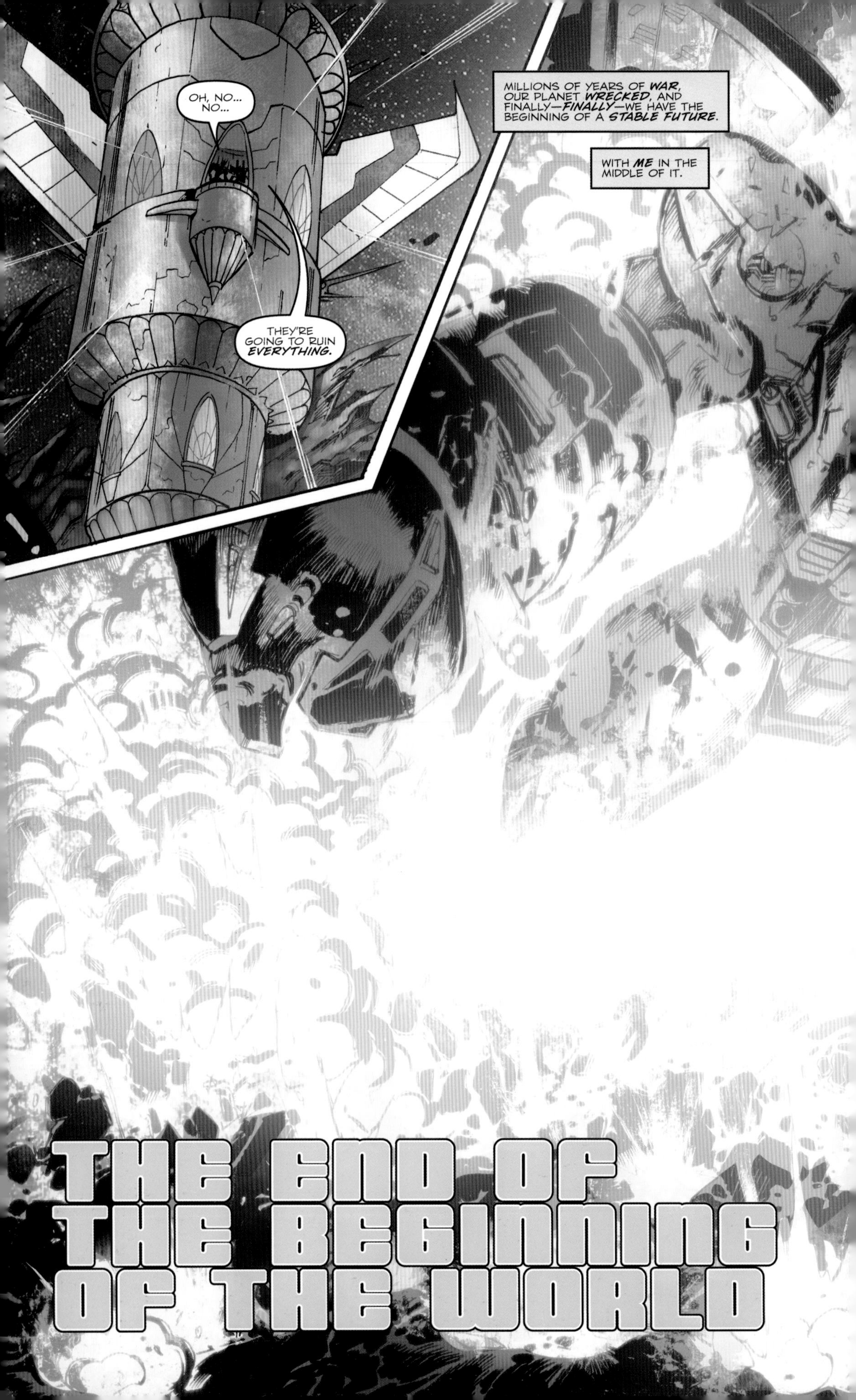
OH, NO... NO...
THEY'RE GOING TO RUIN EVERYTHING.
MILLIONS OF YEARS OF WAR, OUR PLANET WRECKED, AND FINALLY—FINALLY—WE HAVE THE BEGINNING OF A STABLE FUTURE.
WITH ME IN THE MIDDLE OF IT.
THE END OF THE BEGINNING OF THE WORLD

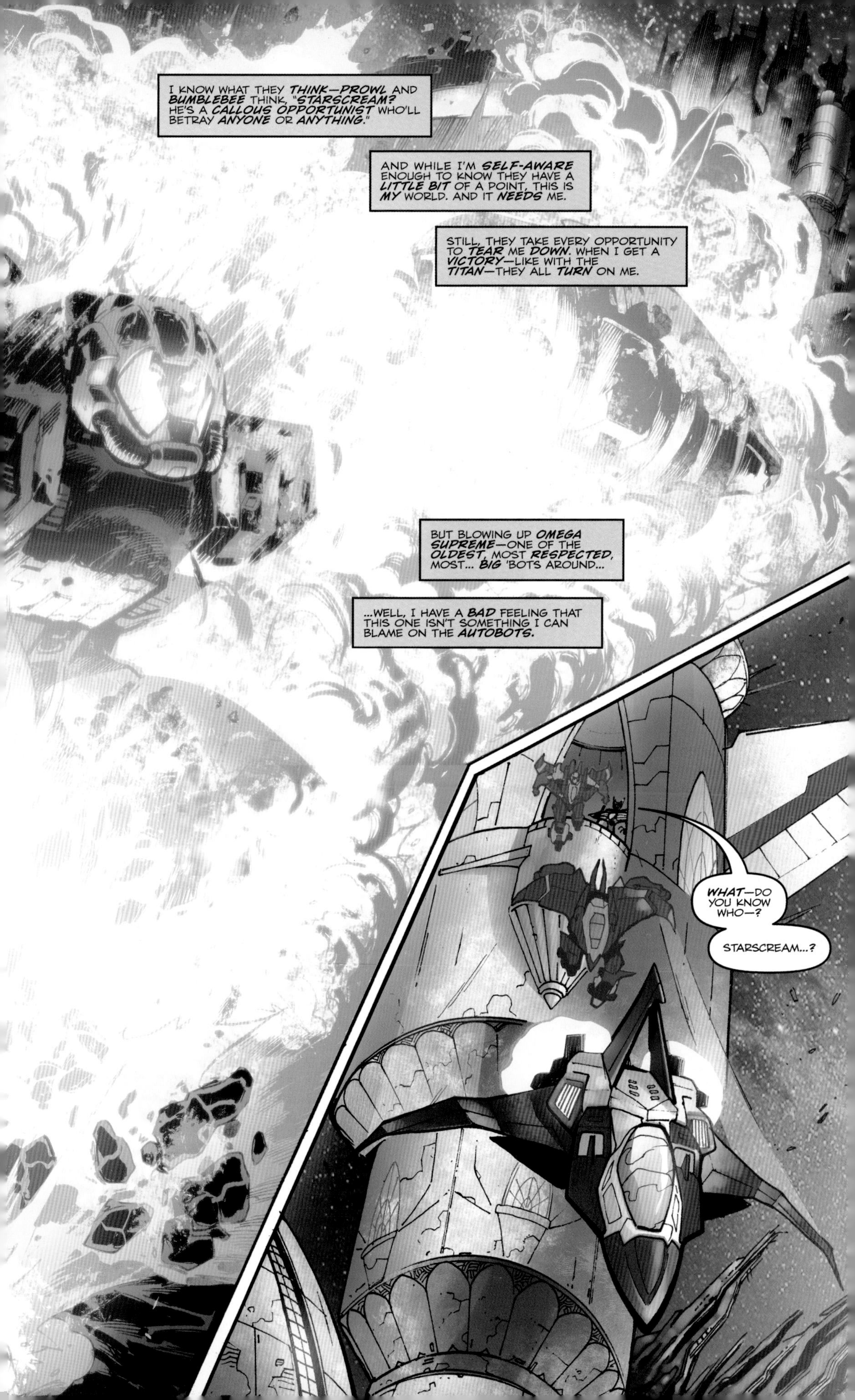

I KNOW WHAT THEY *THINK*—*PROWL* AND *BUMBLEBEE* THINK, "*STARSCREAM?* HE'S A *CALLOUS OPPORTUNIST* WHO'LL BETRAY *ANYONE* OR *ANYTHING*."
AND WHILE I'M *SELF-AWARE* ENOUGH TO KNOW THEY HAVE A *LITTLE BIT* OF A POINT, THIS IS *MY* WORLD. AND IT *NEEDS* ME.
STILL, THEY TAKE EVERY OPPORTUNITY TO *TEAR* ME *DOWN*. WHEN I GET A *VICTORY*—LIKE WITH THE *TITAN*—THEY ALL *TURN* ON ME.
BUT BLOWING UP *OMEGA SUPREME*—ONE OF THE *OLDEST*, MOST *RESPECTED*, MOST... *BIG* 'BOTS AROUND...
...WELL, I HAVE A *BAD* FEELING THAT THIS ONE ISN'T SOMETHING I CAN BLAME ON THE *AUTOBOTS*.
*WHAT*—DO YOU KNOW WHO—?
STARSCREAM...?

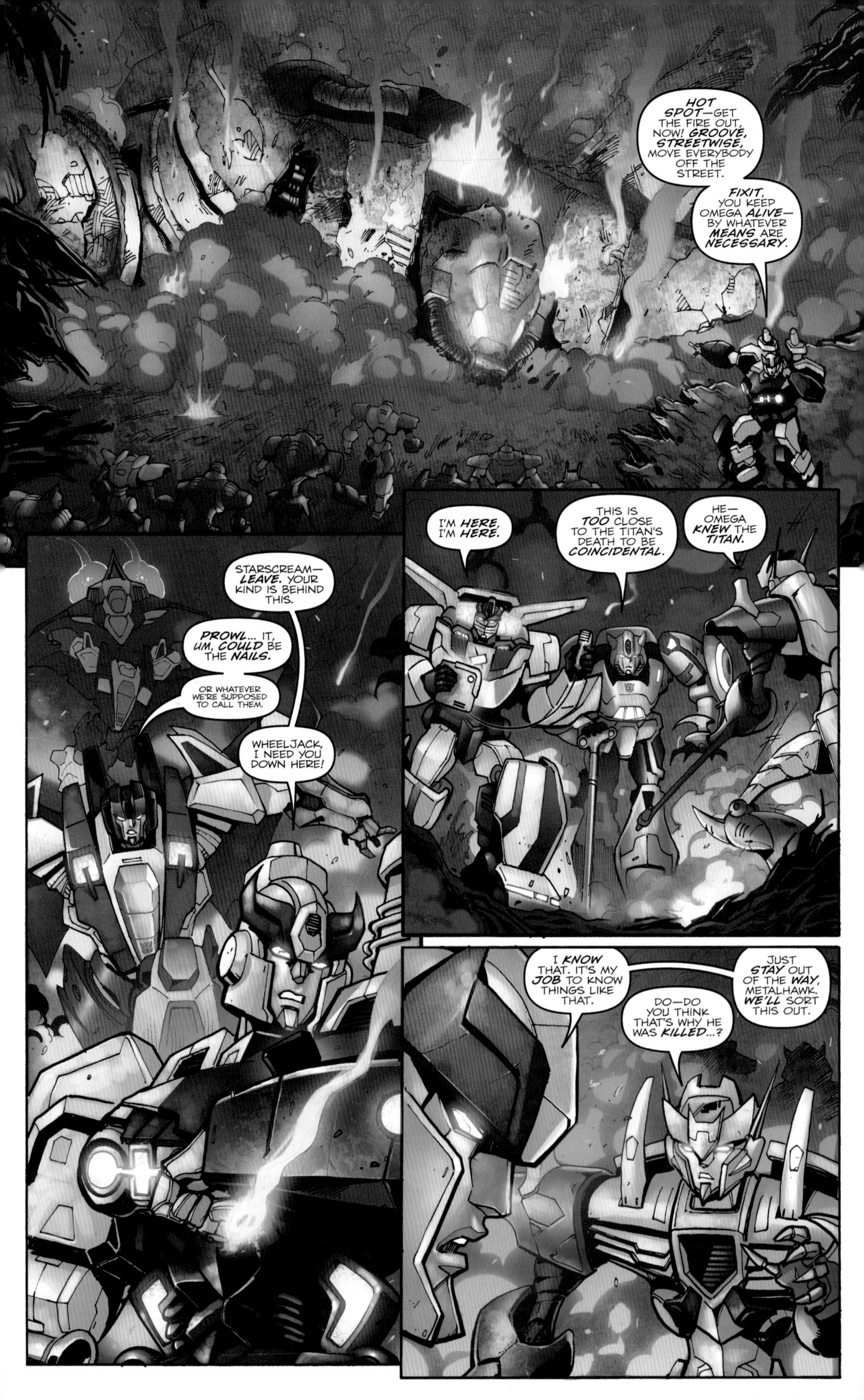
HOT SPOT—GET THE FIRE OUT, NOW! GROOVE, STREETWISE, MOVE EVERYBODY OFF THE STREET.
FIXIT, YOU KEEP OMEGA ALIVE—BY WHATEVER MEANS ARE NECESSARY.
STARSCREAM—LEAVE. YOUR KIND IS BEHIND THIS.
PROWL... IT, UM, COULD BE THE NAILS.
OR WHATEVER WE'RE SUPPOSED TO CALL THEM.
WHEELJACK, I NEED YOU DOWN HERE!
I'M HERE, I'M HERE.
THIS IS TOO CLOSE TO THE TITAN'S DEATH TO BE COINCIDENTAL.
HE—OMEGA KNEW THE TITAN.
I KNOW THAT. IT'S MY JOB TO KNOW THINGS LIKE THAT.
JUST STAY OUT OF THE WAY, METALHAWK. WE'LL SORT THIS OUT.
DO—DO YOU THINK THAT'S WHY HE WAS KILLED...?

STARSCREAM—THIS IS *CIRCUIT*, LIVE FOR THE *I.C.S.*—JUST *ONE HOUR AGO* YOU PASSED THIS WAY AND *OMEGA SUPREME* WAS STILL *ALIVE.*

ANY *COMMENT* FOR OUR VIEWERS?

WELL, IT *SOUNDS* LIKE HE'S STILL *ALIVE*, BUT... COME ON, *FOLLOW ME.*

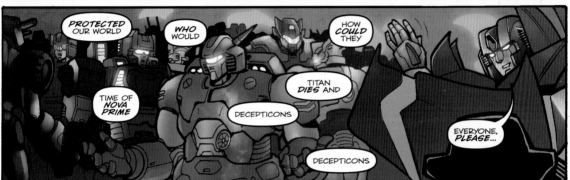

PROTECTED OUR WORLD

WHO WOULD

HOW COULD THEY

TIME OF *NOVA PRIME*

TITAN *DIES* AND

DECEPTICONS

DECEPTICONS

EVERYONE, *PLEASE...*

...LET'S ALL *STEP BACK* AND LET *PROWL* AND HIS *SERVANTS* HANDLE THE SITUATION. THE IMPORTANT THING IS TO MAKE SURE *OMEGA SUPREME*—AND EVERYONE ELSE—IS *OKAY.*

THERE WILL BE *PLENTY* OF TIME FOR *RECRIMINATIONS* LATER.

DECEPTICON

DECEPTICON

DECEPTICON

STARSCREAM— DO YOU CARE TO *COMMENT:*

HOW DID YOU *ALLOW* YOUR FELLOW *DECEPTICONS* TO *BLOW UP* PART OF OUR *CITY* AND ONE OF ITS *OLDEST* AND MOST *REVERED* CITIZENS?

UH.

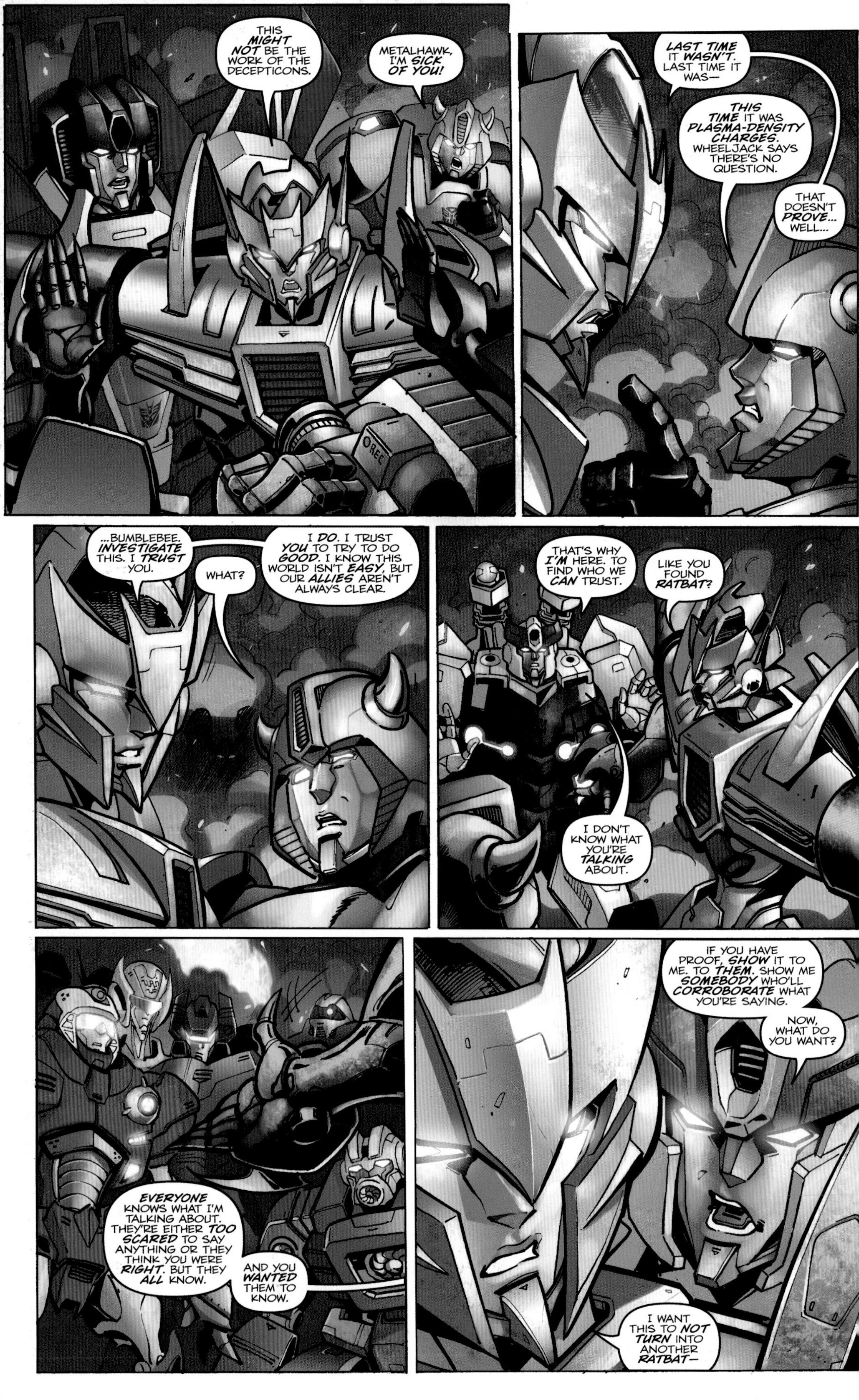
THIS MIGHT NOT BE THE WORK OF THE DECEPTICONS.
METALHAWK, I'M SICK OF YOU!
LAST TIME IT WASN'T. LAST TIME IT WAS—
THIS TIME IT WAS PLASMA-DENSITY CHARGES. WHEELJACK SAYS THERE'S NO QUESTION.
THAT DOESN'T PROVE... WELL...
...BUMBLEBEE. INVESTIGATE THIS. I TRUST YOU.
WHAT?
I DO. I TRUST YOU TO TRY TO DO GOOD. I KNOW THIS WORLD ISN'T EASY, BUT OUR ALLIES AREN'T ALWAYS CLEAR.
THAT'S WHY I'M HERE. TO FIND WHO WE CAN TRUST.
LIKE YOU FOUND RATBAT?
I DON'T KNOW WHAT YOU'RE TALKING ABOUT.
EVERYONE KNOWS WHAT I'M TALKING ABOUT. THEY'RE EITHER TOO SCARED TO SAY ANYTHING OR THEY THINK YOU WERE RIGHT. BUT THEY ALL KNOW.
AND YOU WANTED THEM TO KNOW.
IF YOU HAVE PROOF, SHOW IT TO ME. TO THEM. SHOW ME SOMEBODY WHO'LL CORROBORATE WHAT YOU'RE SAYING.
NOW, WHAT DO YOU WANT?
I WANT THIS TO NOT TURN INTO ANOTHER RATBAT—

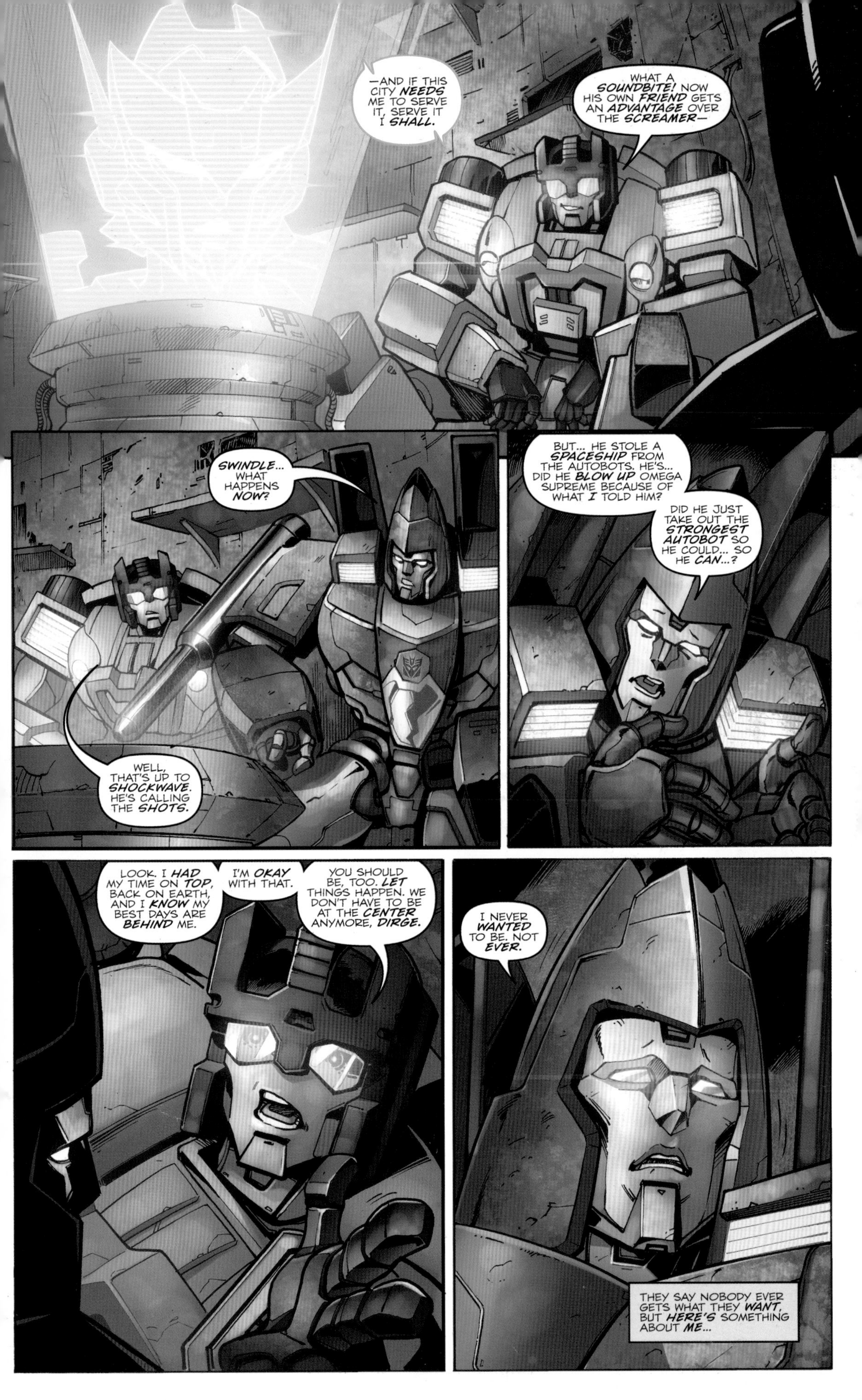
—AND IF THIS CITY NEEDS ME TO SERVE IT, SERVE IT I SHALL.
WHAT A SOUNDBITE! NOW HIS OWN FRIEND GETS AN ADVANTAGE OVER THE SCREAMER—
SWINDLE... WHAT HAPPENS NOW?
WELL, THAT'S UP TO SHOCKWAVE. HE'S CALLING THE SHOTS.
BUT... HE STOLE A SPACESHIP FROM THE AUTOBOTS. HE'S... DID HE BLOW UP OMEGA SUPREME BECAUSE OF WHAT I TOLD HIM?
DID HE JUST TAKE OUT THE STRONGEST AUTOBOT SO HE COULD... SO HE CAN...?
LOOK. I HAD MY TIME ON TOP, BACK ON EARTH, AND I KNOW MY BEST DAYS ARE BEHIND ME.
I'M OKAY WITH THAT.
YOU SHOULD BE, TOO. LET THINGS HAPPEN. WE DON'T HAVE TO BE AT THE CENTER ANYMORE, DIRGE.
I NEVER WANTED TO BE. NOT EVER.
THEY SAY NOBODY EVER GETS WHAT THEY WANT, BUT HERE'S SOMETHING ABOUT ME...

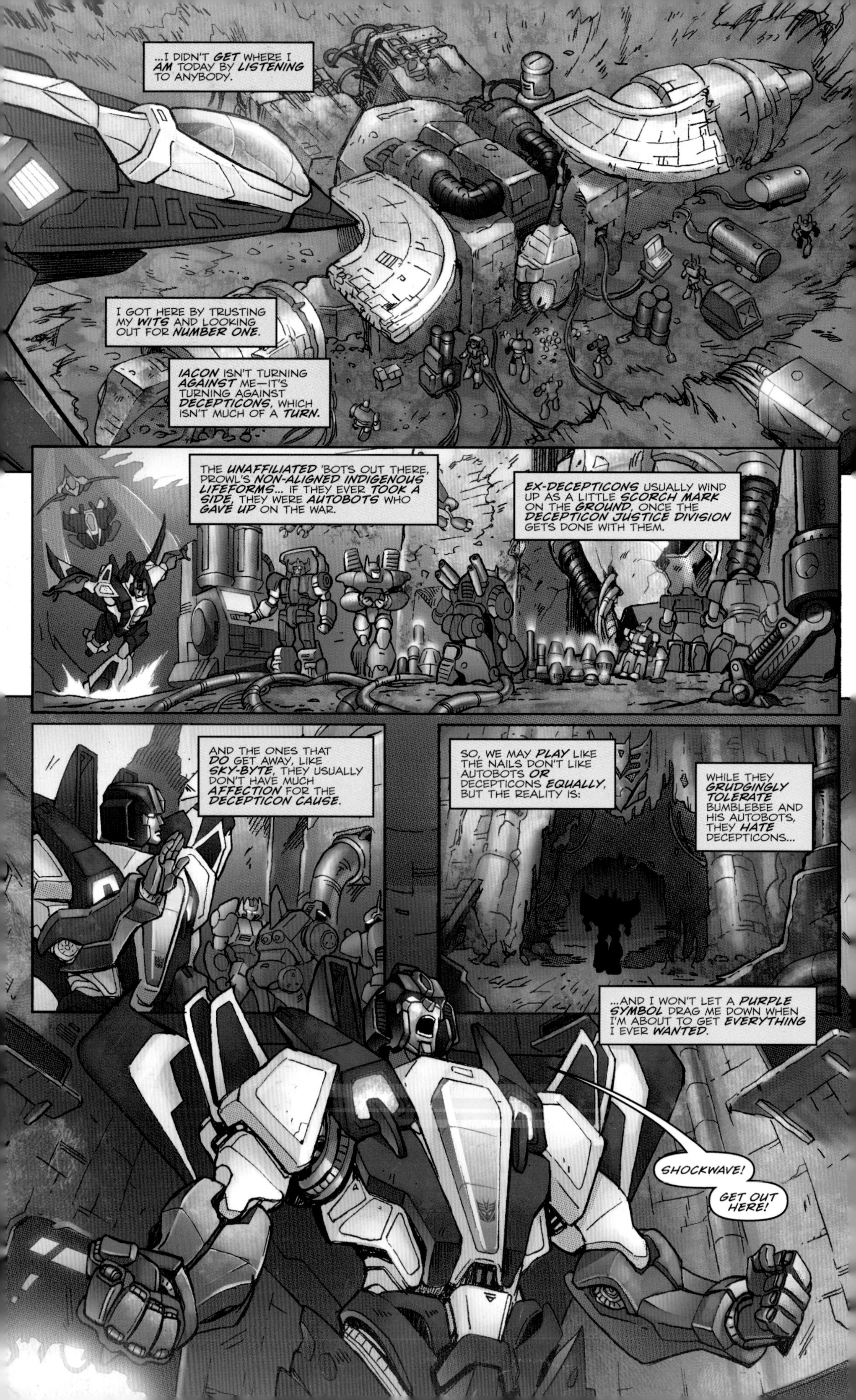
...I DIDN'T GET WHERE I AM TODAY BY LISTENING TO ANYBODY.
I GOT HERE BY TRUSTING MY WITS AND LOOKING OUT FOR NUMBER ONE.
IACON ISN'T TURNING AGAINST ME—IT'S TURNING AGAINST DECEPTICONS, WHICH ISN'T MUCH OF A TURN.
THE UNAFFILIATED 'BOTS OUT THERE, PROWL'S NON-ALIGNED INDIGENOUS LIFEFORMS... IF THEY EVER TOOK A SIDE, THEY WERE AUTOBOTS WHO GAVE UP ON THE WAR.
EX-DECEPTICONS USUALLY WIND UP AS A LITTLE SCORCH MARK ON THE GROUND, ONCE THE DECEPTICON JUSTICE DIVISION GETS DONE WITH THEM.
AND THE ONES THAT DO GET AWAY, LIKE SKY-BYTE, THEY USUALLY DON'T HAVE MUCH AFFECTION FOR THE DECEPTICON CAUSE.
SO, WE MAY PLAY LIKE THE NAILS DON'T LIKE AUTOBOTS OR DECEPTICONS EQUALLY, BUT THE REALITY IS:
WHILE THEY GRUDGINGLY TOLERATE BUMBLEBEE AND HIS AUTOBOTS, THEY HATE DECEPTICONS...
...AND I WON'T LET A PURPLE SYMBOL DRAG ME DOWN WHEN I'M ABOUT TO GET EVERYTHING I EVER WANTED.
SHOCKWAVE!
GET OUT HERE!

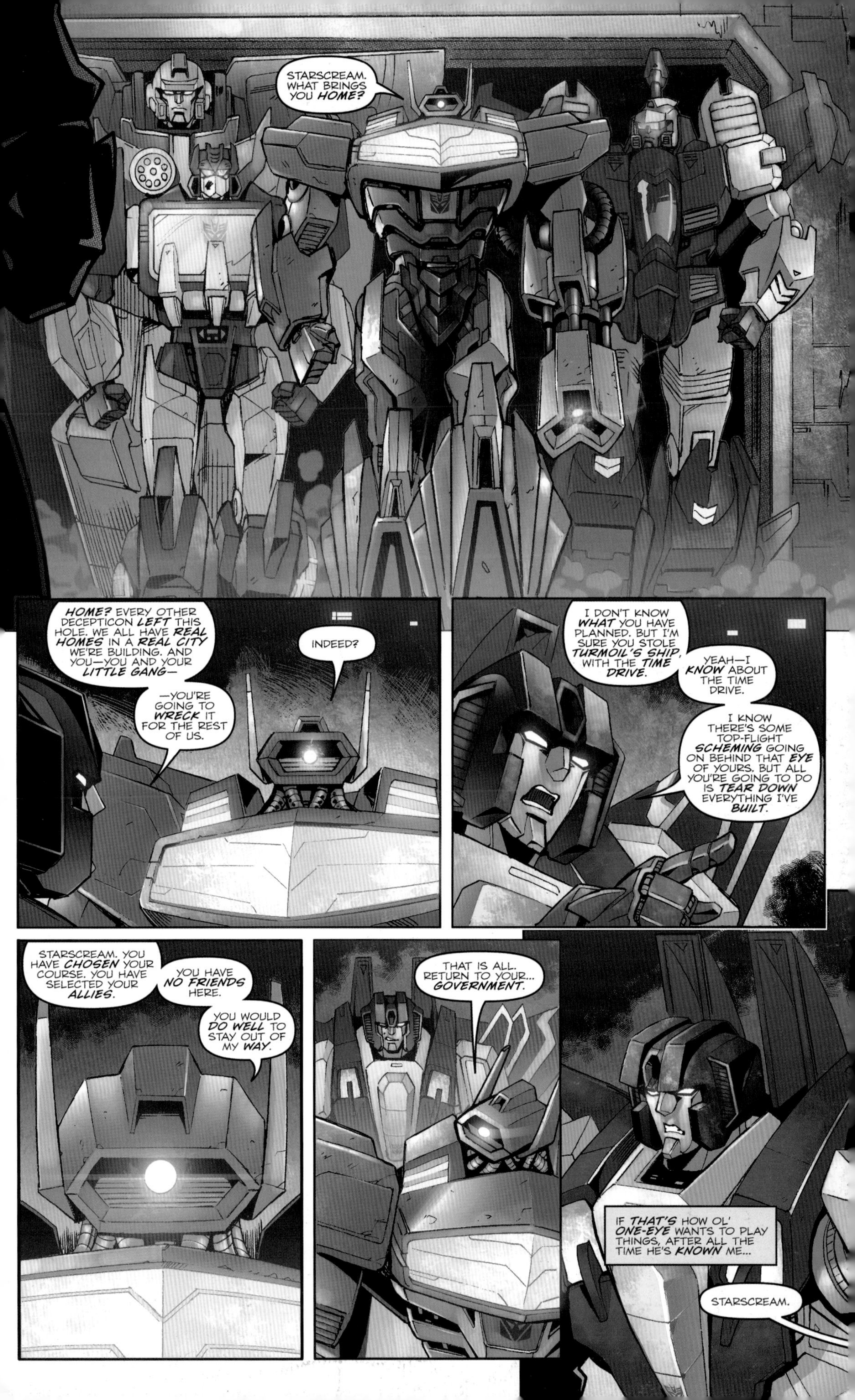
STARSCREAM. WHAT BRINGS YOU HOME?
HOME? EVERY OTHER DECEPTICON LEFT THIS HOLE. WE ALL HAVE REAL HOMES IN A REAL CITY WE'RE BUILDING. AND YOU—YOU AND YOUR LITTLE GANG—
—YOU'RE GOING TO WRECK IT FOR THE REST OF US.
INDEED?
I DON'T KNOW WHAT YOU HAVE PLANNED. BUT I'M SURE YOU STOLE TURMOIL'S SHIP, WITH THE TIME DRIVE.
YEAH—I KNOW ABOUT THE TIME DRIVE.
I KNOW THERE'S SOME TOP-FLIGHT SCHEMING GOING ON BEHIND THAT EYE OF YOURS. BUT ALL YOU'RE GOING TO DO IS TEAR DOWN EVERYTHING I'VE BUILT.
STARSCREAM. YOU HAVE CHOSEN YOUR COURSE. YOU HAVE SELECTED YOUR ALLIES.
YOU HAVE NO FRIENDS HERE.
YOU WOULD DO WELL TO STAY OUT OF MY WAY.
THAT IS ALL. RETURN TO YOUR... GOVERNMENT.
IF THAT'S HOW OL' ONE-EYE WANTS TO PLAY THINGS, AFTER ALL THE TIME HE'S KNOWN ME...
STARSCREAM.

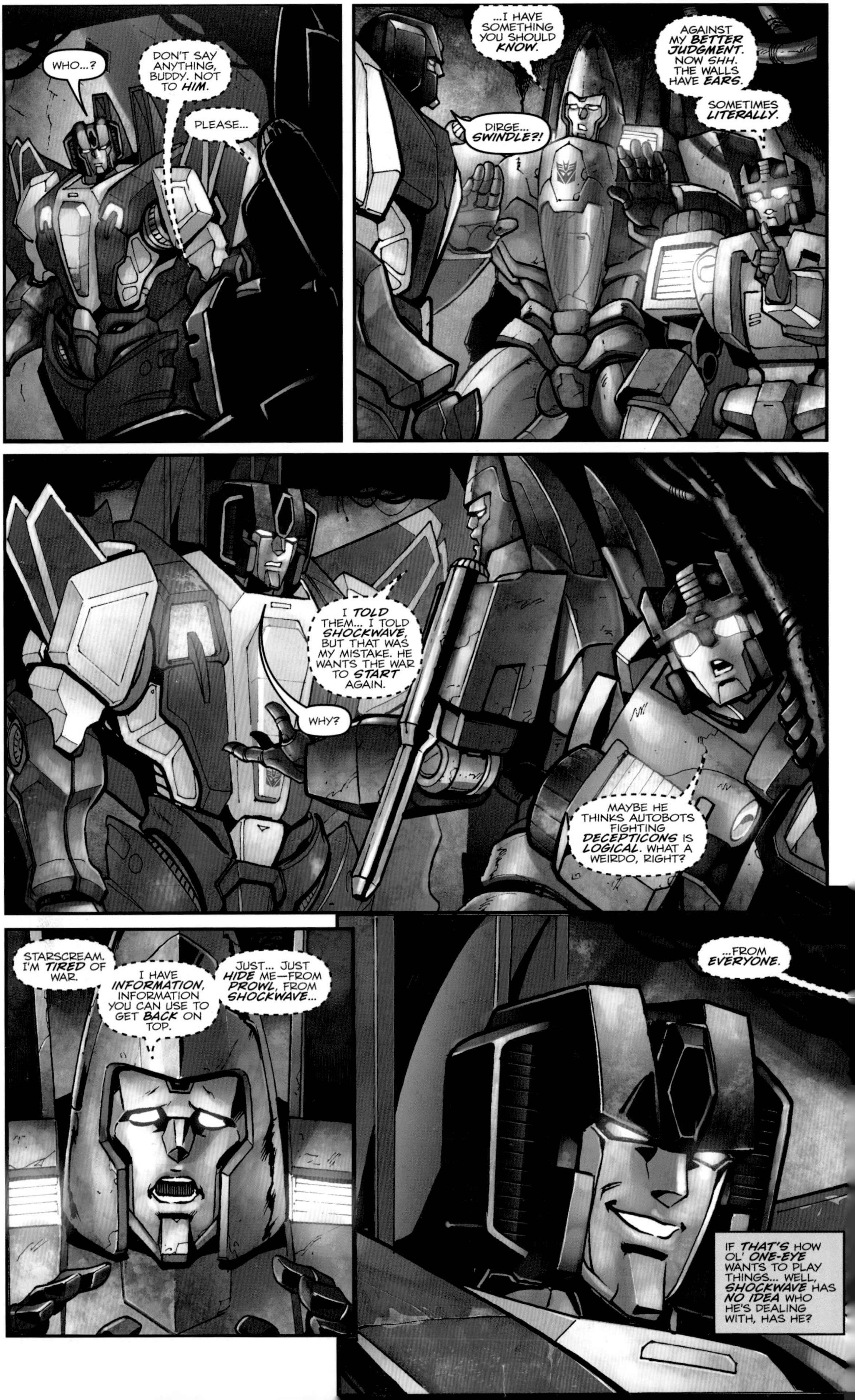
WHO...?
DON'T SAY ANYTHING, BUDDY. NOT TO HIM.
PLEASE...
...I HAVE SOMETHING YOU SHOULD KNOW.
DIRGE... SWINDLE?!
AGAINST MY BETTER JUDGMENT. NOW SHH. THE WALLS HAVE EARS.
SOMETIMES LITERALLY.
I TOLD THEM... I TOLD SHOCKWAVE, BUT THAT WAS MY MISTAKE. HE WANTS THE WAR TO START AGAIN.
WHY?
MAYBE HE THINKS AUTOBOTS FIGHTING DECEPTICONS IS LOGICAL. WHAT A WEIRDO, RIGHT?
STARSCREAM. I'M TIRED OF WAR.
I HAVE INFORMATION, INFORMATION YOU CAN USE TO GET BACK ON TOP.
JUST... JUST HIDE ME—FROM PROWL, FROM SHOCKWAVE...
...FROM EVERYONE.
IF THAT'S HOW OL' ONE-EYE WANTS TO PLAY THINGS... WELL, SHOCKWAVE HAS NO IDEA WHO HE'S DEALING WITH, HAS HE?

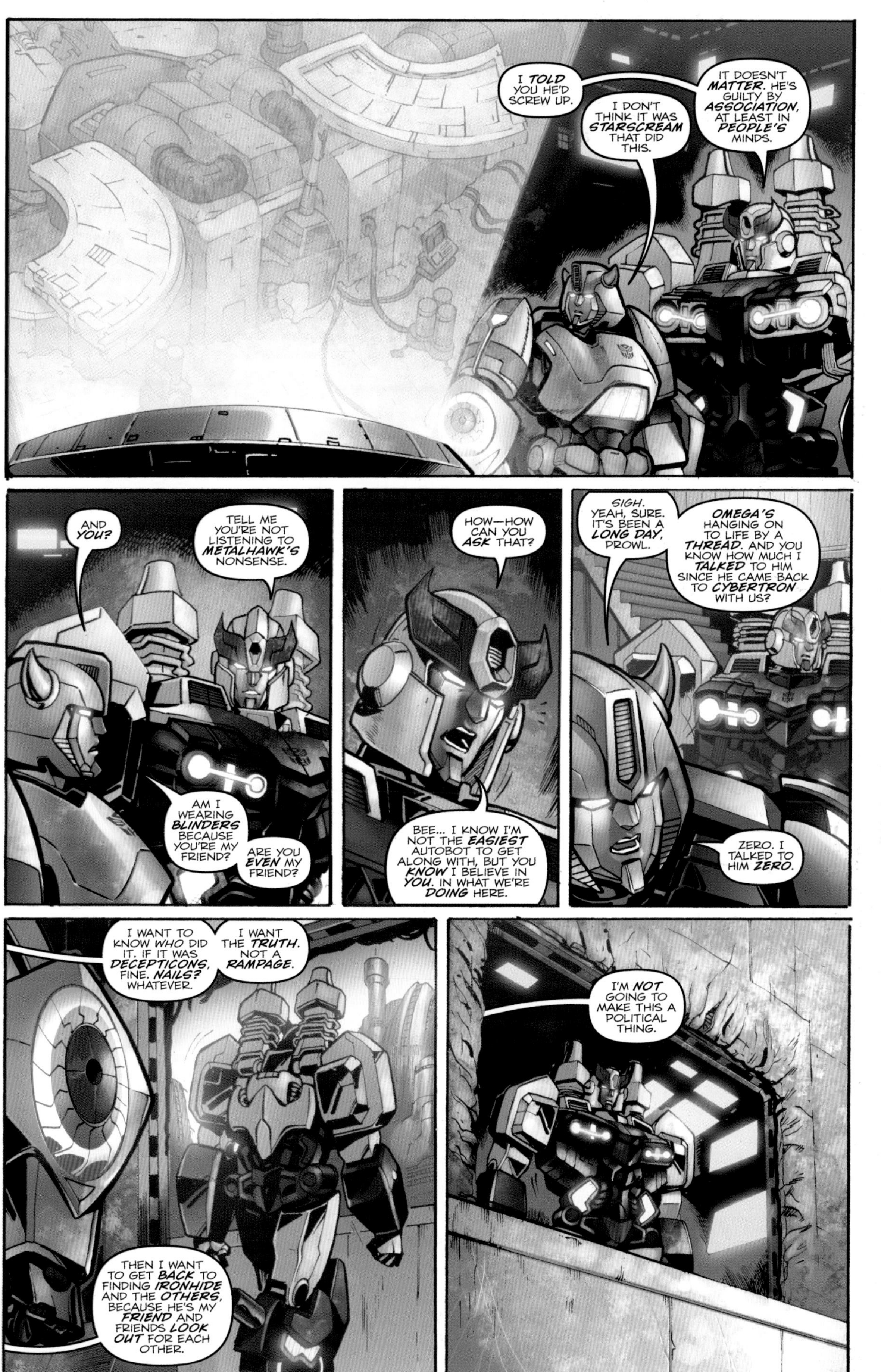
I TOLD YOU HE'D SCREW UP.
I DON'T THINK IT WAS STARSCREAM THAT DID THIS.
IT DOESN'T MATTER. HE'S GUILTY BY ASSOCIATION, AT LEAST IN PEOPLE'S MINDS.
AND YOU?
TELL ME YOU'RE NOT LISTENING TO METALHAWK'S NONSENSE.
AM I WEARING BLINDERS BECAUSE YOU'RE MY FRIEND?
ARE YOU EVEN MY FRIEND?
HOW—HOW CAN YOU ASK THAT?
BEE... I KNOW I'M NOT THE EASIEST AUTOBOT TO GET ALONG WITH, BUT YOU KNOW I BELIEVE IN YOU. IN WHAT WE'RE DOING HERE.
SIGH. YEAH, SURE. IT'S BEEN A LONG DAY, PROWL.
OMEGA'S HANGING ON TO LIFE BY A THREAD. AND YOU KNOW HOW MUCH I TALKED TO HIM SINCE HE CAME BACK TO CYBERTRON WITH US?
ZERO. I TALKED TO HIM ZERO.
I WANT TO KNOW WHO DID IT. IF IT WAS DECEPTICONS, FINE. NAILS? WHATEVER.
I WANT THE TRUTH. NOT A RAMPAGE.
THEN I WANT TO GET BACK TO FINDING IRONHIDE AND THE OTHERS, BECAUSE HE'S MY FRIEND AND FRIENDS LOOK OUT FOR EACH OTHER.
I'M NOT GOING TO MAKE THIS A POLITICAL THING.

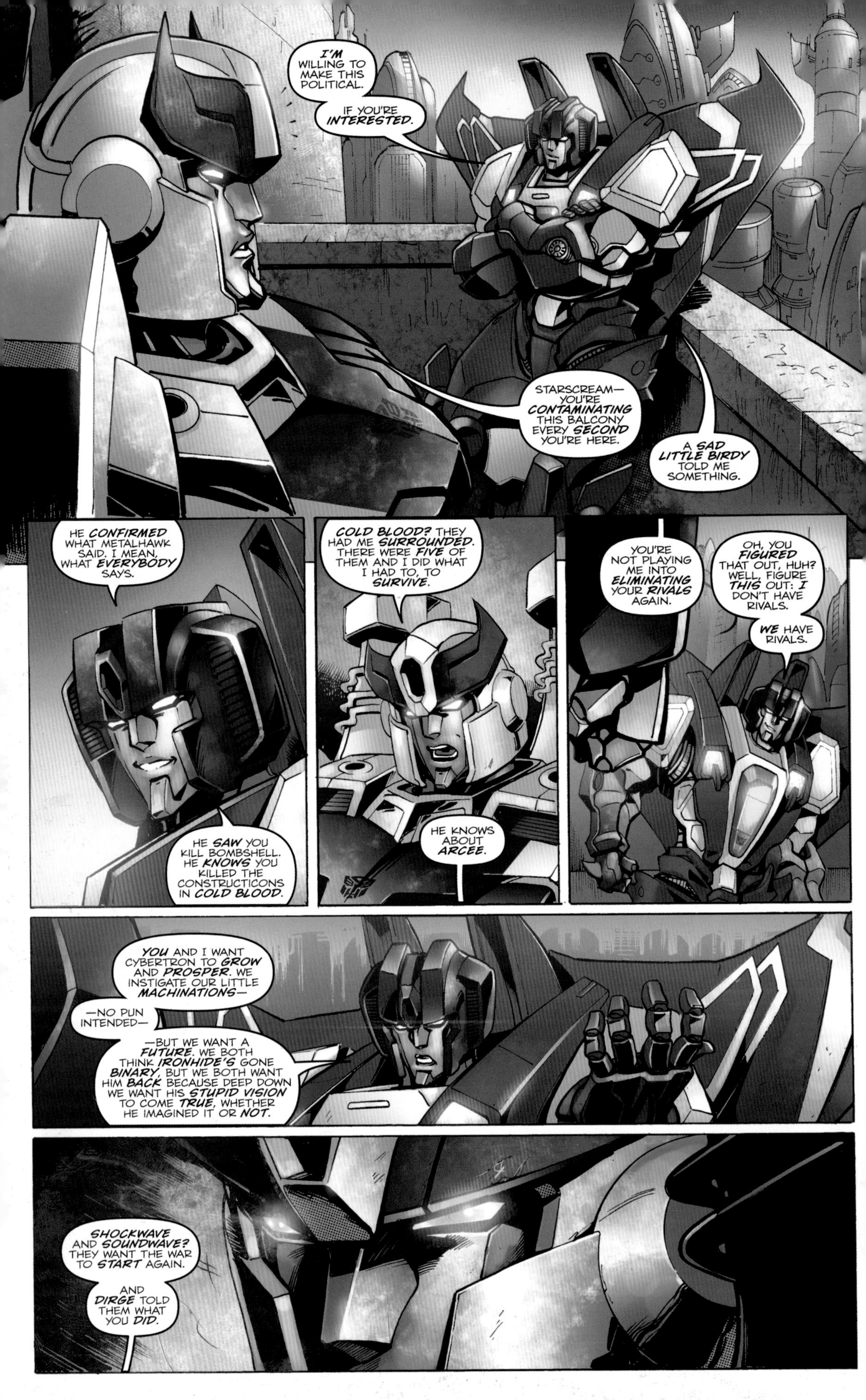
I'M WILLING TO MAKE THIS POLITICAL.
IF YOU'RE INTERESTED.
STARSCREAM— YOU'RE CONTAMINATING THIS BALCONY EVERY SECOND YOU'RE HERE.
A SAD LITTLE BIRDY TOLD ME SOMETHING.
HE CONFIRMED WHAT METALHAWK SAID. I MEAN, WHAT EVERYBODY SAYS.
HE SAW YOU KILL BOMBSHELL. HE KNOWS YOU KILLED THE CONSTRUCTICONS IN COLD BLOOD.
COLD BLOOD? THEY HAD ME SURROUNDED. THERE WERE FIVE OF THEM AND I DID WHAT I HAD TO, TO SURVIVE.
HE KNOWS ABOUT ARCEE.
YOU'RE NOT PLAYING ME INTO ELIMINATING YOUR RIVALS AGAIN.
OH, YOU FIGURED THAT OUT, HUH? WELL, FIGURE THIS OUT: I DON'T HAVE RIVALS.
WE HAVE RIVALS.
YOU AND I WANT CYBERTRON TO GROW AND PROSPER. WE INSTIGATE OUR LITTLE MACHINATIONS—
—NO PUN INTENDED—
—BUT WE WANT A FUTURE. WE BOTH THINK IRONHIDE'S GONE BINARY, BUT WE BOTH WANT HIM BACK BECAUSE DEEP DOWN WE WANT HIS STUPID VISION TO COME TRUE, WHETHER HE IMAGINED IT OR NOT.
SHOCKWAVE AND SOUNDWAVE? THEY WANT THE WAR TO START AGAIN.
AND DIRGE TOLD THEM WHAT YOU DID.

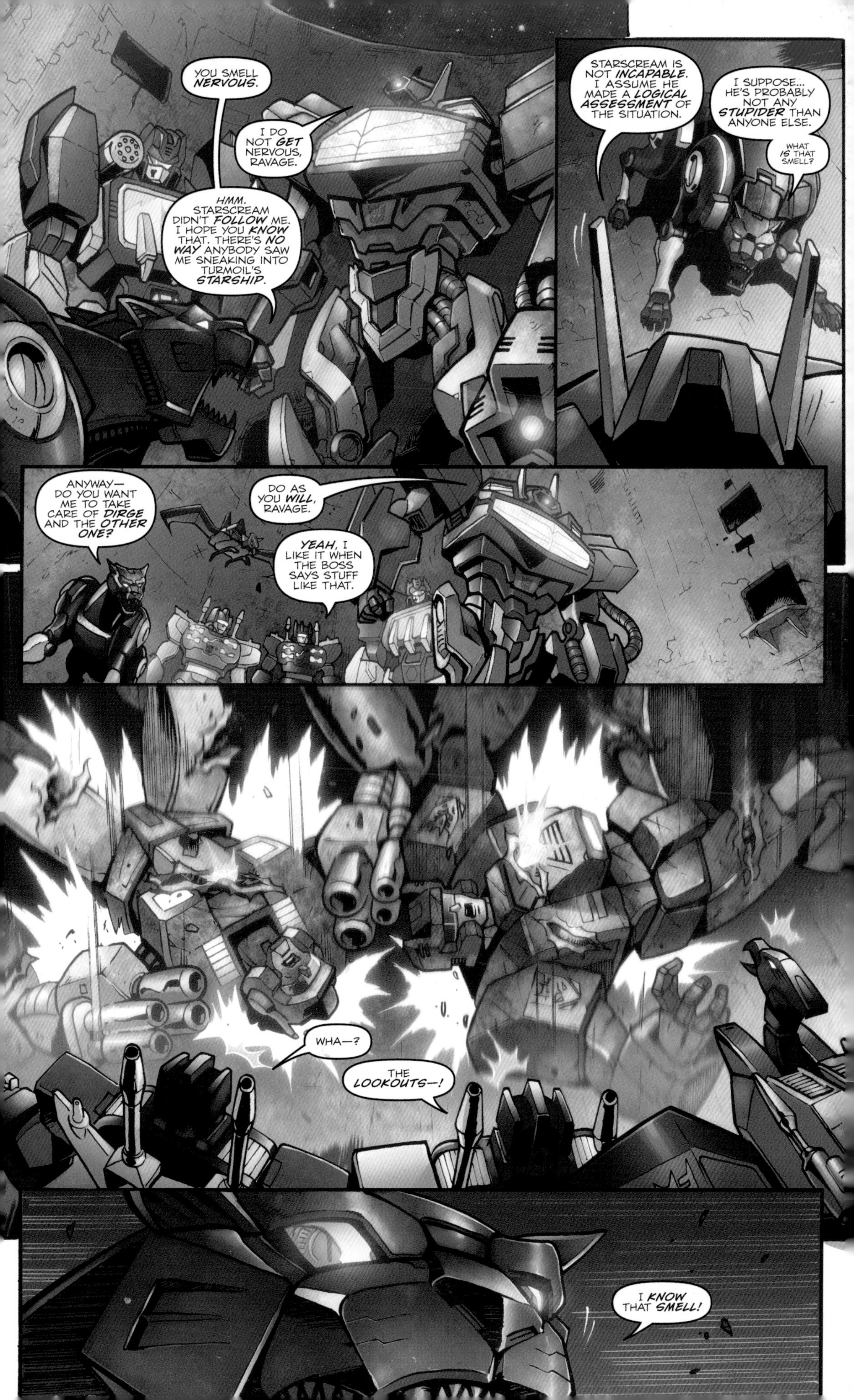
YOU SMELL NERVOUS.
I DO NOT GET NERVOUS, RAVAGE.
HMM. STARSCREAM DIDN'T FOLLOW ME. I HOPE YOU KNOW THAT. THERE'S NO WAY ANYBODY SAW ME SNEAKING INTO TURMOIL'S STARSHIP.
STARSCREAM IS NOT INCAPABLE. I ASSUME HE MADE A LOGICAL ASSESSMENT OF THE SITUATION.
I SUPPOSE... HE'S PROBABLY NOT ANY STUPIDER THAN ANYONE ELSE.
WHAT IS THAT SMELL?
ANYWAY— DO YOU WANT ME TO TAKE CARE OF DIRGE AND THE OTHER ONE?
DO AS YOU WILL, RAVAGE.
YEAH, I LIKE IT WHEN THE BOSS SAYS STUFF LIKE THAT.
WHA—?
THE LOOKOUTS—!
I KNOW THAT SMELL!

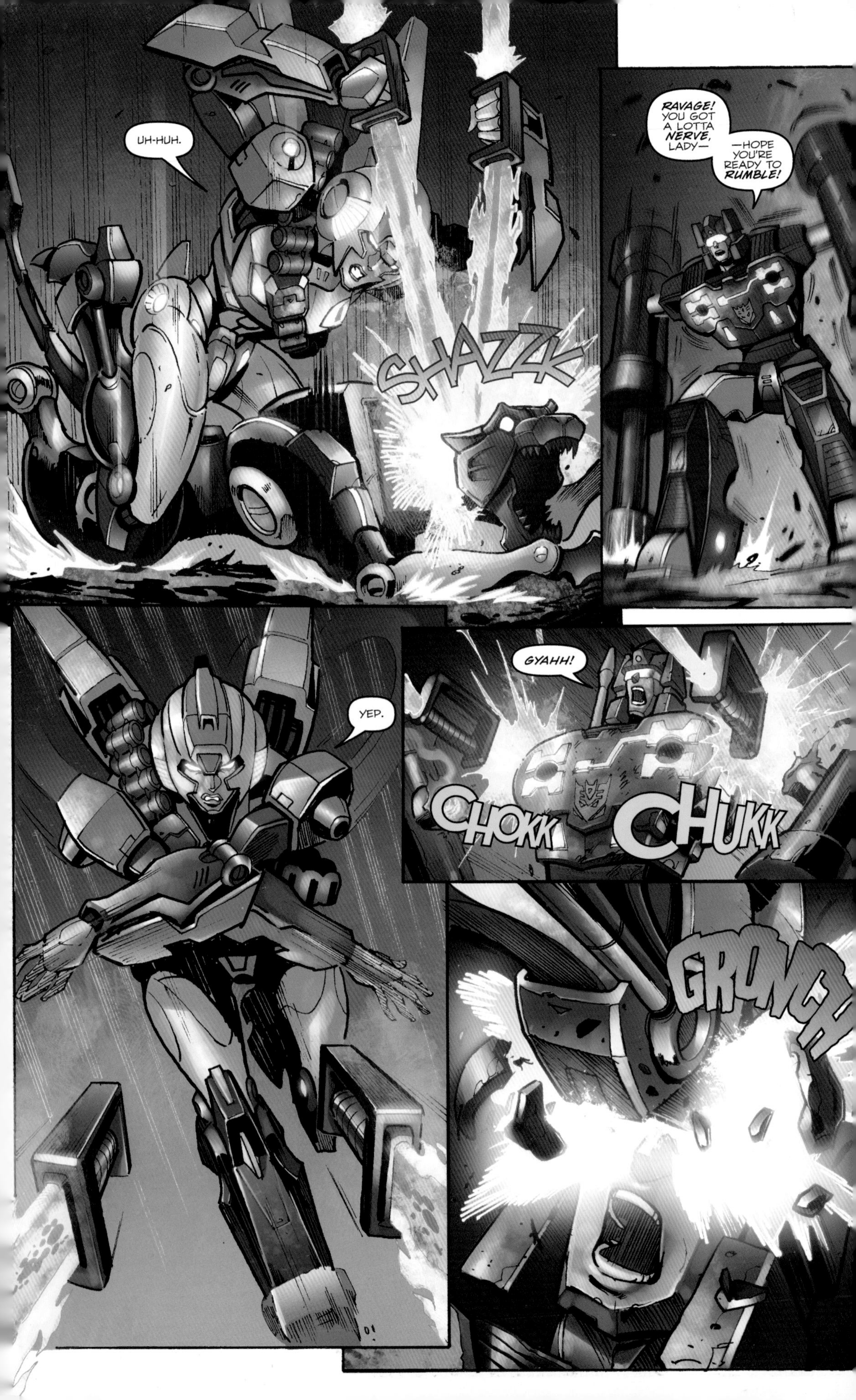
UH-HUH.
SHAZZK
RAVAGE! YOU GOT A LOTTA NERVE, LADY—
—HOPE YOU'RE READY TO RUMBLE!
YEP.
GYAHH!
CHOKK
CHUKK
GRUNCH

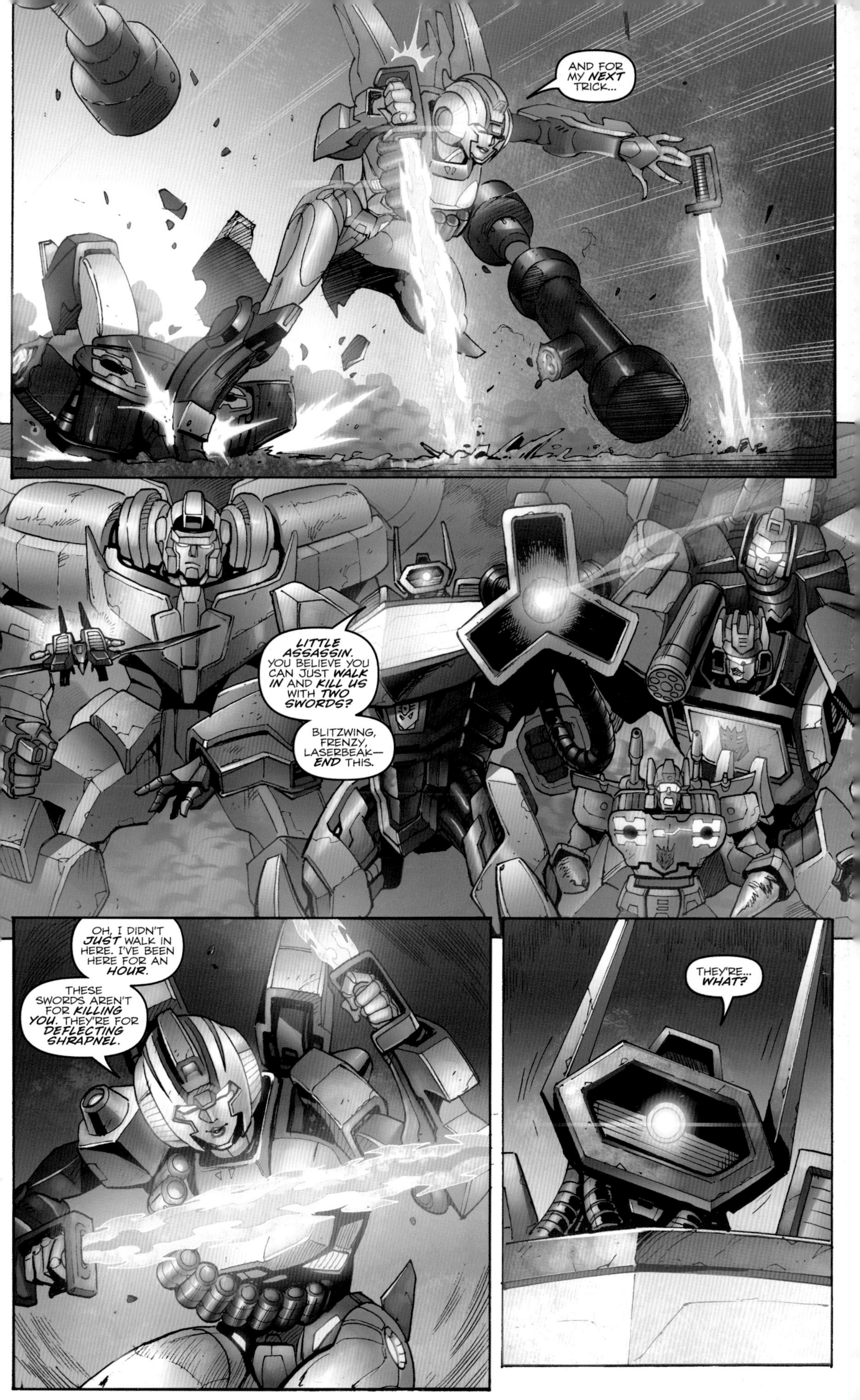
AND FOR MY NEXT TRICK...
LITTLE ASSASSIN. YOU BELIEVE YOU CAN JUST WALK IN AND KILL US WITH TWO SWORDS?
BLITZWING, FRENZY, LASERBEAK— END THIS.
OH, I DIDN'T JUST WALK IN HERE. I'VE BEEN HERE FOR AN HOUR.
THESE SWORDS AREN'T FOR KILLING YOU. THEY'RE FOR DEFLECTING SHRAPNEL.
THEY'RE... WHAT?

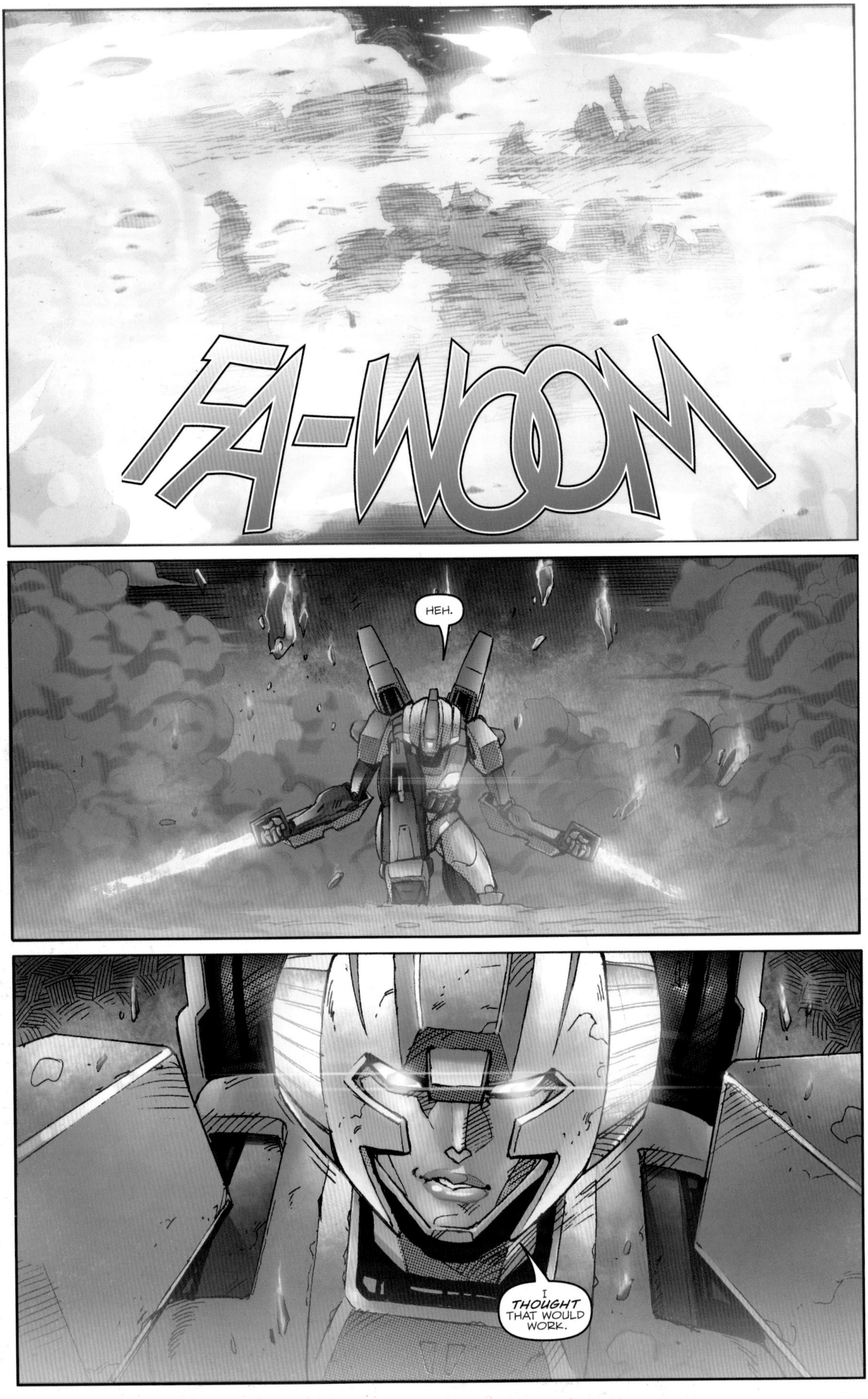
FA-WOOM
HEH.
I *THOUGHT* THAT WOULD WORK.

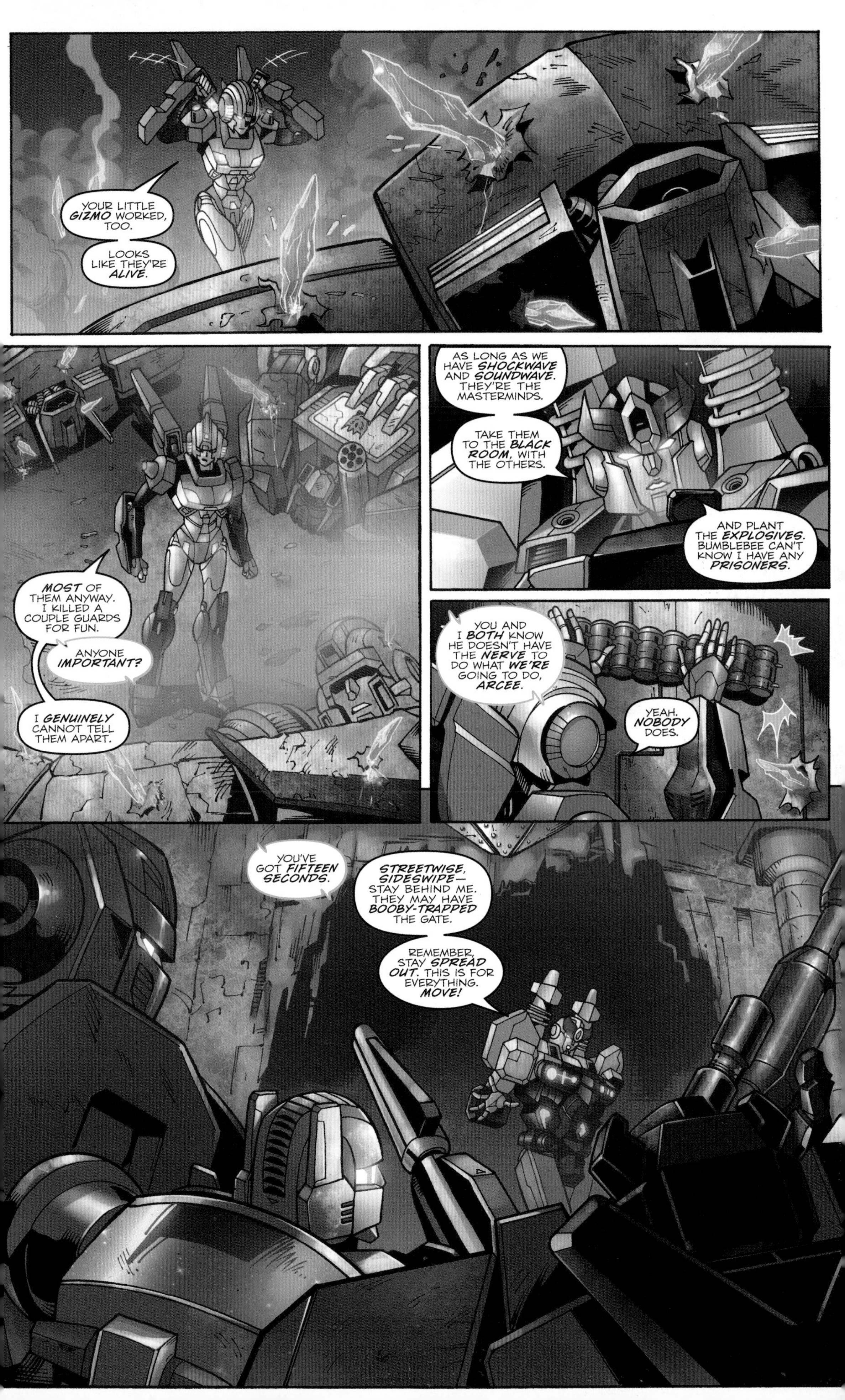
YOUR LITTLE GIZMO WORKED, TOO.
LOOKS LIKE THEY'RE ALIVE.
MOST OF THEM ANYWAY. I KILLED A COUPLE GUARDS FOR FUN.
ANYONE IMPORTANT?
I GENUINELY CANNOT TELL THEM APART.
AS LONG AS WE HAVE SHOCKWAVE AND SOUNDWAVE. THEY'RE THE MASTERMINDS.
TAKE THEM TO THE BLACK ROOM, WITH THE OTHERS.
AND PLANT THE EXPLOSIVES. BUMBLEBEE CAN'T KNOW I HAVE ANY PRISONERS.
YOU AND I BOTH KNOW HE DOESN'T HAVE THE NERVE TO DO WHAT WE'RE GOING TO DO, ARCEE.
YEAH. NOBODY DOES.
YOU'VE GOT FIFTEEN SECONDS.
STREETWISE, SIDESWIPE— STAY BEHIND ME. THEY MAY HAVE BOOBY-TRAPPED THE GATE.
REMEMBER, STAY SPREAD OUT. THIS IS FOR EVERYTHING. MOVE!

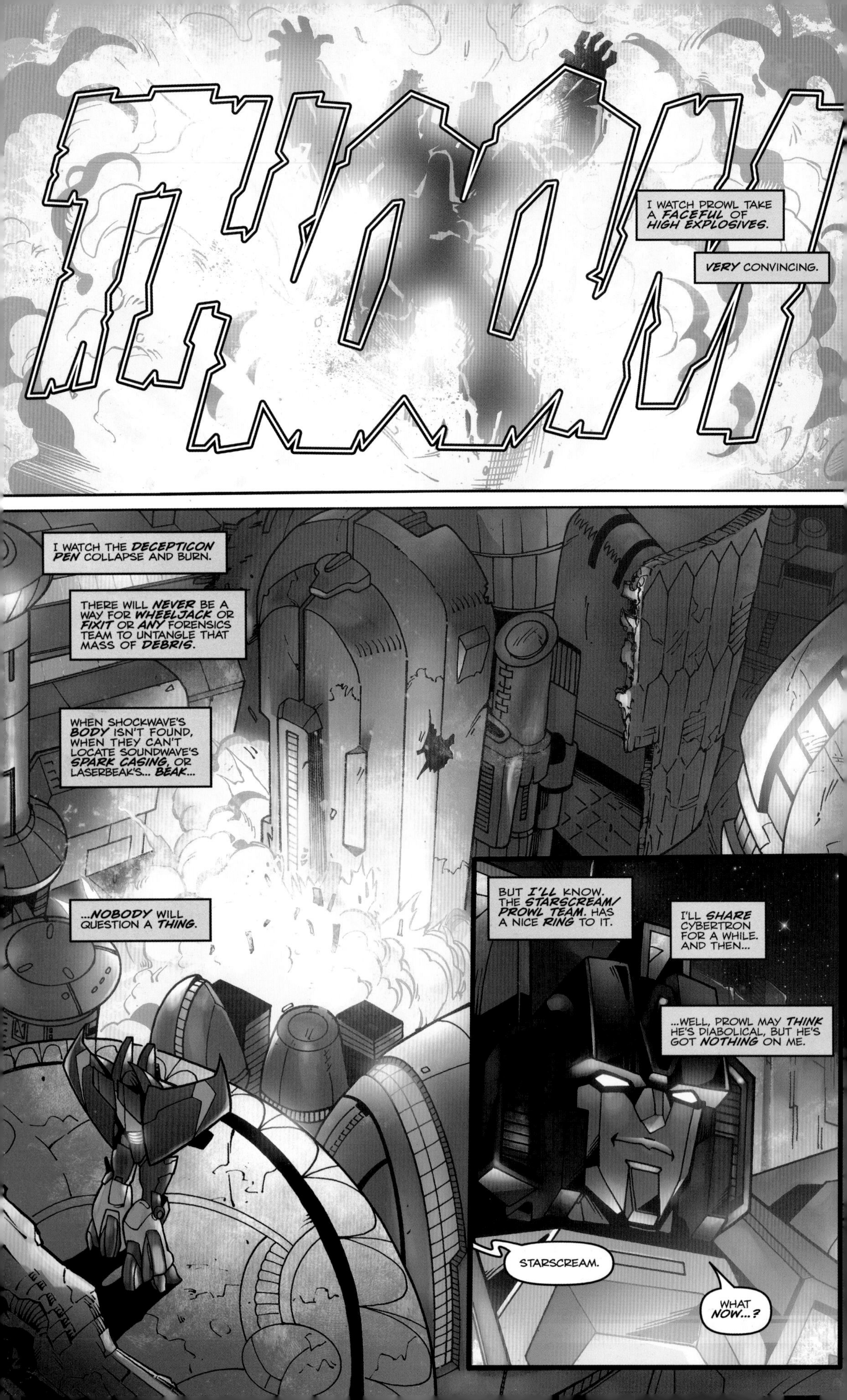
THOOOM!
I WATCH PROWL TAKE A FACEFUL OF HIGH EXPLOSIVES.
VERY CONVINCING.
I WATCH THE DECEPTICON PEN COLLAPSE AND BURN.
THERE WILL NEVER BE A WAY FOR WHEELJACK OR FIXIT OR ANY FORENSICS TEAM TO UNTANGLE THAT MASS OF DEBRIS.
WHEN SHOCKWAVE'S BODY ISN'T FOUND, WHEN THEY CAN'T LOCATE SOUNDWAVE'S SPARK CASING, OR LASERBEAK'S... BEAK...
...NOBODY WILL QUESTION A THING.
BUT I'LL KNOW. THE STARSCREAM/ PROWL TEAM. HAS A NICE RING TO IT.
I'LL SHARE CYBERTRON FOR A WHILE. AND THEN...
...WELL, PROWL MAY THINK HE'S DIABOLICAL, BUT HE'S GOT NOTHING ON ME.
STARSCREAM.
WHAT NOW...?

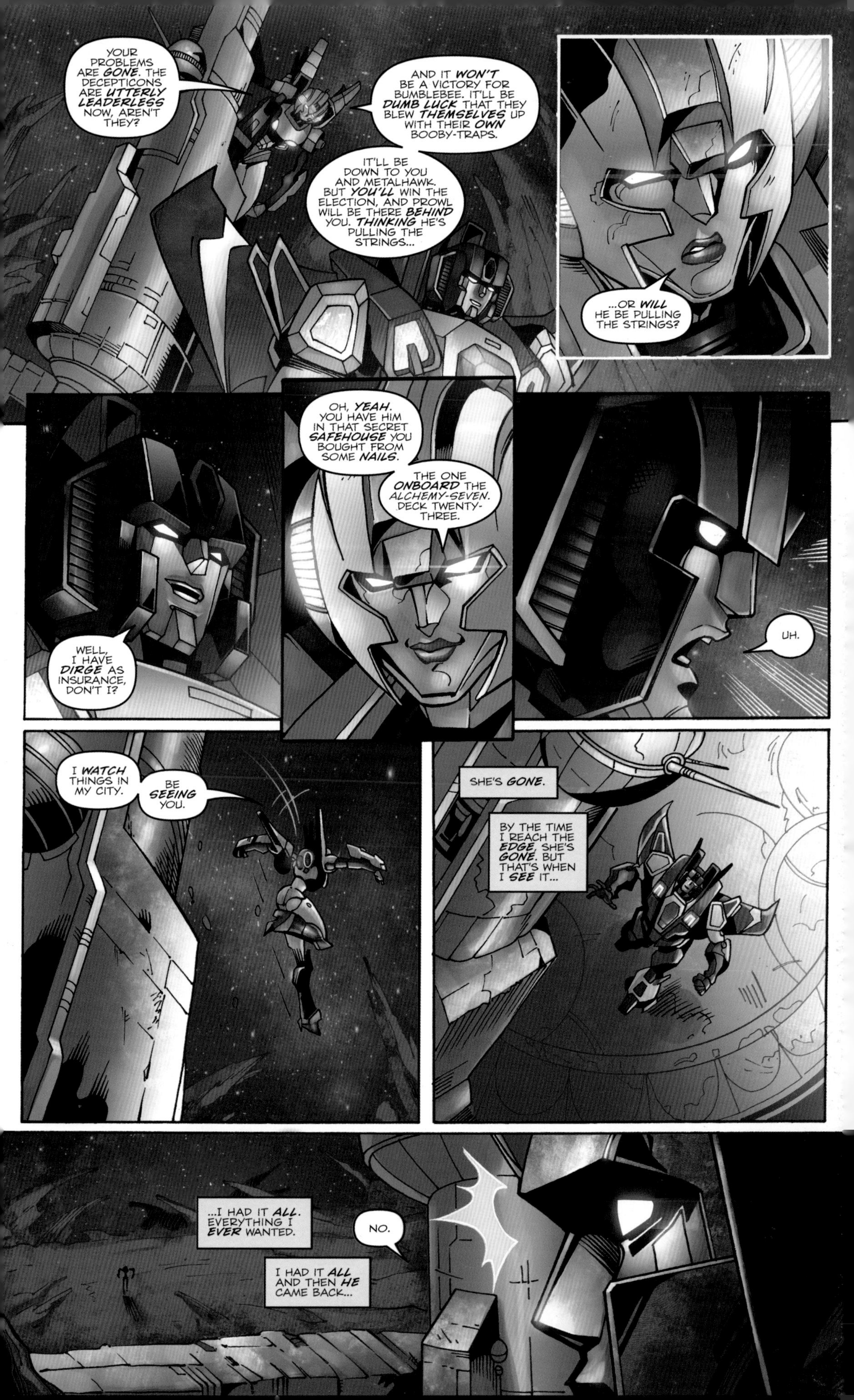
YOUR PROBLEMS ARE GONE. THE DECEPTICONS ARE UTTERLY LEADERLESS NOW, AREN'T THEY?
AND IT WON'T BE A VICTORY FOR BUMBLEBEE. IT'LL BE DUMB LUCK THAT THEY BLEW THEMSELVES UP WITH THEIR OWN BOOBY-TRAPS.
IT'LL BE DOWN TO YOU AND METALHAWK. BUT YOU'LL WIN THE ELECTION, AND PROWL WILL BE THERE BEHIND YOU. THINKING HE'S PULLING THE STRINGS...
...OR WILL HE BE PULLING THE STRINGS?
WELL, I HAVE DIRGE AS INSURANCE, DON'T I?
OH, YEAH. YOU HAVE HIM IN THAT SECRET SAFEHOUSE YOU BOUGHT FROM SOME NAILS.
THE ONE ONBOARD THE ALCHEMY-SEVEN. DECK TWENTY-THREE.
UH.
I WATCH THINGS IN MY CITY.
BE SEEING YOU.
SHE'S GONE.
BY THE TIME I REACH THE EDGE, SHE'S GONE. BUT THAT'S WHEN I SEE IT...
...I HAD IT ALL. EVERYTHING I EVER WANTED.
NO.
I HAD IT ALL AND THEN HE CAME BACK...

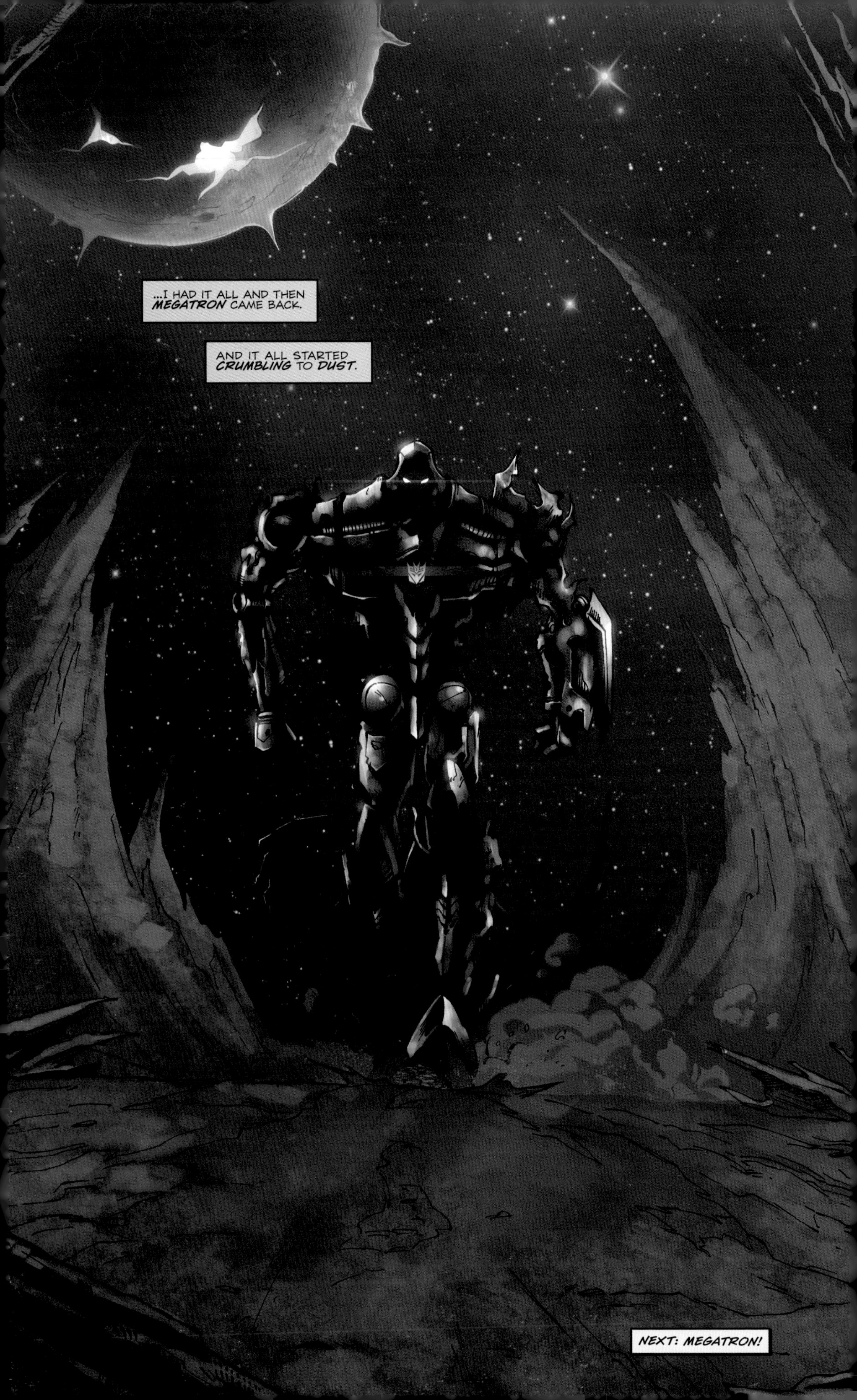
...I HAD IT ALL AND THEN MEGATRON CAME BACK.
AND IT ALL STARTED CRUMBLING TO DUST.
NEXT: MEGATRON!

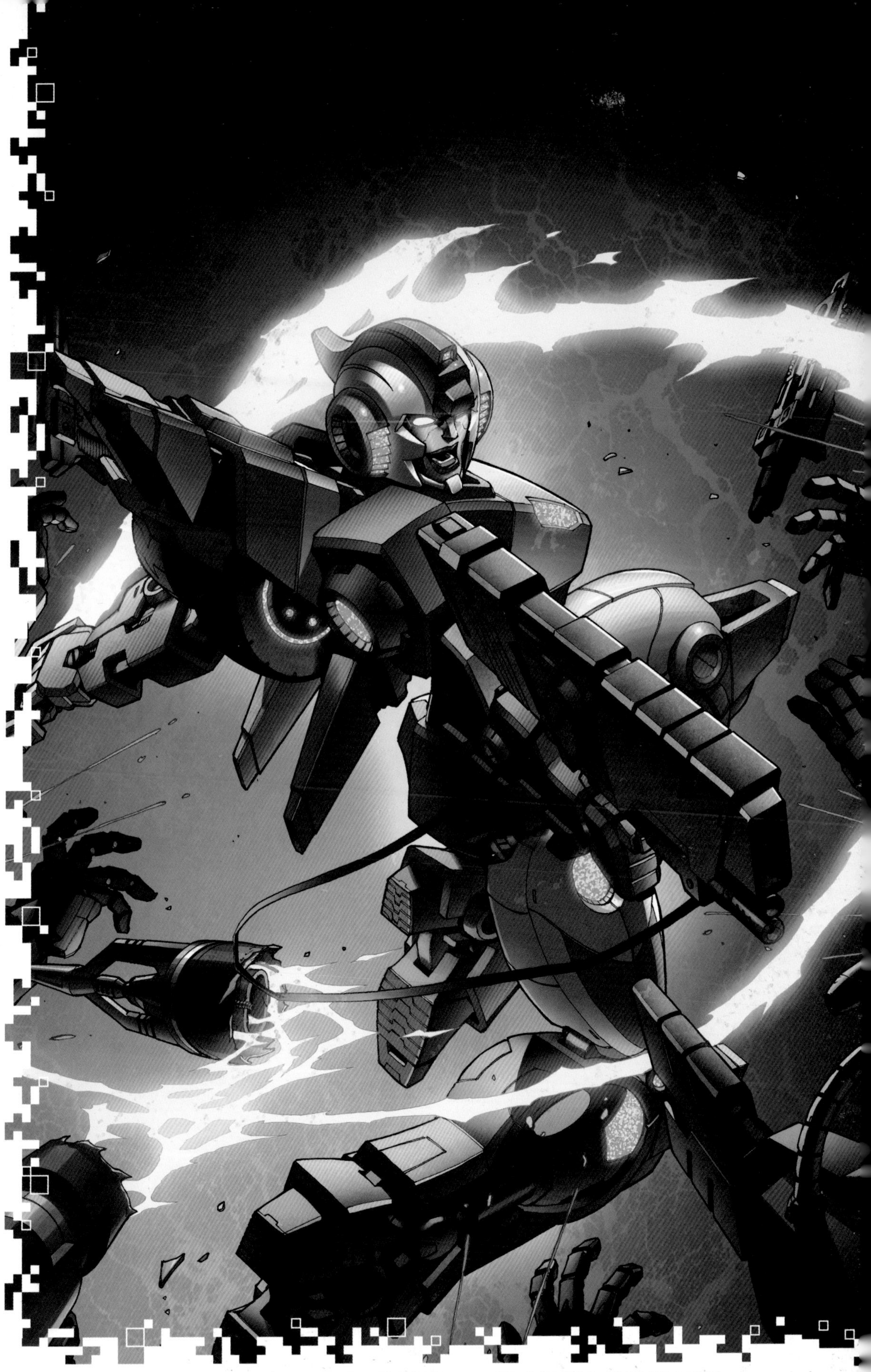

ROBOTS IN DISGUISE #11 COVER B

by **CASEY W. COLLER** Colors by **JOANA LAFUENTE**

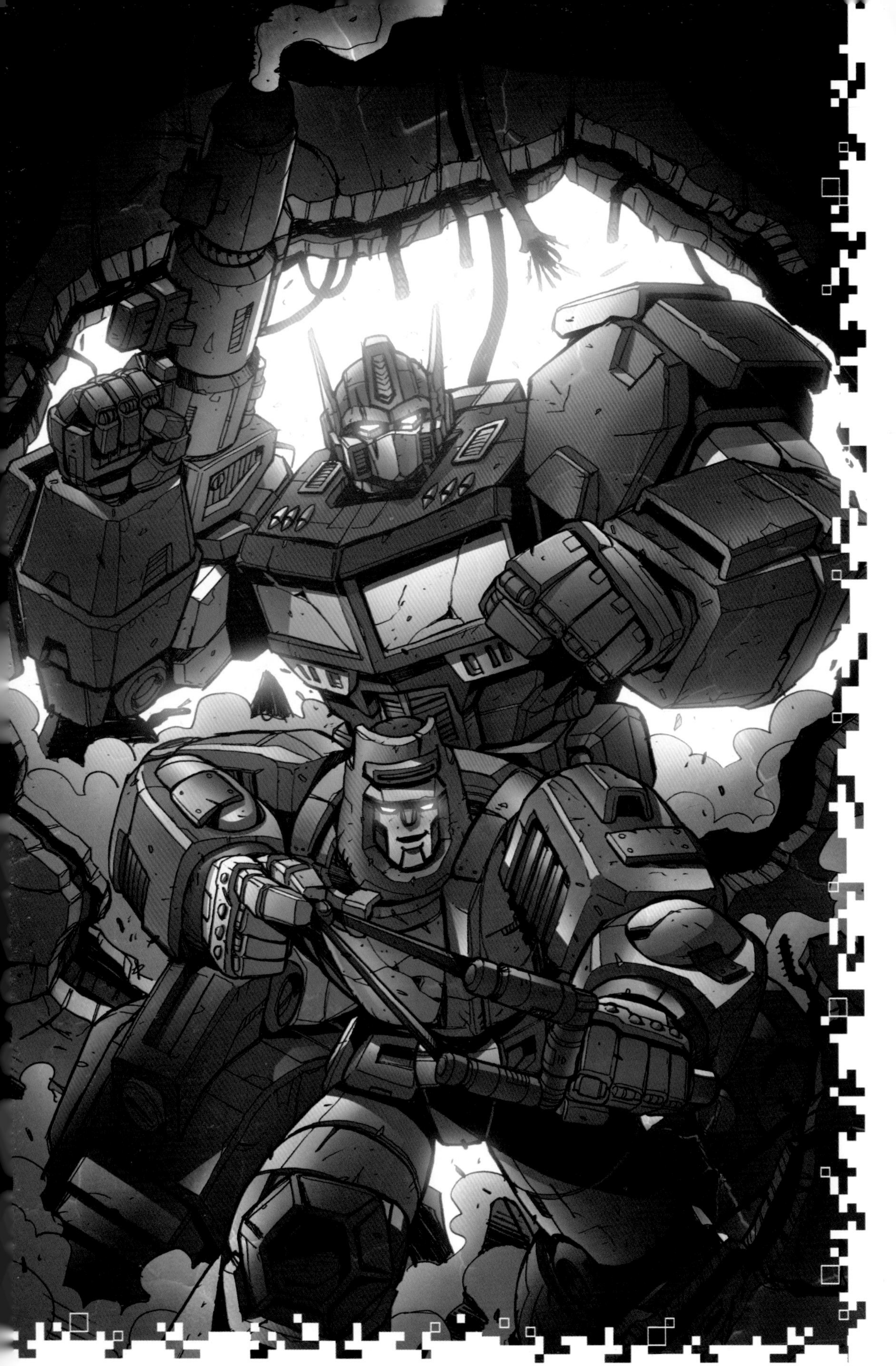

ROBOTS IN DISGUISE #10 COVER RI

by MARCELO MATERE Colors by JOANA LAFUENTE

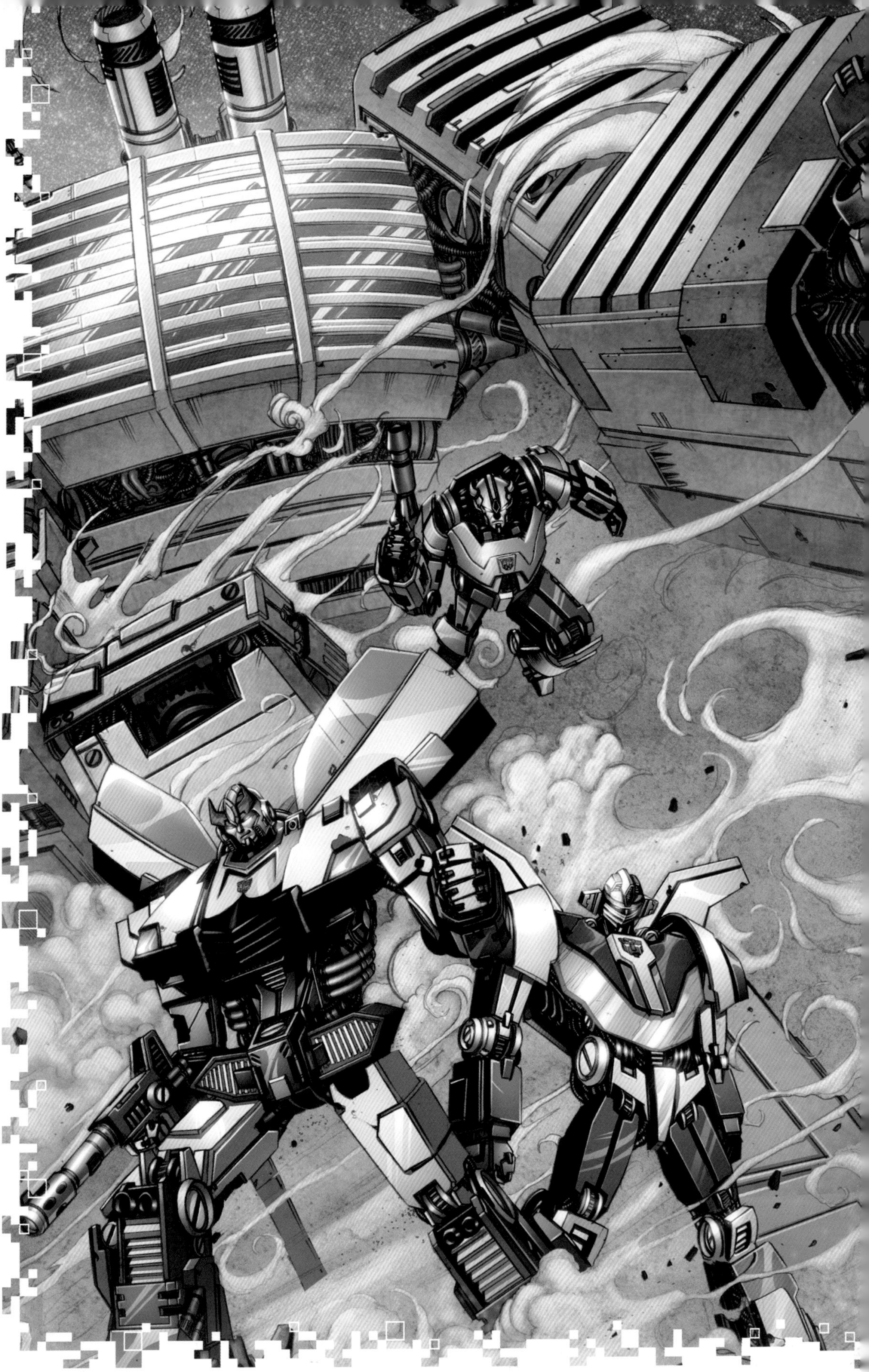

ROBOTS IN DISGUISE ANNUAL COVER RI

by JIMBO SALGADO Colors by JUAN FERNANDEZ

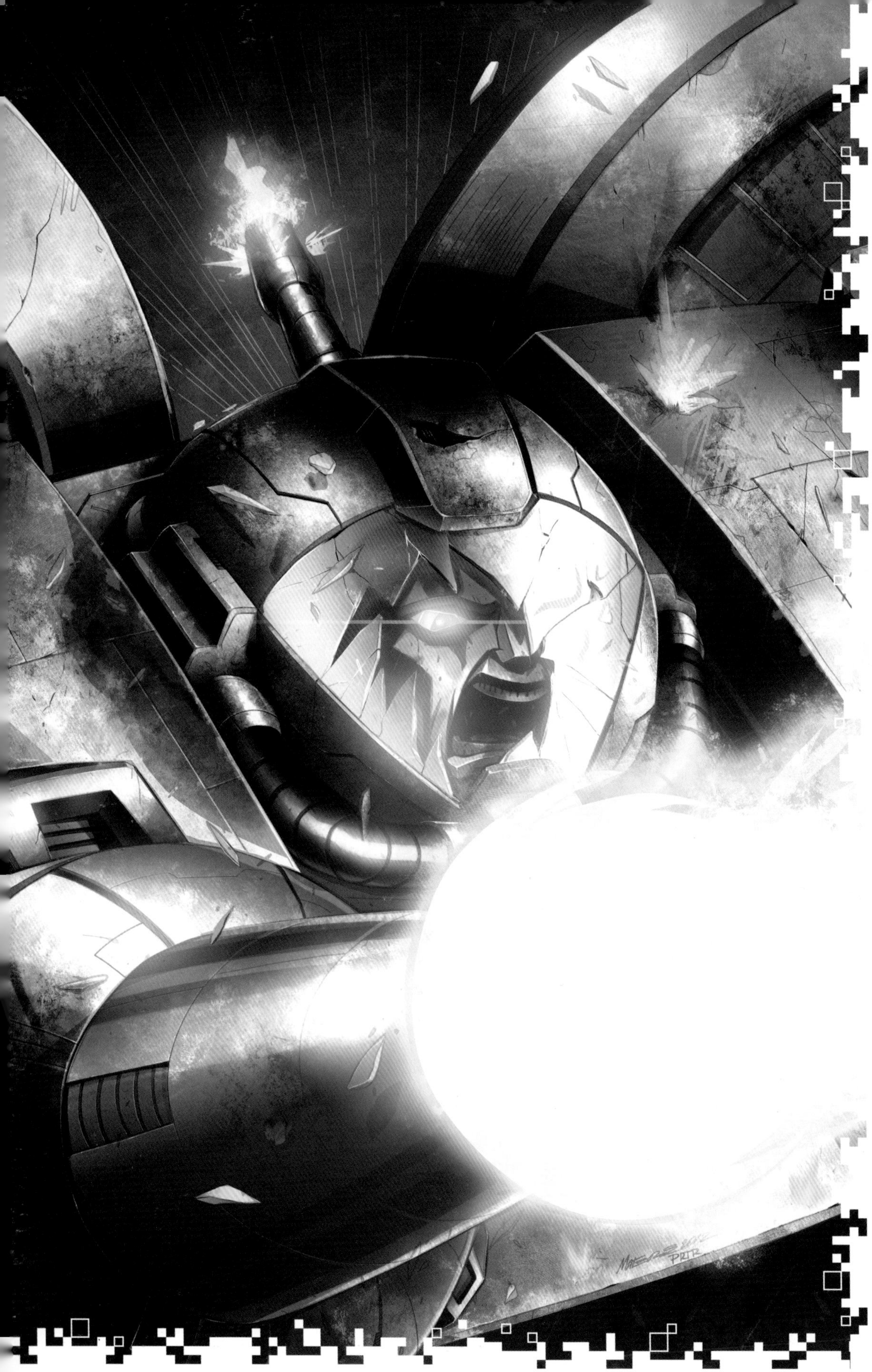

ROBOTS IN DISGUISE #11 COVER RI

by **MARCELO MATERE** Colors by **PRISCILLA TRAMONTANO**

IDW TRANSFORMERS - RID ANNUAL P.28 (14/46)

GUIDO GUIDI 2012

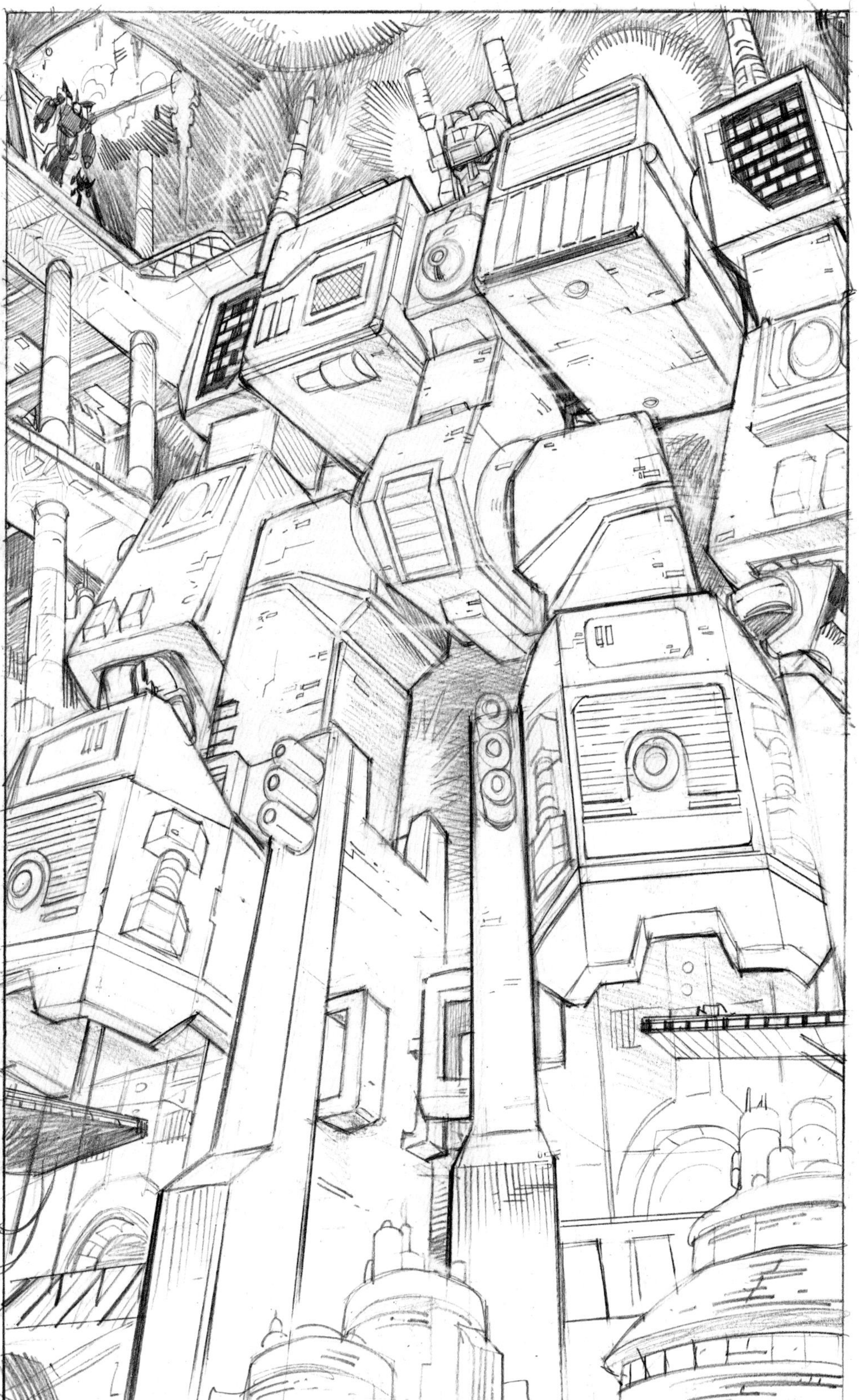

28

Pencils by **GUIDO GUIDI**

*TRANSFORMERS: ROBOTS IN DISGUISE*
**Annual 2012: Primus**
Script by John Barber
Draft 1 (5/10/12)

*Notes: Here's the idea with these retro pages: The plan is to evoke issue 1 of
Transformers--very specifically that issue. It was the first piece of TF fiction, so there's a
certain weirdness and foreign-ness to the thing that necessarily was never repeated. But
I'd like to try to get that feeling here--this isn't a time we've ever seen in this particular
iteration of the TF universe, so I think we can get this feeling of new-ness or the shock of
the new or whatever. None of the panels (even the ones I call out specifically tied to other
panels) need to be direct homages--probably better if they're not--just evocative of it.*

## PAGE ONE

1/ Echo page 1 of issue one of Marvel's Transformers series: 5 widescreen panels. We're in deep
space, a star gleaming against a tiny Cybertron. This is Cybertron of the distant past--at the dawn
of the "Golden Age". The planet looks more like it does in current RID issues than in older
comics--it's not built up yet; there aren't cities covering the surface. And it has 2 moons. A flare
comes off the star it orbits--encircling the planet in a ring of light.

*[handwritten: — as Guido noted— no, it doesn't in the real-time of the rest of the flashback panels, but this one is way in the past.]*

*[handwritten annotation, circled: "And it has 2 moons"]*

1 CLASSIC CAPTION:        In the far reaches of the <u>cosmos</u>, circling a burning
                          <u>yellow dwarf star</u> spins a <u>planet</u>--as <u>unusual</u> as it is
                          <u>dangerous</u>!

2 CLASSIC CAPTION:        <u>Cybertron</u>--a <u>tarnished jewel</u> embedded in a <u>ring of light</u>
                          worn on the universe's <u>clenched fist</u>!

2/ Closer to the planet, like panel 3 of *Transformers #1*, we're over the surface of the planet,
seeing metal hills and plateaus--but unlike *Transformers #1*, the planet is covered by the remnants
of a just-ended war. Scorch marks and dead bodies--and wrecked vehicles--litter the surface.

3 CLASSIC CAPTION:        Its <u>hilltops</u>--once-glistening of <u>steel</u> and <u>chrome</u>--now
                          <u>blackened</u> by endless millennia of <u>civil war</u>.

4 CLASSIC CAPTION:        Its <u>inhabitants</u> evolved--not from <u>cells</u> into <u>muscles</u> and
                          <u>bones</u> but from <u>metal</u> into <u>gears</u> and <u>levers</u>.

3/ Closer to the surface again, we can see living Transformers on the surface, some in vehicle
mode some in robot. Maybe some random bot changing modes?

5 CLASSIC CAPTION:        A <u>unique ability</u> arose among them--the ability to <u>change</u>
                          <u>shape</u> at will, to <u>better suit</u> their <u>surroundings</u>.

6 CLASSIC CAPTION:        Across the <u>galaxy</u> their kind would come to be <u>known</u>
                          and <u>feared</u> as--<u>the Transformers</u>.

4/ Close in on a hilltop, with our set of heroes (see next page) barely visible, facing away from
us--maybe silhouetted?

7 CLASSIC CAPTION:        <u>War</u> is the lot decreed upon them by <u>fate</u>--<u>endless war</u>…

8 CLASSIC CAPTION:        …until there came a <u>leader</u>. One <u>Cybertronian</u> who
                          <u>united</u> the planet--who <u>ended</u> the fighting--

9 CLASSIC CAPTION:        --who gave these <u>metal giants</u> a <u>new beginning</u>.

5/ Close on the back of the leader of our heroes--NOVA PRIME--from the back--we can't make
out who it is yet, even if we know him.

10 CLASSIC CAPTION:       They called him <u>Prime</u>--

IDW TRANSFORMERS RID ANNUAL 2012 P.1 -RETRO PAGE- GUIDO GUIDI

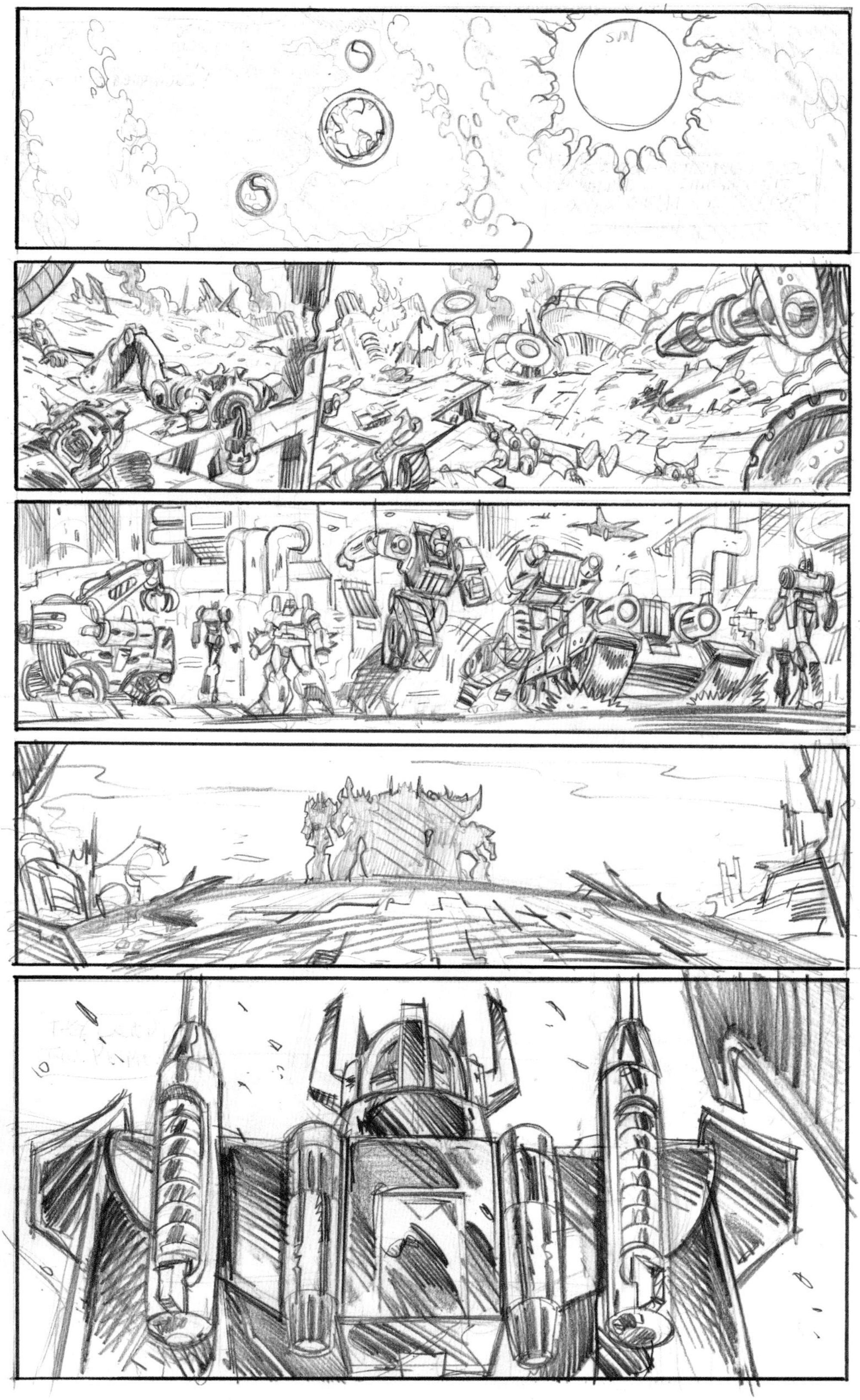

Pencils by **GUIDO GUIDI**

**PAGE TWO**
**Guido retro page**

SPLASH/ Big image of our heroes, Nova Prime in front, looking heroic at something we can't see. Behind him are: GALVATRON, JHIAXUS, CYCLONUS, and DAI ATLAS. All of them in their classic looks--will Dai Atlas look okay? He's got the oddest look compared to the others, but I think it'll be cool to see him in a retro-80s style. Nobody has Autobot or Decepticon symbols.

1 CLASSIC CAPTION (BIG): --NOVA PRIME!

2 NOVA PRIME: Here! At last--our search ends, old friends!

3 NOVA PRIME: We've found it--the legendary lair of great Primus himself--the bestower of life upon all our kind!

4 GALVATRON: I hope you're right, Nova! Because looking at that place—

5 LOGO: THE TRANSFORMERS

Keep?

IDW TRANSFORMERS: RID ANNUAL 2012 - P2/40 - RETRO PAGE

Pencils by **GUIDO GUIDI**

## PAGE TWELVE

1/ Big panel. Shot of all the heroes--this is meant to be evocative of those 3 pages in *Transformers #1* where everybody absurdly and at length announces who they are, real casual-like. Especially the Deception one, where it's only the top half of the page. So leave a ton of room for the intentionally lengthy dialog here. And try to arrange the guys so the balloons can flow in order! Sorry, Guido!

1 NOVA PRIME:    Forgive me, <u>great one</u>--for we come in <u>peace</u>! I, <u>Nova Prime</u>, trace my <u>lineage</u> to the great <u>Primus</u> who <u>you</u> once <u>served</u>!

2 NOVA PRIME:    And I see you have served <u>well</u>, and <u>loyally</u>! My <u>friends</u> and I are here to <u>relieve</u> you, <u>noble warrior</u>!

3 GALVATRON:    <u>Galvatron</u> welcomes you into our <u>new world</u>! Perhaps your <u>military prowess</u> is a match for my <u>own</u>! Whatever the case--I'm sure we will find ourselves <u>fast friends</u>!

3 CYCLONUS:    <u>Indeed</u>--one such as <u>you</u>, who has witnessed <u>so much</u>, will be able to teach <u>Cyclonus</u> of the <u>ancient legends</u> of <u>Cybertron</u>!

4 JHIAXUS:    It is not <u>legends</u> that interest <u>Jhiaxus</u>! Only the <u>cold truth</u> of <u>science</u> sways <u>my</u> thinking--but even in <u>this</u>, Omega, you will surely prove a <u>boon</u>.

5 DAI ATLAS:    My friends are <u>overzealous</u>--what matters <u>most</u> is the <u>peace</u> we will share <u>together</u>! I, <u>Dai Atlas</u>, wish to step into this <u>bold future</u> with <u>you</u> at our <u>side</u>!

2/ Close on Omega.

6 OMEGA SUPREME:  So long… so <u>long</u> have I stood guard. <u>Alone</u>…

7 OMEGA SUPREME:  You talk of <u>Primus</u>, and of <u>peace</u>. What has <u>happened</u> on the world, since the <u>Guiding Hand</u> left us?

3/ Nova and Atlas, as Nova delivers an impassioned speech.

8 NOVA PRIME:    <u>War</u>, great Omega. War seemingly without <u>end</u>--

9 NOVA PRIME:    --but <u>we</u> have <u>ended it</u>!

10 NOVA PRIME:   We stand on the <u>precipice</u> of a <u>Golden Age</u>. And as the heir to the <u>throne</u> of <u>Primus</u>, my friend, I bid you-- <u>freedom</u>…

4/ Omega considers.

NOVA PRIME (OP):   …the <u>right</u> of all <u>sentient beings</u>!

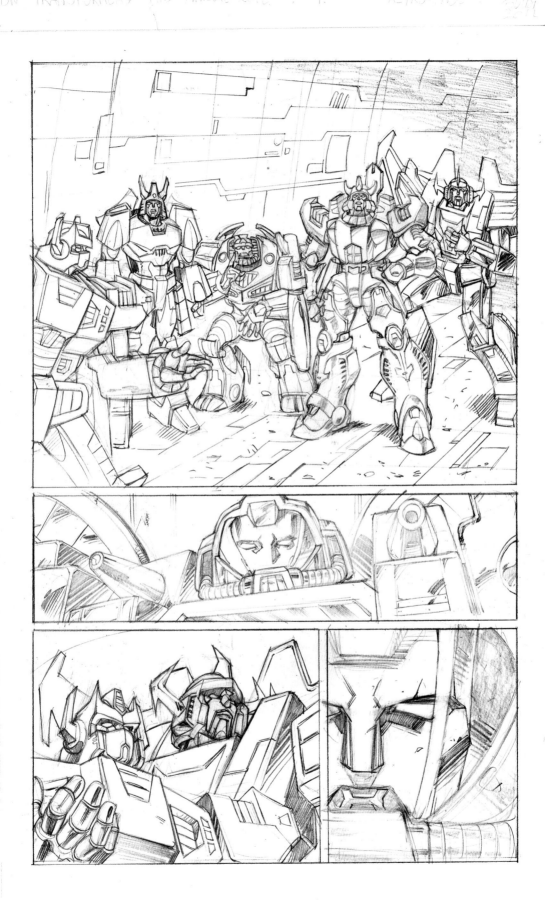

Pencils by **GUIDO GUIDI**

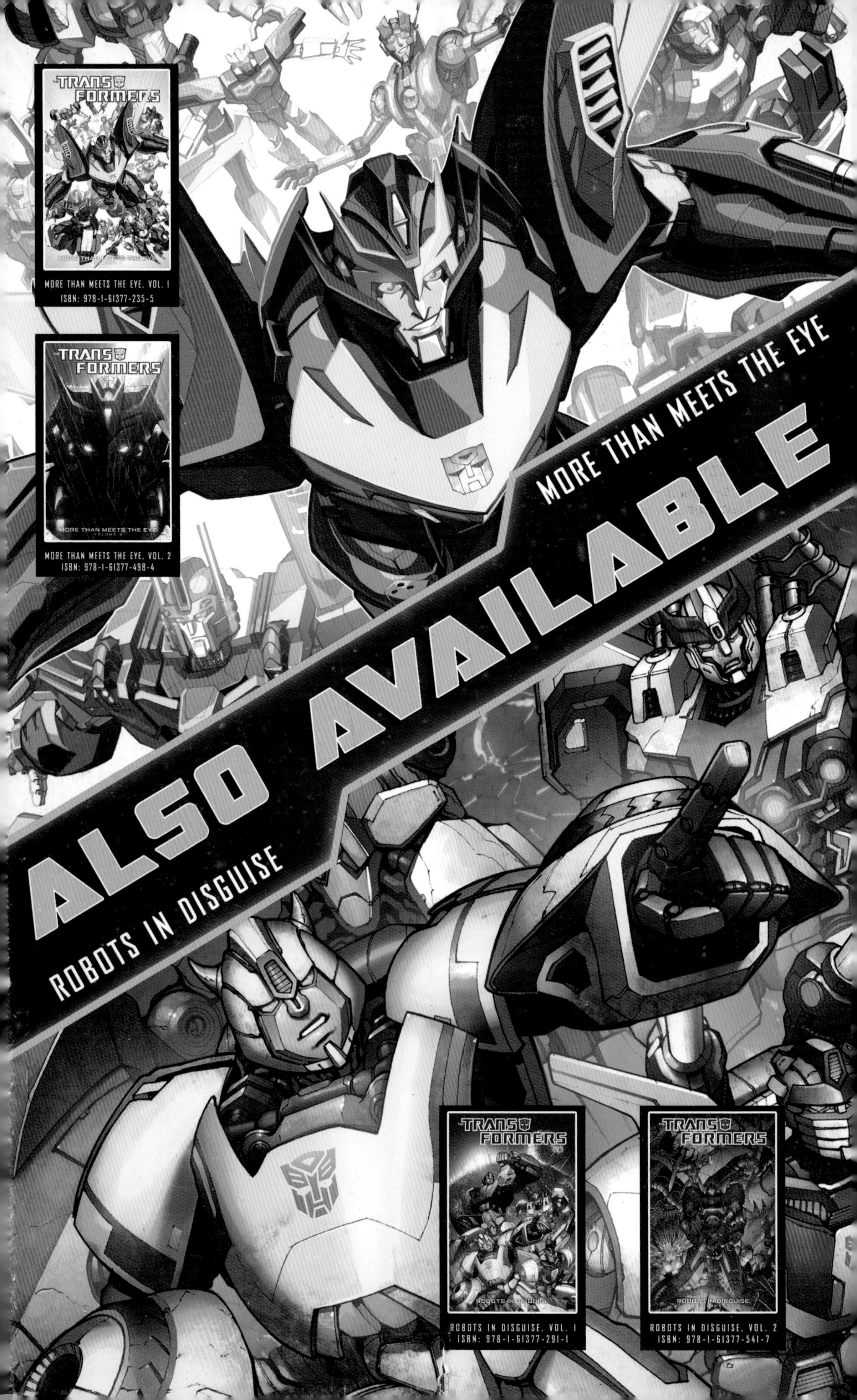
TRANSFORMERS
MORE THAN MEETS THE EYE, VOL. 1
ISBN: 978-1-61377-235-5
TRANSFORMERS
MORE THAN MEETS THE EYE
MORE THAN MEETS THE EYE, VOL. 2
ISBN: 978-1-61377-498-4
MORE THAN MEETS THE EYE
ALSO AVAILABLE
ROBOTS IN DISGUISE
TRANSFORMERS
ROBOTS IN DISGUISE
ROBOTS IN DISGUISE, VOL. 1
ISBN: 978-1-61377-291-1
TRANSFORMERS
ROBOTS IN DISGUISE
ROBOTS IN DISGUISE, VOL. 2
ISBN: 978-1-61377-541-7